THE TRAVELER'S GUIDE
to the
Hudson River Valley
From Saratoga Springs to New York City

BLACK·DOME

Also by Tim Mulligan

The Traveler's Guide to Western New England
and the Connecticut River Valley

Virginia: A History and Guide

The Battle of Hampton Roads:
New Perspectives on the USS Monitor
and the CSS Virginia (co-editor)

THE TRAVELER'S GUIDE
——— to the ———
Hudson River Valley
From Saratoga Springs to New York City

20th Anniversary Edition

TIM MULLIGAN

Illustrated by Stan Skardinski

BLACK·DOME

Published by
Black Dome Press Corp.,1011 Route 296, Hensonville, New York 12439
www.blackdomepress.com Tel: (518) 734–6357

Fifth edition 2007. Earlier editions of this work were published by
Random House, Inc., in 1985, 1991, 1995 and 1999.

ISBN-13: 978-1-883789-49-7
ISBN-10: 1-883789-49-4

Library of Congress Cataloging-in-Publication Data

Mulligan, Tim, 1938-
   The travelers guide to the Hudson River Valley : from Saratoga Springs to New York
City / Tim Mulligan. -- 25th anniversary ed., 5th ed.
      p. cm.
   Includes index.
   ISBN-13: 978-1-883789-49-7
   ISBN-10: 1-883789-49-4
   1. Hudson River Valley (N.Y. and N.J.)—History. 2. Hudson River Valley (N.Y.
and N.J.)—Guidebooks. 3. Historic sites—Hudson River Valley
(N.Y. and N.J.)—Guidebooks. I. Title.

   F127.H8M884 2006
   917.47'30444—dc22
                                          2006018497

Cover photograph: Vanderbilt Mansion, Hyde Park
© James Bleecker. www.jamesbleecker.com

Design: Toelke Associates, www.toelkeassociates.com

Printed in the USA
10 9 8 7 6 5 4 3

For John O'Keefe

C O N T E N T S

TO THE READER

This book has now been in continuous print since 1985, and each edition has had its innovations, additions, etc.

Now the book has its own website: **hudson-river-valley-travelers-guide.info.** I hope you will feel free to e-mail me your comments, criticisms, suggestions, questions, complaints … in short, whatever you want to tell me. In the past, your comments were invaluable and have had no little influence on the book's contents, and I look forward to hearing from you in the future. Particularly relevant suggestions will be added to the web site. And don't be hesitant—past suggestions have added immeasurably to the diversity of what is in the book and not a little to my own enjoyment of the Valley.

If, on the other hand, you would like to write to me, please feel free to do so. The address:

Tim Mulligan
Hudson River Guide
10 Montague Terrace
Brooklyn, NY 11201

AUTHOR'S NOTE

The distance covered by this book, from New York City to Saratoga, is one that can be done in a five-hour drive. It is relatively easy, therefore, to go from any place mentioned in the Upper Hudson section to, say, one listed in the Lower Hudson. I suggest that, if you can, you consider taking the train. The ride from New York to Albany offers unparalleled views of the river, making it one of the country's great train trips, because most of the track runs along the east bank.

I do not list motels—see one, you've seen them all—but they are there, in run-of-the-mill abundance, if you cannot get a reservation at one of the inns, Bed & Breakfasts or hotels mentioned in this book.

Two other things. First, I have decided to follow the Hudson from Saratoga south to New York City for the purely arbitrary reason that to me it feels right going with the flow of the river rather than against it, and that the logical culmination for the book is in New York City, where the Hudson disappears under the great harbor.

Second point: Hours may vary as well as schedules. If you are operating on a tight timetable, it would be wise to call in advance.

Finally, this is a personal book that reflects my tastes and opinions. It is not a compendium of everything in the Valley; moreover, as you will see, I do not pretend to like every place I describe—and I will tell you why. I have written this book as I would talk to a friend, giving information that I hope will be enjoyed. And you have responded by sending me information that, in this new edition, I am happy to pass along.

ACKNOWLEDGMENTS

An extraordinary number of people extended themselves to help, counsel and guide me in the creation of this book. Several of these deserve a formal acknowledgment.

I would like to thank Jerry Aiello, a longtime devotee of the river, who was always ready for yet one more visit on the Hudson and whose gentle perceptions added a great deal to my own observations.

Frank Gilligan and Fernanda Kellogg gave me their home in the Valley several times to serve as a "base of operations" and were hospitality itself, as was the late Lillian Phipps, who made a visit to Saratoga among my most memorable stays in the Valley.

Fred Johnston, who appears in these pages, was among the first to open my eyes to the depth and splendor of the Valley and was also a loyal supporter of my efforts to capture something of the feel of the Hudson River Valley. His death leaves the Valley bereft of one of its main supporters.

Pamela Fiori, former editor of *Travel & Leisure* and now editor of *Town & Country,* gave me the opportunity to write extensively on the Hudson and has long been not only one of my favorite people but also a superb and wise editor.

The wisdom and interest of my original editor, Cheryl Merser, can still be felt on every page, and she has become a much-valued friend. And now my new editors, Deborah Allen and Steve Hoare, also have provided wonderful help and support.

Finally, I would like to thank all the people who are involved with the sites, buildings, places and so forth about which I have written. Almost all have provided help, advice and commentary that have served to improve and deepen what I have written. To them and to all the others who were in one way or another involved in this venture, thank you. Needless to say, the good things come from all of them; the bad are mine alone.

INTRODUCTION

I have lived near the Hudson many, many years, and throughout that time I have watched the life on this great river—freighters and tugs, the last of the great ocean liners, fireworks on the Fourth of July, sunsets that could have been painted by Turner or Monet or Church, great cakes of ice clustering around the piers in winter, sailboats and yachts in summer.

Familiarity has made the Hudson central to my life. It is the one timeless and unchanging part of New York City, the anchor that, to borrow from Gertrude Stein, lets you know there is a "there" there. It is comforting to know that there still are places from which the Hudson looks exactly the same as it did to the first settlers: from the Cloisters, for example. And the Palisades, those wonderful walls of the Hudson, remain relatively unspoiled, the most beautiful natural feature left near the city. But this is only the mouth of a river whose beauty is so great that the first cohesive group of American artists, the Hudson River School, formed to paint it and its surroundings in every mood and season.

The Hudson is an ancient river whose beginnings go back 75 million years. About 65 million years ago, as the land rose, the river began cutting its valley between the Catskill and Taconic mountains, down to the splendid Hudson Highlands, and flowed first west, then east to empty into the Atlantic Ocean. About 10 million years ago, theory has it, a smaller river moved northward and there, in the Highlands, joined the Hudson, which abandoned its old course and now flows south to the sea. More recently, during the Ice Age, the sea level was lower than it is today, and the continental shelf was exposed; the Hudson then flowed through this plain for 120 miles until it reached the sea. Today you may think the river ends in the harbor, but it really is flowing onward, to the end of the shelf, where it finally disappears into the Hudson Canyon and the vastness of the Atlantic.

Because the Hudson's channel is below sea level from, roughly, Troy on, ocean tides run up to Troy, making the river an estuary. According to Robert H. Boyle, author of the brilliant book *The Hudson River: A Natural and Unnatural History,* "More properly, the Hudson is a drowned river; after the last glacier melted, rising seawater moved in and flooded the old course of the river. Because of this, the lower Hudson is unusually deep and is suitable for navigation by ocean-going vessels up to Albany."

As great rivers go, the Hudson is relatively small, only 315 miles long from its source to the ocean—by comparison, the Mississippi is 2,348 miles long, the Seine 482 miles and the Rhine 820 miles—and what most people see is simply that part from Albany south, a distance of only 150 miles. But what extraordinary beauty it encompasses along this length. And what an extraordinary amount of life it supports. Millions of fish live here, both marine and freshwater species, making it, according to Mr. Boyle, "the greatest single wildlife resource in New York State."

It was only in 1872 that the true source of the Hudson was located when Verplanck Colvin, an official surveyor for the state of New York, discovered a tiny pond on the slopes of Mount Marcy in the Adirondacks and knew that there was the beginning of the river. In his report to the state legislature Colvin wrote, "Far above the chilly waters of Lake Avalanche, at an elevation of 4,293 feet, is Summit Water, a minute, unpretending tear of the clouds, as it were—a lovely pool shivering in the breezes of the mountains, and sending its limpid surplus through Feldspar Brook and to the Opalescent River, the well-spring of the Hudson." So moved were the legislators by Colvin's eloquence that they changed the name of Summit Water to Lake Tear of the Clouds.

From there, for 161 miles until the river joins the Mohawk, it flows southeast, mainly through unspoiled wilderness. Oddly enough, this, one of the world's most famous rivers, is almost unknown for a good part of its length, and yet in this seldom-visited stretch is found some of its greatest drama—for instance, where the river rushes for a mile, churning and violent, through the Hudson Gorge, a series of great cliffs that rise, in some places, to eminences of more than 800 feet. Then, once out of the Adirondacks, it grows placid, a gentle river flowing through pretty fields on its way to Albany.

From Albany the river passes through scenery so diverse and appealing that many people find it the most beautiful river valley in the world. "Perpetually interesting," Henry James said of the Hudson, and so it is, with the stunning Catskill Mountains, the brooding intensity of the Hudson Highlands, the greatest city in the world at its mouth and an extraordinary bounty of things to see and do that can keep you going back for years to revel in them.

The river was first discovered in 1524 by Giovanni da Verrazano, who was exploring the coast of North America for Francis I, king of France. But it was not until 1609, when Henry Hudson sailed as far north as Albany on a voyage sponsored by the Dutch (and mistakenly thinking the river might lead to the Orient), that it truly entered our history. Since then, millions upon millions of immigrants have arrived in America on the Hudson's waters, and almost every ethnic group has left its distinguishing mark on the river valley. In the eighteenth century, control of the river, the colonists' most important "highway," meant control of the country, and during the American Revolution one third of the battles were fought along its shores. Indeed, arguably the most important conflict of the war took place here, the Battle of Saratoga, which decided once and for all that the British would not gain control of the vital waterway.

Then, in the nineteenth century, with the opening of the Erie Canal, the development of the West could move ahead in earnest, helping to make New York a world metropolis and the economic center of the nation. It was the Hudson that provided the foundation for the Empire State.

It was in the nineteenth century, too, that the river experienced its most brilliant development. The steamboat got its start when Robert Fulton first sailed the Clermont—"a boat driven by a teakettle," some said—from New York to Albany in 32 hours. Great estates appeared, a long line of them along both banks of the river, that made the Hudson into America's own Loire Valley. Cities arose, grew, and prospered. Trade flourished. And the painters sent out their impressions of the Valley, first to the nation, then to the world, while thousands came to see and share the magnificence.

Today the Valley is tinged with an aura of romance and wrapped in that famous, unique light still so much admired by artists and travelers alike. Like America, the Hudson River Valley has matured, even grown old—many canals are graceful ruins, the towns are in the throes of restoration, the estates have mostly become public institutions of one sort or another, the great families have either died out or retreated behind their walls as their wealth, like the early prosperity of the Valley, has declined. But also like America, it has a new vitality stirring. And with prosperity and time and maturity have come a new awareness of the river and what it means to all of us.

Four final mentions. **River Valley Tours, Inc.,** has summer tours of the Valley by boat that last seven nights and eight days. They go from New York City to the gateway to the Erie Canal. Nights are spent in inns along the way, while buses meet the boat for sightseeing trips. For complete information, phone 800-836-2128 or e-mail rivervalleytours.com. For information on one of the more interesting annual ventures—a festival of guided hiking and walking tours of the Valley as well as of the Catskill Forest Preserve and the Shawangunk Mountains—phone **Hudson River Valley Ramble** at 800-453-6665 or visit hudsonvalleyramble.com. Many of the tours have cultural or historical themes, such as the Hudson River Artists' Landscape tour. And there is a marvelous cookbook devoted to regional food, *The Hudson River Valley Cookbook,* which is available in paperback ($16.95), by Waldy Malouf, one of New York City's better known chefs, with Molly Finn. Using Valley ingredients, this cookbook is a wonderful addition to anyone's kitchen and will help prolong memories of your visit. One other book well worth your consideration: *Hudson Valley Harvest: A Food Lovers Guide to Farms, Restaurants and Open-Air Markets* by Jan Greenberg ($18.95).

HUDSON VALLEY WINERIES

The seyval blanc that **Clinton Vineyards** specializes in is discussed at another point in this book (see page 148), but there are a few other vineyards that make good wines and are particularly appealing to visit.

Perhaps the father of the Valley's burgeoning reputation as a wine region is Mark Miller, who founded the **Benmarl Wine Company** in Marlboro, near New Paltz (phone: 845-236-4265, web site: www.benmarl.com). Benmarl offers daily tours and tastings.

Certainly one of the best-known vineyards is **Millbrook Vineyards,** in Millbrook (phone: 845-677-8383, web site: millbrookwine.com). It also offers daily tours. Owner John S. Dyson has sunk a great deal of money into making the vineyard a success and, indeed, his wines are, I think, among the best reds in the Valley.

One of the more pleasant vineyards to visit is **Cascade Mountain Vineyards,** north of Amenia in Dutchess County (phone: 845-373-9021, web site: cascademt.com). It was founded by William Wetmore, who has been known to bless his wines with such names as Pardonnez-moi because it is, he says, a wine for social emergencies, and Le Hamburger red. The vineyard is in an extremely pleasant setting, and there is a restaurant, open Thursday–Sunday, where you can enjoy a pleasant—and excellent—lunch while tasting his wines (see page 176).

And then there's the **Shawangunk Wine Trail** (phone: 845-255-2494, web site: www.shawangunkwinetrail.com). This is an organization of nine vineyards in Ulster County located between the Shawangunk Mountains and the Hudson. They are an active and creative group offering tours of their wineries as well as special events, all of which can be great fun; one spring event that I remember was called "Pasta Primo—Vino!", in which the vineyards' wines were accompanied by pasta recipes.

Finally, there are several Hudson River Valley winery maps on the web. I think this is about the best: www.travelenvoy.com, then click on USA Winery Index.

LIGHTHOUSE LOVERS AND OTHER IMPORTANT MATTERS

Here, in absolutely no order, are odds and ends, many of which will appeal to you.

Seven lighthouses still grace the Hudson River, and access to almost all can be arranged. Go to the web site www.ulster.net/~hrmm/lighthouses/frame.html for information. In addition, the **Saugerties Lighthouse is a Bed & Breakfast** offering two bedrooms. Go to www.saugertieslighthouse.com or phone: 845-247-0656.

For many years **Sotheby's,** the world-famous auction house, had its restoration center in Claverack, a delightful village near Hudson (see page 68). It closed in 2001, but many of the craftsmen—they hired only the best—had worked there for at least a decade, and this part of the Valley had become home. So they stayed, and now their services are available to us all. And, from personal experience, their work is splendid. There is **John Dunham** (515-392-6136; www.dunhamwoodcraftsman.com), primarily a woodworker who, for the past three decades, has been building and restoring furniture. His reproductions were so good that Sotheby's used him to build custom pieces, extend dining sets, etc. **Sharon Cohen** (518-851-7589; chairseats@webtv.net) specializes in all styles of woven chair seats—cane, rush, splint, and Shaker tape—and she has done work for museums, auction houses and collectors. She is particularly skilled at weaving complicated patterns and shapes. **Margaret Saliske** (518-822-0855; Margaretsaliske@hotmail.com) restores and conserves painted finishes on furniture, folding screens and other decorative objects and architectural pieces, Asian and European lacquer and Japaning. She, too, has worked with major collections and collectors. **Neil Van Alstyne** (518-758-6353; neilvanalstyne@yahoo.com) is a finisher, particularly versed in shellac finishes, English and French polishing and faux finishes. He is known for his innovative solutions to solving unusual problems, such as restoring complex Japanese pieces. **Julie Rutschmann** (518-392-5997) is an expert at gilding objects including carved wooden and composition frames, furniture, and decorative objects, and then antiquing them to match. She does water and oil golding as well as gilding on glass. And finally there is **John Hanna** (518-943-3058; rnjhanna@yahoo.com) who is an expert at finishing and refinishing, with the ability to match colors and apply a variety of finishes. He, too, has a great deal of experience with English and French polishing as well as a variety of varnishes and lacquers. I, obviously, haven't used all of these people, but those I have have been wonderful to work with and, I think, reasonably priced. As for their work, it's superb.

If you are interested in **bird watching for bald eagles** in the Valley—and they are spectacular to see in the wild—go to: www.dec.state.ny.us/website/dfwmr/wildlife/endspec/eaglehud.htm.

Hudson Valley Raptor Center, South Road, Stanfordville. Open: Weekends, May–October. Phone: 758-6957.

This is one of the few designated hospitals and temporary sanctuaries in this country for wild birds of prey, including hawks, owls, eagles and falcons. Visiting here is a lot of fun. There's a good video in the center's building, with Joanne Woodward as an effective narrator. Then Zsa Zsa is introduced to the assembled group. Zsa Zsa is a Eurasian Eagle Owl (whose scientific name is Bubo bubo) whose range covers Europe, Asia and northern Africa. It is one of the largest owls in existence and has a wing span of five to six feet. Zsa Zsa, who is very beautiful, horned, and has brown/black and white feathers, has imprinted on humans and stares at you in a calm, fixed way that, if it goes on long enough, can be rather disconcerting.

The next stop is to see the raptors currently being cared for at the Center, and at each cage there is a short talk on the birds themselves and their habits. ("Cage" makes it seem so small. In fact, the cages are very high, so the birds can roost comfortably, and they are deep—for the American eagle cage, for example, the depth is extensive enough to enable the bird to fly to its roost.) All in all, this part of the visit takes about an hour.

Next is my favorite part—a falconer demonstrates his art using a hawk and a falcon. Hawks perch on trees and swoop down on their prey. Falcons catch their prey in the air. Using three tiny, longhaired dachshunds as his assistants, the falconer demonstrates how each bird hunts. It is fascinating.

Who doesn't enjoy shopping at a **farmers' market?** For a list of all those in New York State, go to www.ams.usda.gov/farmersmarkets/States/NewYork.htm.

There are very good **hiking trails** throughout the Valley. To get started, go to: www.newyorkheritage.com/rvw/hudson.html.

I think the best web site for **pick-your-own farms** is www.bearsystems.com/farms/farms.html.

Calling all **chocaholics.** Two great places for you to raid: Krause's Chocolates in Saugerties (41 South Partition Street; Phone: 845-246-8377; Web site: www.krauseschocolates.com) and Vasilow's Confectionery in Hudson (741 Columbia Street; Phone: 518-828-2717; Web site: www.vasilows.com).

Old books, prints, autographs. No one can resist going through piles of books in the hope of finding some unexpected treasure. There really is something irresistible about these stores. In the list below, some only carry books. Others have prints and/or autographs as well. I write about the Lyrical Ballad Bookstore on page 28, the Hudson Rogue Company on page 188, and the Pickwick Bookshop on page 199. Here's a smattering of a few others located around the Valley that, over the years, I've found pleasurable.

- **Rodgers Book Barn,** 467 Rodman Road, Hillsdale.
  (Phone: 518-325-3610; web site: www2.Taconic.net/~bookbarn/)
- **Editions,** 153 Route 28, Ashokan. (Phone: 914-657-7000)
- **Main Street Books,** 4 Church Avenue, Germantown.
  (Phone: 518-537-5878 or 4559; web site: www.abebooks.com)
- **Riverrun,** 7 Washington Avenue, Hastings-on-Hudson.
  (Phone: 914-478-1339; web site: www.riverrunbooks.com)
- **The Brown Bag Bookstore,** 127A Main Street, Dobbs Ferry.
  (Phone: 914-693-2322)

Hope Farm Press & Book Trader Located at 252 Main Street in Saugerties, this excellent bookshop specializes in regional books—the Catskills, the Hudson River Valley, counties and towns, hiking, folklore, Indians and so forth—that can be extremely hard to find elsewhere. Pleasant browsing, indeed, and you are bound to walk away with something. Phone: 845-246-3522. Website: www.hopefarm.com.

For the **best coffee** in the Valley—and in most other places, too—look for Schapira's Coffee & Tea Company bags, either beans or ground. (Phone: 518-398-7100; Web site: www.schapira.com.) The company is in Pine Plains, and the product is used in many of the best restaurants not only in the Valley but in New York City as well. Delicious.

Ballooning is big in the Valley. I must be honest and tell you that this is one adventure I've allowed to pass me by, but if you want to check out sources, go to www.blastvalve.com.

Tubing on the Esopus, a creek on the west bank that drains into the Hudson and also is good for trout fishing, is a lot of fun. It's a five-mile course that takes you through the Catskills. You go to Phoenicia, where you can rent tubes from The Town Tinker Tube Rental on Bridge Street. They rent as many as 20,000(!) tubes a summer. (Phone: 845-688-5553; Web site: www.towntinker.com)

One man's junk is another man's treasure. Zaborski Emporium for architectural salvage, antiques and used items can be amazing. How to describe Zaborski's? Well, for one thing you'll definitely find more "used items" than antiques in what is, at least in part, a junkyard. But if you're lucky you'll find just what you've been looking for but can't find anywhere else. Clawfoot tubs are reasonably common. The occasional Stickley chair shows up. I have a friend who found a lock that matched the hardware in her 100-year-old house. That's Zaborski for you. But don't expect bargains. Stan Zaborski, the father, knew how to price his wares and was no fool, and the sons are chips off the old block (which you also may find here). Zaborski Emporium is at 27 Hoffman Street, Kingston. Open: Wednesday–Saturday, 11–5; Sunday, 1–5. The hours can be erratic, so be sure to call in advance. No credit cards. Phone: 845-338-6465. Web site: www.stanthejunkman.com.

In my opinion **Augustus Saint-Gaudens** (1848–1907) was the finest American sculptor of the nineteenth century. Imagine my delight, then, to read of three of his sculptures in the magazine "Hudson Valley." The first, a bronze Jesus, is part of the George F. Baker Memorial in Kensico Cemetery in Valhalla (914-949-0347); the second, a stone angel commemorating John Hudson Hall, is in Sleepy Hollow Cemetery (914-631-0081); and the third, a grouping of a large bronze cross with, on opposite sides, two women, hands raised in supplication, is a memorial for Hamilton Fish and can be seen just north of St. Philip's Church in the Highlands on the west side of Route 9D in Garrison.

Christmas in the Valley is a wonderful time to visit the great houses. All of them have special activities ranging from candlelight tours to sleigh rides. Check their web sites for complete details. (All the web sites are listed in the text.)

Auctions Many people's favorite seems to be **Absolute Auctions and Realty Inc.** (phone: 845-635-3169; web site: wwwabsoluteauctionrealty.com) on South Avenue in Pleasant Valley. It is 7 miles east of Poughkeepsie, a sharp right off Route 44 at Dutchess County 47, and 4 miles from the Taconic, going west on Route 44 for 3 1/2 miles to South Avenue (Dutchess County 47) and then left. The auction hall is a quarter-mile in from 47.

The venture has been a family business since 1946, and it can be a pleasant, fun way to spend an evening. The family handles estates, antiques, paintings, collectibles, glass … in short, something for everyone.

I, personally, am fond of **Copake Auction** (phone: 518-329-1142; web site: www.copakeauction.com), a small organization run by a father and son team, Michael and Seth Fallon, that is off Route 22 on Route 7A in Copake. Copake itself is very near the Connecticut/Massachusetts border in Columbia County. They specialize in Americana, and each year they have a bicycle auction that draws people from all over this country and even abroad, as well as a textile auction that can be very special.

The Bakery, 13A North Front Street, New Paltz 12561. Phone: 845-255-8840. No credit cards. Web site: www.ilovethebakery.com.

This is not as special as Bread Alone (see below), but it's pretty darn good, and on Sunday mornings you will see customers lined up, patiently waiting to get to the counter. In addition, the bakery has a full coffee bar and sandwich menu. There also is an outdoor garden where you can sit and enjoy it all.

Bread Alone, Route 28 (8 miles above the 375 turnoff), Boiceville. Phone: 845-657-3328. Web site: www.breadalone.com.

People, literally, come from miles away to sample these breads, which now are sold in the most select shops in New York City. You can even have your choices delivered anywhere in the country by UPS (12-loaf minimum). Bread Alone uses only organically grown products and bakes in a wood-fired oven. (The pile of wood at the side door is proof of this.) So if you're in the area, make a special point of checking them out. And now there's one in Rhinebeck as well as in Woodstock and Kingston.

Hammertown Barn, Route 199, Pine Plains 12567. Phone: 518-398-7075. Web site: www.hammertown.com.

To visit one of the most attractive shops in the Valley, see page 152.

THE
UPPER HUDSON

*From Saratoga County
to Dutchess County*

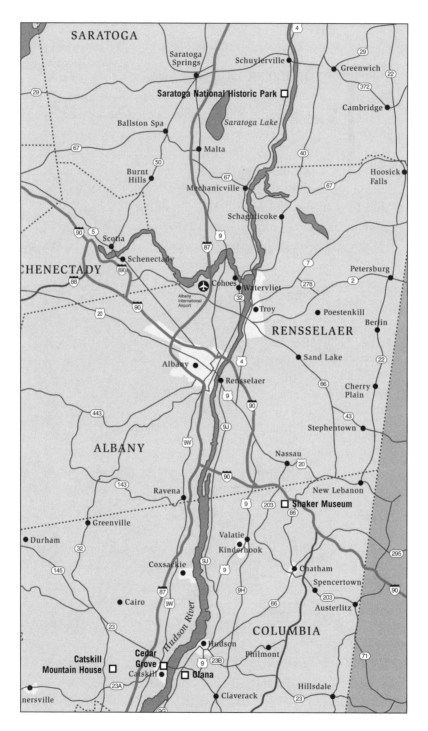

THE UPPER HUDSON communicates a series of vibrantly colored and diverse impressions: jockeys in their brilliant shining silks entering the handsomest of racing courses at Saratoga; at the Catskill Mountain House site looking at blues and greens and browns and russets spreading out for miles to the horizon, defining one of the more spectacular views in the nation; the cold formality of the Albany Mall, looking surreal in its essentially rural environs; gray-white cloud shadows, scudding like ghosts of soldiers above the battlefield of Saratoga; a museum dedicated to the Shakers—this area was their original home—set deep in the countryside within barn-red buildings and filled with exquisite creations echoing a simpler, more direct past. And through it all the Hudson, narrow and placid near Saratoga, vast and filled with traffic at Albany, blue and tranquil and looking rather gentrified at the old estate of Clermont at the southern tip of Columbia County.

The whole area builds like a pointillist painting. Each new experience or sight or building or museum adds another dot to the canvas and finally, once you've seen and felt it all and stand back, there it is, revealed in all its glory: a composition as lovely and complex as you could imagine, the Hudson at its heart, giving it, in many instances, its very reason for being.

The reader might think that, precisely because the Upper Hudson is so diverse, the distances must be great, too. Not so. You can easily drive from Saratoga Springs, the farthest point north, to Clermont in about two hours.

SARATOGA COUNTY

Saratoga Springs

Saratoga Springs, a town of slightly over 26,000 people, is the quintessential American resort. It always has been. By that, I mean that everyone—with money, without money, socially on top or at the very bottom, racing tout or culture buff—did and does come here. They eat in the same restaurants, stay at the same hotels, ignore each other or mix as the mood moves them. It works beautifully. In fact, it's one reason the Springs is so alluring.

Today, more than ever before, it offers something for every taste: ballet, concerts, the baths, all kinds of sports, theater—and, of course, the world-famous track. I love to come here; it has a certain raffish charm quite unlike any other place.

HISTORY

The mineral springs were what originally made the village famous, but although the Indians had known about them for years, it was not until 1771 that the first white man of importance arrived. He was Sir William Johnson, the British general superintendent of Indian Affairs, who was suffering from a wound in his leg that refused to heal. The Iroquois, who were fond of him, bundled Johnson off to what would become known as High Rock Spring, and he later wrote of his "cure."

Nothing much happened after that until the end of the Revolutionary War—people had been too busy fighting to think about "taking the waters"—when Philip Schuyler, member of one of the most prominent families in the area, who had a country estate in what today is Schuylerville but then was the original town of Saratoga, cut a trail through to the spring in 1783 and brought to it such luminaries as Washington (he considered buying property there), Alexander Hamilton (he married Schuyler's daughter Betsy) and New York State governor George Clinton. Other prominent men of the time were soon to follow.

Then, in 1789, Gideon Putnam arrived and saw right away that he was sitting on a gold mine. He bought land near the recently discovered Congress Spring (named that because it was discovered by a member of

A door is a door is a door—except when an imaginative late Victorian decided he wanted it to make a statement.

Congress) and built the Springs' first hotel in 1802. Almost from its start it proved a success, so in 1805 Putnam purchased an additional 130 acres and laid out a village, donating land for a church, school and graveyard. Later would come the elm trees—which throughout the nineteenth century were to be a distinguishing feature of Saratoga—along Broadway, the avenue which Putnam had designed to run by his hotel.

The next big break for Saratoga came in 1826 when Dr. John Clarke, operator of the first soda fountain in New York City, began bottling and shipping water from the springs. By 1830, over 1,000 bottles a day were going out into the world. Saratoga was well on its way to becoming a household word, and the number of visitors began to increase proportionally. (By the end of the 1830s, 12,000 guests were arriving annually.) Dr. Clarke was also responsible for laying the foundations of one of the most pleasant spots in Saratoga, Congress Park. That was the plus side. On the minus end, according to some viewpoints (but not Saratoga's), the 1830s brought the introduction of heavy gambling, and in 1842 a man named Ben Scribner opened the first formal gambling parlor, starting a tradition that would last until the 1950s and for which Saratoga became as well known then as Las Vegas is today.

Two other events around this time helped immensely in the development of Saratoga: the use of steamboats on the Hudson and the introduction of the railroad. Together they changed the trip to the Springs from one that definitely required a cure at its end to a pleasant and relatively relaxing journey. By the 1850s, then, Saratoga was it; no other resort could touch its popularity. It had even caused the invention of the Saratoga trunk, a cavernous object large enough to hold a month's clothing.

In those days, too, a Saratogan made a major contribution to American cuisine. It was fashionable to repair to nearby Lake Saratoga in the late afternoon to dine, and the most famous of the establishments there was called Moon's Lake House, reasonably enough. The chef, George Crum, son of a mulatto jockey and an Indian, was a man with a ferocious temper. He considered himself a superb cook—which he apparently was—and went into a rage if anyone ever dared complain about one of his delectable dishes. On a hectic night in 1853, a man sent back his French fried potatoes demanding they be cut thinner and fried crisper. George was not pleased. He proceeded to slice some potatoes paper thin, wrapped them in a napkin, and then covered them with chunks of ice. After letting his customer cool his heels for half an hour, George threw the equally cool potatoes into boiling oil. Once they were fried to a crisp, he sent them out to the table. A gesture of pure contempt that backfired—for lo and behold, the customer loved them! George had just invented the potato chip, which for many years afterward was known as the Saratoga chip.

The greatest and most flamboyant period of the Springs began with the end of the Civil War and continued until the close of the century, when it seemed that everywhere throughout the nation the opportunities to make vast amounts of money were endless, and those who did usually could think of no better place to spend it than here. They came in droves, and many of their descendants are still returning today.

This was the period of the great hotels, two of which—the Grand Union and the United States—are still talked about. The Grand Union was a five-story behemoth that covered seven acres. Its 450-foot-long façade faced Broadway while at each end was a wing that extended back

The Adelphi Hotel, one of the last remnants of the great nineteenth-century hotels on Saratoga's Broadway whose primary ornaments were their great columned piazzas and fantasy-laden Victorian decorations.

for a whole quarter of a mile. The wings enclosed gardens, shaded by those famous Saratoga elms, and an opera house. There were 824 guest rooms, a main dining room that could serve a thousand at a clip (an additional room could take an overflow of up to 400 diners) and a mile of piazzas filled with hundreds of wicker armchairs.

The United States Hotel wasn't much smaller, but its 50-foot pillars were distinguished by capitals of a singularly ugly Victorian design, some carver's nightmarish vision of jungle foliage. This hotel had "cottages" with as many as seven bedrooms for its better-heeled clientele, but its overall length was only a quarter of a mile. Both the United States and the Grand Union devised a myriad of diverse activities for their guests, including lawn games and concerts every morning, afternoon and evening. (Victor Herbert, among others, conducted here.) It was grand, all right, but it's all gone, like Ozymandias' kingdom in Shelley's poem. ("Look on my works, ye Mighty, and despair! Nothing besides remains . . .") The United States was razed in 1946, the Grand Union in 1952. To add insult to injury, where the Grand Union once stood is now the site of an indescribably boring shopping center.

This was also the era of the great show-offs, some of whom took flamboyance to heights—or depths—rarely rivaled since. Probably the most outrageous in creative vulgarity was Diamond Jim Brady, who made $12 million by the time he was forty selling railroad equipment and whose close companion—they probably were never lovers—was the beauteous, amply endowed Lillian Russell. The stories about Brady are legion. Item: Diamond Jim had thirty sets of jewels, one for (well, almost) each day of the month, that flashed out from everywhere on his person; even his underclothes sported jeweled buttons. In the most fabulous set—all to be worn at the same time, naturally—were more than 2,500 diamonds. Item: One year Brady arrived at the Springs in a silver-plated railroad car with 27 Japanese houseboys. Item: Enormous in girth as well as fortune, Diamond Jim was the possessor, it was said, of a stomach six times the normal size. (I imagine this is why contemporaries figured he wasn't doing much with Miss Lillian.) Brady never drank liquor or wine, but could easily down four gallons of freshly squeezed orange juice during a meal. To very special friends Diamond Jim often proved as generous as Maecenas. Consider the bicycle he gave Lillian: it was gold-plated, the handlebars studded with diamonds and emeralds that formed her initials. It must be said, the actress and the financier fitted in very well with the general Saratoga tone.

WHAT TO SEE AND DO

Racing ■ The racecourse at Saratoga, the oldest in the country, is the Queen Dowager of American tracks. During August, the racing season here, it turns the Springs into the capital of the race world and sets off a whirl of social activities that few other resorts can match.

The course was founded in 1863, when a track was built for thoroughbreds. Almost from the beginning three millionaire turf experts—stockbroker William R. Travers; John Hunter, a famous sportsman of the day; and Leonard Jerome, Winston Churchill's grandfather—were involved. The first season, a four-day, eight-race meeting, was a success, but the partners felt the track was too narrow and the grandstand too small, so they bought 125 acres across the road, landscaped them lavishly, erected a handsome grandstand—and, a year later, they were off and running. (The old course is still in use though, as a training track, and is now known as Horse Haven.) In that year, too, 1864, the Travers Stakes, the oldest and certainly one of the most prestigious racing events in America, was first run.

The track and all the surrounding buildings leave you with a vivid series of impressions: Petunias and flaming red geraniums in boxes everywhere ... The elaborately carved horsehead decorations ... The red-coated outriders escorting the horses and jockeys to the starting gate each day just before the 2:00 p.m. post time ... The canoe in the lake in the infield, painted each year with the colors of the stable whose entry has captured the Travers Stakes ... The elegant grandstand with its peaks and gables giving it a particularly jaunty air ... The stables flying famous racing colors from all over the country ... The thrill of watching the horses go through their early morning workouts while you enjoy breakfast at the track on red-and-white tablecloths, a color combination that seems to especially epitomize this track. (This breakfast ritual at the track anyone can share and no one should miss.) By post time the excitement is palpable. There is a sense of ceremony here, a long tradition that separates this course from all others. You don't even have to like racing to enjoy it. It is indeed the Dowager Queen.

Web site: www.saratogaracetrack.com

The National Museum of Racing and Hall of Fame ■ This museum, located on Union Avenue right across from the track, is unique in the nation. It was formed in the early 1950s to interpret the history and convey the excitement of thoroughbred racing in America. They're well along in their goal; there is, for example, the auctioneer's gavel that closed the sale of Man o' War, the most famous horse of this century, for $5,000 (he went on to win almost $250,000); a re-creation of the studio of the noted nine-teenth-century equine artist Edward Troye; a cane given to a jockey by King Edward VII; a Rembrandt Peale portrait of George Washington, who liked to officiate at race meets; and dozens of other artifacts. There even are examples of the furniture that once graced the Grand Union and United States hotels, as well as an excellent reference library.

The museum underwent a $6 million renovation, completed in 1988, and although the old version was well done, if a trifle stodgy, the new is nothing short of brilliant—a must for any visitor to Saratoga. In fact, the museum now is to thoroughbred racing what Cooperstown is to baseball. Even if you aren't a racing fan you'll enjoy yourself.

Entering the museum, you are immediately aware of the roar arising from the crowd as the horses break away from the starting gate. And there in front of you is a life-size starting gate complete with horses. Put your entrance token in the slot and you, too, are off.

The first two galleries, filled with trophies, prints, paintings, bronzes and other memorabilia, take the history of racing in this country from its beginnings (in the eighteenth century, horses shipped from England stood throughout the more than two-month voyage supported by slings that also protected them in rough weather) through the Civil War. In the next gallery, the visitor learns about the thoroughbred horse. There is a skeleton of a thoroughbred to show its anatomy. There is a discussion of what makes a thoroughbred, and a TV screen that illustrates what we have learned about the horse and movement. Particularly interesting is the fiber-optic board based on *The Stud Book,* kept by the Jockey Club, which demonstrates through thousands of moving lights and dozens of horses' names, the lineage of all thoroughbreds back to the three Arab stallions from whom all thoroughbreds are descended. Simply touch the name of a horse and then watch as his bloodlines are traced back to one or more of the three progenitors.

At the center of the museum is an exhibition called The Racing Day, a splendid evocation of the track with five-minute audio sets describing the professions of America's top trainers, cutout figures of racing types, descriptive texts, wax figures, a replica of the paddock at Hialeah, a wonderful case of racing buttons and badges … in short, fascinating material that covers the race-goer, betting in its various forms, the jockeys, officials, other people who work there and so forth. It is the most pleasurable learning experience possible, and I should point out that labels and text panels

here, as everywhere in the Museum, are models of their kind and antici-
pate all your questions.

Behind this gallery is the Hall of Fame, an auditorium with a large
movie screen at the far end. On each side of the auditorium are television
monitors. Here, through your own selections, you can get complete information on all horses, jockeys and trainers in the Hall of Fame. Running
around the top of the side walls are cases containing racing colors. On the
walls, too, are metal plaques providing a citation for each honoree. (The
one thing I miss from the old museum is a display of more than 200 racing silks belonging to every famous name in this country. Racing colors
originated in Newmarket, England, when it was agreed in 1762 that owners should choose specific colors to be worn by their jockeys and that these
colors would then be reserved for their exclusive use. In this country, most
colors are registered with the Jockey Club.)

Each year between five and eight new Hall of Fame members are chosen by the votes of 100 turf writers throughout the country, and the colors
of the new inductees are placed at the front of the auditorium.

A short film—a little more than 15 minutes—is shown here on a regular basis. Called *Race America,* it is a brilliant, impressionistic montage of
racing from coast to coast that is so well done you must not miss it.

The remaining galleries are equally interesting. There is one, for example,
on The Triple Crown, the winner of which earns America's ultimate racing
accolade. (The Triple Crown consists of the Kentucky Derby, the Preakness
and the Belmont Stakes.) Another gallery deals with famous American racing
families, but my favorite in this last section is a gallery devoted to Saratoga in
the nineteenth century, when she was "Queen of Spas," and includes a superb
realization of a Saratoga bar of the period. Finally, and aptly, the last gallery
explores the August races of today, with witty black-and-white cutouts in the
stands against the walls, and a model of the track in the center of the room
complete to the canoe in the infield lake.

As you leave, be sure to visit the gift shop, which has a selection of
material so complete on racing and horses and related material as to make
browsing here an education in itself.

**Open: During the season, 9–5 daily; other times of the year,
Monday–Saturday 10–4, Sunday 12–4:30. Phone: 518-584-0400.
Web site: www.racingmuseum.org**

The Casino and Congress Park ■ In 1861, John Morrissey, ex-boxer and "enforcer" for Tammany Hall, the notoriously corrupt Democratic machine that ran New York City, opened a gambling casino in Saratoga on what is now Woodlawn Avenue. Born in Troy, New York, Morrissey made his first real money—$5,000—in a boxing match in California during the Gold Rush. Once back in New York, he rejoined the Tammany organization and served it so well that he was rewarded with his own gambling parlor. It proved a success, and soon John was the leading gambler of New York City. But it was to Saratoga that he turned his full attention and talents; he was shrewd enough to recognize that here was the greatest potential moneymaker of his career. He was right.

In 1863, Morrissey helped to start thoroughbred racing; by that time he was a well-established figure on the Saratoga scene. With the end of the Civil War and the influx of the new rich, though, Morrissey saw an even bigger opportunity and bought land adjoining Dr. John Clarke's Congress Spring estate. He then proceeded to build a Club House and landscape the grounds, creating the most impressive gambling establishment in the country. It's still there and is known now as the Casino.

The Club House opened in 1870 and immediately was the rage. It also included an elegant small parlor where women could sip ices, doubtless another reason why the Club House soon became the major center of Saratoga's social life. (To keep the natives from getting restless, Morrissey contributed heavily to local charities and would not allow them to gamble in his establishment—no chance of sour grapes if they couldn't lose their shirts.)

But Morrissey's days of wine and roses and cascading piles of gold were doomed. He made the mistake of taking thoroughly poor financial advice from Commodore Vanderbilt, of all people, and quickly lost $1 million. Added to which, his health was failing. In 1878, at the age of 47, John Morrissey died.

The Club House then passed on to Albert Spencer and Charles Reed for several uneventful years until, in 1894, Richard A. Canfield, "Prince of Gamblers," bought and completely renovated the building, changing its name to the Saratoga Club. By 1900 Canfield was the most famous—and richest—gambler in the nation. Like Morrissey, Canfield had a colorful background. A man of little formal education, he was once thrown in prison for six months for illegal gambling. To while away the hours, he began to read and educate himself. This—and collecting works of art—became Canfield's passion and would remain so for the rest of his life. (James McNeill Whistler and Canfield later became friends, and the artist painted his portrait, slyly calling it "His Reverence.")

In 1902, Canfield bought the land adjoining the Casino and landscaped it into an Italian garden, which is now part of Congress Park. At the same time he also added the stunning restaurant, still the most beautiful room in the Casino building, with its barrel-vaulted ceiling set with octagonal stained-glass windows. Unfortunately, though, the glory days for gamblers were coming to an end as reform sentiment swept across the country. The Casino did not open for the 1904 season, much to everyone's shock and chagrin, and, even worse, Canfield put it up for sale in 1907. No buyers were interested, and in 1911, the village trustees purchased it for $150,000, combining it with the adjacent section of Congress Park,

A section of the Saratoga Casino, once the most elegant and fabulous gambling establishment in the nation and now a fading memory set in a pretty park.

which they had already acquired. Canfield himself died in 1914 in New York City after a fall down a subway stair.

Today the Casino is a pleasant museum displaying the history of Saratoga Springs, including a particularly handsome Victorian parlor with an excellent sampling of furniture by John Henry Belter, the German-born cabinetmaker whose New York City shop turned out some of the finest examples of Victorian furnishings produced in this country. In addition there are other historical rooms, including, on the second floor, the restored private high-stakes gambling parlor complete with table and original interior features, as well as changing art exhibits and a museum gift shop.

**Open: All year. Phone: 518-584-6920 for times,
or e-mail historicalsociety@spa.net**

Saratoga Performing Arts Center (SPAC) ■ In the early 1960s, a group of Saratogans suggested to then-Governor Nelson Rockefeller that a performing arts center would make the perfect addition to Saratoga and could be placed in Saratoga Spa State Park (see below). Rockefeller was enthusiastic and, on June 30, 1964, the official groundbreaking ceremonies took place. The Saratoga Performing Arts Center was completed two years later. Since then it has become one of the major summer festival sites in the nation, each year serving as summer home for the New York City Ballet (July) and the Philadelphia Orchestra (August). In addition, SPAC also presents the Lake George Opera and has a Little Theatre seating 500, which hosts the Chamber Music Festival. From June to September, SPAC presents a broad range of today's top popular entertainers, including the two-day Freihofer's Jazz Festival. This enormously successful formula now attracts more than 450,000 people during the season.

The amphitheater that houses the two major companies lies at the base of a gentle hill. It covers 150,000 square feet and can seat more than 5,000. (The surrounding hillside can absorb thousands more.)

One of my favorite stories about SPAC was told to me by a prime mover in getting the center off the ground, Mrs. Lillian Phipps, who also was prominent in the Saratoga racing world. The first time the Philadelphia Orchestra held a rehearsal, she said, Eugene Ormandy mounted the podium, tapped his baton to call the orchestra to order, and then gave the downbeat. After a few bars he stopped, cocked his head and waved over an assistant. "What's that noise?" he asked. The assistant looked puzzled. "That gurgling," Ormandy elaborated. "That's a stream behind the amphitheater, Maestro." "Stop it at once!" Ormandy ordered. Thousands of dollars later, the offending stream was silenced.

For information, phone: 518-584-9330. Web site: www.spac.org

Saratoga Spa State Park ▪ The park covers 2,200 acres and includes: the Saratoga Performing Arts Center; the Roosevelt baths (the Washington Baths is now the National Dance Hall of Fame [see below]); two golf courses, one with 18 holes; two swimming pool complexes, including one Olympic-sized pool, that can accommodate thousands of people; plus tennis courts, bridle trails and picnic areas. (As for the baths, the Roosevelt is open all year. Reservations required. Phone: 518-583-2880.) During the winter season, the park offers 6.3 miles of marked cross-country trails, ice hockey and ice-skating rinks.

In the early 1900s, so many millions of gallons of the precious waters were being withdrawn by companies who extracted the carbonic gases for carbonating beverages that the citizens of the town began to worry that they might eventually exhaust their major natural resource. So they petitioned the state legislature to create a Saratoga Springs Reservation, which the state did, eventually taking over most of the wells in the Springs.

Then, in 1929, Franklin D. Roosevelt, governor at the time, created a special commission to develop the spa and appointed financier Bernard Baruch as chairman. (Baruch was a particularly apt choice; his father, whom he adored, had long advocated that the spa be developed into a European-style health resort. Today his name is honored by the Simon Baruch Research Laboratory in the park.) Bernard Baruch was not used to doing things in a small way—neither, for that matter, was FDR—and so by 1935 he had created the vast park and spa pretty much as it looks today, including the Gideon Putnam Hotel. Web site: saratogaspastatepark.org.

National Museum of Dance ▪ This, the newest museum on the Saratoga scene, opened in 1986 at 99 South Broadway. It is located in the handsome 1909 Arts and Crafts–style Washington Bath Pavilion at Saratoga Spa State Park and is the nation's only museum dedicated exclusively to professional American film, theater, ballet and modern dance.

Each year exhibitions related to the history of dance are mounted that feature visionary leaders from the dance world.

The highlight of the museum is the Mr. and Mrs. C. V. Whitney Hall of Fame, where masters of American dance are honored. Here you will find everyone from Fred Astaire and Busby Berkeley to George Balanchine and Martha Graham to Ruth St. Denis, Hanya Holm, Jerome Robbins, Agnes de Mille, Alvin Ailey and Bill Robinson. In addition, at the Lewis A. Swyer School for the Performing Arts, visitors can see rehearsals and classes during sessions of the New York State Summer Institute's School of Dance. For a calendar of events, write them at 99 South Broadway, Saratoga Springs 12866.

There also is a gift shop.

Open: Year-round, Tuesday–Sunday 10–5. Phone: 518-584-2225. Web site: www.dancemuseum.org

Yaddo ▨ Of all the glories of Saratoga, this certainly ranks among the most honorable.

In 1881, Spencer Trask (1844–1909), a New York banker who had made a considerable fortune, and his wife, Katrina (1853–1922), purchased several hundred acres just outside the village for a summer home. In 1893, the 55-room Victorian mansion that still stands there today was completed and the Trasks moved in. Then an extraordinary series of tragedies struck. The Trasks' eldest son had died some years before, but now they lost their two remaining children over a short period of time to diphtheria.

Devastated, Spencer and Katrina Trask planned to sell the estate, but then changed their minds and decided to leave it—and their entire fortune—to establish a retreat that today invites writers, visual artists, composers, choreographers, performance artists and film and video artists to work free from all distractions. Yaddo, as it is today, opened in 1926, four years after Katrina Trask's death, and has been a monumental success ever since, harboring at various times such members of the American cultural hierarchy as John Cheever, Aaron Copland, Eudora Welty, Truman Capote, Philip Roth, Milton Avery and Leonard Bernstein. Patricia Highsmith was also a resident there and completed her most famous novel, Strangers on a Train, at Yaddo. When she died, she left her entire estate of about $3 million to the colony, as well as furniture and many of her own books. A welcome surprise, indeed. The public can visit the rose gardens, and the estate grounds are so lovely that it is worth taking the extra time to see them. (The entrance is on Union Avenue, about two miles southeast of the village.)

Web site: www.yaddo.org

A Saratoga Walking Tour ▪ The Springs is not only a treasure trove of Victorian architecture but contains fine examples from other periods, too. You should plan on spending some time just wandering about. North Broadway, for instance, is still a prime street for the great racing families and has house after wonderful house to enjoy. You should certainly see Union Avenue, a wide, formal thoroughfare, with its mansions. Then there's Circular Street, with my favorite Victorian architectural fantasy, the 1873 Batcheller Mansion at No. 20. I'm also very fond of Franklin Square

Saratoga, renowned for its Victorian buildings, can also boast of some remarkably handsome homes from earlier in the nineteenth century.

(take Division Street off Broadway) with its handsome Greek Revival homes. In addition, there are many antique shops in the area, and while you're wandering, you may want to stop in at the Regent Street Art & Antique Center at 153 Regent Street, which is just off Union Avenue in the downtown area. A variety of dealers offer a wide range of antiques. (Open 10–5 daily; closed Monday, Tuesday, Jan., Feb., March.) I'd also strongly recommend an antiquarian bookstore that I defy you to walk away from without at least one purchase. It's called the Lyrical Ballad Bookstore and it's at 7–9 Phila Street, just off Broadway. There is a wonderful selection of old and out-of-print books as well as a nice selection of artwork. Phone: 518-584-8779.

Skidmore College ■ Founded in 1903 by Lucy Skidmore Scribner, the wife of publisher Charles Scribner, the college has now moved to a new 1,200-acre campus off North Broadway. Skidmore also is the home of The Frances Young Tang Teaching Museum and Art Gallery.

For current exhibition information go to www.tang@skidmore.edu or phone 518-580-8080.

Saratoga Lake ■ Three miles east of the village, on Route 9P, Saratoga Lake offers boating, swimming, picnicking and amusement rides in summer, ice-skating and skiing in winter.

Saratoga Gaming and Raceway ■ Open throughout most of the year.

Call 518-584-2110 for exact schedule and times of events. Web site: www.saratogaraceway.com

ENVIRONS OF SARATOGA SPRINGS

The Hyde Collection ■ Located at 161 Warren Street in Glens Falls, 15 miles north of Saratoga Springs, this exceptional little treasure is worth a detour. To whet your appetite, consider that the artworks here range from the late Gothic period to the twentieth century and include everyone from Botticelli and Raphael to Rubens, El Greco and Rembrandt to Ingres, Degas and Renoir to the Americans, Eakins, Homer and Ryder.

The Hyde collection was the lifelong work of Charlotte Pruyn Hyde (1867–1963), who founded the museum in 1952, and her husband, Louis Fiske Hyde (1866–1934). Mrs. Hyde's father was the cofounder of a highly successful paper company in Glens Falls, and that was the source of the family's wealth.

You enter the museum through the Education Wing, designed by Edward Larrabee Barnes and built in 1989. This is the museum's space not only for educational activities but also for concerts and temporary and permanent exhibitions. To the right of this wing is Hyde House, which houses the greater part of the permanent collection. To the left is the administrative building, Cunningham House, the home of a sister of Mrs. Hyde's. (To the right of Hyde House is the home of yet another sister. Originally, all three were connected by walkways and formal gardens.)

Immediately to the left of the main foyer in the Education Wing is the Orientation Gallery and museum shop. To the left and off the center of the foyer are two additional galleries used for temporary exhibitions, approximately eight annually.

On through the connecting corridor and into the house itself, you enter a charming covered courtyard inspired, perhaps, by the more famous house (Fenway Court) and collection of Isabella Stewart Gardner in Boston. Surrounding the courtyard are the dining room, library, reception room and foyer and a guest room. Upstairs, where all but one bedroom open onto the courtyard, are a total of three bedrooms and the music room, the last being the heart of the house and the collection.

The collection consists of approximately 3,000 objects with about 40 percent of this on view at any given time. In addition to the superb collection of paintings and sculpture, Hyde House also is furnished with outstanding examples of Italian Renaissance and French eighteenth-century furniture. Yet with all this splendor, the feeling is one of intimacy and repose; you are drawn in by the human scale and informed taste of the selections rather than overwhelmed by objects demanding, "LOOK AT ME!"

For example, who could forget the wonderful Thomas Eakins in the East Bedroom ("In the Studio—Girl and Dog," ca. 1884), a study in which the white dress of the girl spills down her body like the spume of a waterfall, to spread out at her feet in an agitated pool. Or "The Dance of Salome" (Matteo di Giovanni di Bartolo, 1480) in the outside corridor, with its strictly compartmentalized grouping of Salome, her face a blank study in concentration on her physical movements, while Herodias, at the center, content-edly smiles as she looks at the horror-stricken Herod, cringing before the head of John the Baptist as it is presented to him by a kneeling servant.

The first-floor guest room has a wonderful Childe Hassam, "Geraniums" (1888), the flowers a flickering crimson framing the still fig-ure of a woman reading in a window, and the library, with its floor of rich red hexagonal tiles, has an intensely dramatic "Man in Armor" (ca. 1615) by Peter Paul Rubens. This same room has one of the dopier paintings by Jean-Auguste-Dominique Ingres, a "Paolo and Francesca" (ca. 1855–60) in which Paolo has a neck as long and swanny as Dorothy Parker could have wanted, and a Francesca who simpers fatuously (Is she ticklish?) as she receives the fatal kiss. What a contrast to the Ingres in the dining room ("Study for the Odyssey," ca. 1826–27 and 1866) with its female figure the quintessence of dignified and pensive elegance.

And there's more. Always more. A strangely disturbing "Portrait of Christ" (ca. 1655–57) by Rembrandt that is both deeply human and deeply divine at the same time; a Botticelli "Annunciation" (ca. 1492) that, even though not in the best condition, still radiates power through its strong architecture of verticals and arcs framing the entering angel and the shrinking Mary; the fine kneeling "Virgin Mary" (ca. 1480) of Andrea della Robbia; the "Dancer with Red Stockings" (ca. 1883–85) of Edgar Degas; the small, romantically charged "Landscape Near Castle Bentheim" (ca. 1653) by Jacob van Ruisdael. ... This is a collection to savor at leisure.

Before leaving, be sure to stop in at the small but imaginatively stocked gift shop.

Open: Monday–Saturday 10–5; Sunday 12–5. There are daily tours at 1 and 4. Closed: Monday and national holidays. Admission: Free. Phone: 518-792-1761. Web site: www.hydecollection.org

An Interesting Drive
in Saratoga County and Nearby

This drive is among the most important, historically, in the Hudson Valley. It also offers long stretches of serene mountain beauty, a dreamland of timeless scenery, and enough diversity to satisfy the most avid tourist. I particularly like to take it in the fall; all of the "leaf people" are out in full cry—but mostly in nearby Vermont and, consequently, I can enjoy basically the same beautiful colors and scenery at my own leisurely pace here. On the other hand, if it's your first time, I suggest your doing it in the summer when everything along the route is open to the public.

Start from Broadway, right in the center of Saratoga, and take along a picnic basket as there are no good restaurants to stop at for lunch on this trip. Turn from Broadway onto Route 29 East. This will take you through the outskirts of the town and then you will be out in flat, uninteresting countryside. Not to worry. Soon enough the landscape will gently, almost imperceptibly, turn hilly, with pines and clumps of woods and pretty farms to delight the eye.

After 12 miles you will see the **Saratoga Monument** off to your right, and a sign will direct you to turn here to approach it. This 155-foot granite memorial, completed in 1883, could only have been created in the high Victorian era—it combines wildly disparate Gothic and Egyptian elements fighting for your attention, but time has somehow made it endearing and touching rather than grandiose—and was built to commemorate the surrender of the British commander, General John Burgoyne, to General Horatio Gates on October 17, 1777. It makes a perfect introduction to the whole **Saratoga National Historical Park,** site of the historic Revolutionary battle that marked the turning point of the war. The monument stands on a summit 300 feet high, right where Burgoyne had his camp, and from its top you can take in a good part of the surrounding Hudson Valley and the flats where the surrender took place. The three statues in the outside niches, by the way, represent General Philip Schuyler (east), commander of the American forces during much of Burgoyne's campaign, General Horatio Gates (north), and Colonel Daniel Morgan (west) who led the famous Riflemen. On the south the niche is vacant, in symbolic tribute to Benedict Arnold, the fourth commander, who helped carry the victory but later became a traitor to the American cause, a course of action that may have begun right here, as you will see.

Open daily 9–5. Admission: Free.

Continue down the road that brought you to the monument and you will come into **Schuylerville,** right on the banks of the Hudson, where you will turn right on combined Routes 4 and 32. This was the original town of Saratoga, and it was called Old Saratoga until 1831. By 1702, the Schuyler family had an estate here, and in 1763, Philip Schuyler, the general-to-be, began to develop his property, building the first linen mill in America, among other things; the settlement prospered and grew until Burgoyne and his army approached in 1777, causing a mass exodus.

Today the **Schuyler House** is owned and run by the National Park Service and is on your left just as you cross the bridge leaving the village proper. (Open: Memorial Day to Labor Day, Wednesday–Sunday. Admission: Free. Phone: 518-664-9821.) Rebuilt by Philip Schuyler after the British burned it to the ground during the Saratoga campaign, it's a simple colonial house, though large enough for its time, that provides an

In late summer the entwined scents of new-mown grass and stacked bales of hay perfume the air and have the same yearning appeal as the Sirens' call to Ulysses' men.

interesting insight into local history and further information on the life of Schuyler, but it is by no means as important architecturally as Schuyler's town house in Albany (see page 51).

From here you continue south for about 8 miles to the entrance of the battlefield area itself, and this is a fascinating visit. To tell the truth, I'm not a person who finds it enthralling to examine in detail the various sites of ancient campaigns—I find the maneuvering of the different armies well beyond my comprehension—but this one is extremely well presented, quite clear in the way it is set forth, and stretches out over countryside that is subtly and undeniably lovely.

You should first go to the **Visitor Center** and museum, located on top of Fraser Hill and offering an extensive view of the surrounding landscape that gives you an overall idea of what you will later on see in detail. The museum part of the center features a large topographical map that uses 6,000 fiber-optic lights to illustrate the campaign and battlefield action. A timeline exhibit depicts highlights of the Revolutionary War through archival images and original artifacts, and a short, 20-minute film clearly explains the park's story and sets the proper mood for your tour through this most important site. After this you're ready for the 10-mile drive, which can take anywhere from 30 minutes to four hours. I suggest that you plan on an hour, two at the most. First, though, an explanation of the campaign and what it meant to the course of the American Revolution.

The campaign was the idea of John Burgoyne, called "Gentleman Johnny" by his admiring troops, who convinced the political powers in England that the capture of the Lake Champlain–Hudson River waterways would split the colonies in two, allowing the British to pick up the remaining pieces at their leisure. This was not a new idea; throughout the colonial period this route had been fought over by everyone from the Indians to the French as the most important "highway," strategically and economically, in America.

As Burgoyne wrote, "I have always thought Hudson's River the most proper part of the whole continent for opening vigorous operations. Because the course of the river, so beneficial for conveying all the bulky necessities of any army, is precisely the route that an army ought to take for the great purposes of cutting the communications between the Southern and Northern provinces, giving confidence to the Indians and securing a junction with the Canadian forces. These purposes effected, and a fleet upon the coast, it is to me morally certain that the forces of New England must be reduced so early in the campaign to give you battle upon your own terms, or perish before the end of it for want of necessary supplies."

Burgoyne's general plan was to sweep south from Canada, advancing to Albany, where he would then link up with General Sir William Howe, who had captured New York City in 1776 and would now advance from there up the Hudson.

Howe, though, had other ideas. He was more in favor of a campaign in Pennsylvania to capture Philadelphia, ultimately choosing a sea-route invasion via the Chesapeake Bay. This decision had disastrous results from Burgoyne's point of view because, for various reasons, it delayed the British from starting north from New York until October 3, 1777, and because it allowed General Washington to send men northward without having to worry any longer about the main force of British troops. In retrospect, Howe just didn't seem too interested in this invasion from the north and abandoned it before it was well under way.

In the meantime, Burgoyne was making a brave start with his 8,000-man army, moving south from the St. Lawrence at the beginning of June 1777. At first all went well, the army taking Crown Point, 10 miles north of Fort Ticonderoga, easily enough, and then moving on Ticonderoga itself, which commanded the southern end of Lake Champlain and Lake George and was held by a small number of troops under the American Major General Arthur St. Clair. The fort fell to the British on July 6.

By mid-July, Burgoyne was at Fort Edward. In early August he heard that the Americans had a supply depot at Bennington, Vermont, that would, if captured, solve the problem of his dangerously lengthening supply lines. He promptly sent off troops to capture it. They never even reached the Vermont border. General John Stark and 1,500 of his New Hampshire Green Mountain Boys met the advancing British a few miles west of Bennington. On August 16, they roundly defeated them, killing or capturing more than 900 British soldiers. This defeat, important in itself, of course, also gave a great boost to American morale when it was most desperately needed and helped to bring hundreds of volunteers to General Horatio Gates, who took command of the American army from General Schuyler on August 19. (Another British failure at this same time, on the Mohawk River at Fort Stanwix, caused the loss to Burgoyne of fresh troops coming from Canada who were to join him in Albany.)

Not at all daunted, Burgoyne marched south and crossed to the west bank of the Hudson, where American actions slowed his progress to about a mile a day. By now it was early September and Gates had evolved his own strategy: He moved his troops to Bemis Heights, near Old Saratoga and above the Hudson just where the river turns and forces the Albany road to go along the base of the commanding bluffs. Here Gates waited, with an army that now outnumbered Burgoyne's by about 2,000 men.

On September 19, Burgoyne made his decision; he would attack and force his way through to Albany. The battle raged on all day, but Burgoyne was unable to achieve his objective and thereby lost this round while handing the Americans an important victory.

For more than two weeks now the armies warily faced each other with only minor skirmishes, but the British position was growing weaker by the day. (Benedict Arnold particularly distinguished himself at this time and was furious when Gates failed to single him out in his report to Congress. Some say jealousy was the motive. Whatever the reason, a quarrel developed that led to Gates removing Arnold of his command—and that in turn may have planted the first seeds of treasonable thoughts in Arnold's vain and extremely proud head.) On September 21, the British learned that retreat to Canada had been cut off by troops under Colonel John Brown who had retaken the outworks at Fort Ticonderoga. On October 4 rations were reduced. And over all loomed the threat of the oncoming and, especially for the footsore and weary British, devastating weather of an Adirondack fall and winter.

On October 7, Burgoyne took a gamble and attacked. Once again he failed. It was all over, but still he refused to surrender. Instead, he began to retreat. On the 11th he ordered the buildings on the Schuyler estate to be burned, by now a useless act of destruction. Finally, on October 17, he capitulated and formally surrendered, the first such action by a British army commander on American soil.

The Battle of Saratoga was an extremely important victory for the Americans, one that strongly influenced the entire course of the war. Among other things, it convinced France, at last, to openly join the American side, an event that helped ensure our ultimate victory at Yorktown.

Enough history. Now you're ready for the drive through the battlefield itself. Each stop along the route has its own recorded narration explaining what happened there; stop and listen as you choose. I would suggest, though, that you do visit at least a few of these sites if only because the surrounding countryside and the views are so lovely—the land is mostly open here so you can often see for miles to the mountains in Vermont—and the narration is remarkably good. And then it's quite pleasant to walk along any of the numerous trails, sometimes surprising grazing deer (if you're lucky) and just generally enjoying yourself.

I do have a few favorite stops. I particularly like the Revolutionary monuments—one put up by the Poles to honor Thaddeus Kosciuszko who built the trenches, another to Colonel Daniel Morgan, whose Rifle Corps was so important to the American success, this one erected by a descendant—all of which are simple and have a calm dignity that brings you closer in human terms to the actual meaning of the battles than any history book possibly could. I suppose my favorite stop of all, though, is near the end of the drive where you can get out of your car and look down on the Hudson, smallish and unimpressive here, and then suddenly you

The golden onion domes of the Russian church at the Monastery of New Skete, a startling yet somehow appropriate apparition in a basically New England landscape.

realize how central this river is to our history—and it doesn't look so unimpressive after all. (Tour roads are open from April 1 through November, weather permitting.

The Visitor Center is open daily 9–5. Closed January 1, Thanksgiving and Christmas Day. Phone: 518-664-9821 x224. Web site: www.nps.gov/sara

When you leave the park, turn left and, after about 500 feet, you will see a sign on your right for River Road. Take it. For about two miles it runs along the banks of the river, and the houses alongside have little docks for their speedboats. Who from New York City or lower on the Hudson would believe it? There's even a small farm with cows grazing on the bank, for all the world a seventeenth-century Dutch landscape transported out of time.

At the end you will rejoin the highway and go back into Schuylerville. Here you will turn right on Route 29 East and, once across the river, stay on 29 to **Greenwich,** where you will get on 372. (If you have time, explore Greenwich; it has some stunning houses.)

Once you leave Greenwich you will find yourself in unspoiled country that is entrancing for its rapidly changing views of hills and valleys, handsome farms and general aura of undisturbed tranquillity. It is a twentieth-century version of the "Peaceable Kingdom" come to life. This wonderful road will eventually bring you into **Cambridge,** but if you have the time, turn right at the sign for Center Cambridge and drive for a while, drinking it all in.

Cambridge is a charming, totally unspoiled village—you're in Grandma Moses country here; her hometown of Hoosick Falls is only a few miles farther south. There are a few antique shops on the main street, nothing special, but this gives you a nice excuse to walk around, and they're fun to look through. Then continue on to the traffic light and go straight. Next is a stop sign. Go straight again, and you are on County Route 67. This will take you, in a few miles, to a sign for the singular monastery of the Monks of New Skete. This Russian Orthodox monastery has a small, beautiful church with gold-leaf onion domes; inside are darkly glowing icons. It seems strange to come across such a place of worship in this so-American setting, but for that very reason it is well worth a visit. The monks also operate a gift shop on the grounds with, in particular, handsome icons and delicious foodstuffs. They probably are most famous for breeding, raising, and training German shepherd dogs and have published two books on the subject. The nearby nuns of New Skete operate the kitchens, paint icons and, among other things, sell hand-crafted dog beds and a sinfully delicious chocolate cheesecake.

For information and a catalogue of their offerings, phone: 518-677-3928, web site: www.newskete.com

ALBANY COUNTY

Albany

For its size, and despite what you may have heard about it, Albany is a surprisingly interesting city. A pleasant old Dutch town in the nineteenth century—"Antique Albany," Henry James called it; his grandfather made the family fortune there and James always had a soft spot in his heart for the city—but it was definitely on the skids by the time World War II ended. It still remains the butt of gibes and jokes, in much the same way as W. C. Fields thought of Philadelphia. But, also like Philadelphia, people were laughing so hard at all the jokes they didn't notice that the city has suddenly been revived and is blossoming. The Empire State Plaza, for one example, has had a genuine revitalizing effect on Albany's downtown core, and many of the down-and-out city blocks are being reborn as handsome urban dwelling areas as people buy and restore the houses. But there's more, much more, than that. Albany, as you'll see, has a lot to offer.

HISTORY

With a population of slightly more than 100,000, Albany wouldn't exist without the Hudson. It lies at the head of the navigable part of the river, about 145 miles from the Atlantic Ocean, and is, after New York City, the river's greatest port and this country's sixth largest.

It is possible that French traders were trafficking with Indians here well before Henry Hudson sailed up the river in 1609. But it was his "discovery" that gave impetus to settling the area, which was accomplished by 1614, making it the second oldest permanent settlement in the original thirteen colonies. The reason for this interest on the part of the Dutch: Beaver and other skins were brought here by the Indians from as far distant as Lake Superior over the ancient Iroquois trail, and the Dutch West India Company could smell the potential profits all the way from Amsterdam. (The Dutch West India Company, which operated from 1621 to 1791, was chartered by the Dutch government and controlled all trade in New York—or New Netherland—until the English conquered the colony in 1664.)

In 1629, the Dutch West India Company came up with an idea to gain more stability for the settlement, then known as Fort Orange. This was a new version of the feudal manorial concept that became known as the patroon system, the patroon being the lord of the manor. Very briefly, it meant that extensive land and manorial privileges would be granted to the patroon for settling a colony of 50 or more people.

The family that became most famous as patroons were the Van Rensselaers, and their first patroon was Kiliaen. By the mid-seventeenth century, this patroonship—called Rensselaerswyck—was so vast that it extended over 700,000 acres and included what today is Albany County as well as parts of Columbia and Rensselaer counties. The tenants on Kiliaen Van Rensselaer's lands—immigrants and settlers—were required, among other duties, to give him one-third of their crops in rent. When the English arrived they continued the system, and it wasn't until the 1840s that it finally ended. The last patroon, Stephen Van Rensselaer III, known as Stephen III, founded Rensselaer Polytechnic Institute (1824) and also played a key role in the development of the Albany Institute (see page 48). When Stephen III died in 1839, his heirs tried to realize the monies owed the estate—about $400,000, an enormous fortune at the time—in uncollected rents. Open resistance followed, involving land tenants as far south as the town of Hudson, and the whole affair became known as the Anti-Rent Wars. Finally, in 1846, the state outlawed the feudal practice of land-lease that could claim rent or service. Samuel Eliot Morison, in his *Oxford History of the American People*, points out that this system made New York the most aristocratic of the colonies and caused it to be the most Tory of the 13 during the Revolution.

The settlement prospered on its fur trade, and the only change the English instituted when they captured the colony was to change its name of Fort Orange to Albany in honor of its new proprietor, James, duke of Albany and of York and later James II, king of England. In 1686 Albany was chartered as a city—after settling the Van Rensselaers' claims to owning the place outright—and from then until the Revolution it slowly grew, with agriculture eventually replacing the fur trade.

Once independence was gained, the city entered into a new era and, thanks to its excellent turnpike system and central location, quickly became the gateway to the West for New Englanders as well as capital of the state in 1797. Then, with the completion of the Erie Canal in 1825, linking Lake Erie and the other Great Lakes with the Hudson and the Atlantic Ocean, the city boomed, its population doubling in a few years. And, as the railroads developed, Albany became a nerve center for this form of transportation, too, tying together the Northeast with the rapidly expanding West. By the mid-nineteenth century, Albany was the financial center of upstate New York and a major link between east and west, two positions the city still holds today.

As I mentioned at the start of this section, Albany fell on hard times after World War II when the population moved out to the suburbs and

Albany's famous (or infamous) Mall, with the State Capitol at the end. To the right is The Egg. The false story—but accurate description—is that Nelson Rockefeller designed it by placing a grapefruit half on a container of cream.

began avoiding downtown for the more convenient malls. Unlike other cities, though, Albany got Nelson Rockefeller as resident governor, and he soon decided he was going to convert this sow's ear into a magnificent silk purse. In fact, he repeatedly said that his plans would make Albany one of the most beautiful capitals in the world.

WHAT TO SEE AND DO

The Nelson A. Rockefeller Empire State Plaza (The South Mall) ▪ In 1959, as part of the celebration of the 350th anniversary of Henry Hudson's discovery of the Hudson, Governor Rockefeller received Princess Beatrix of the Netherlands in Albany. Driving her to the Executive Mansion, he was so embarrassed by the tawdriness of their surroundings that he decided, then and there, that the city must be revitalized—and thus the concept for the South Mall was born.

It makes a wonderful story, and it is true that the governor was mortified every time an important visitor came to Albany—but contrary to what you may be told, this was only one factor in Rockefeller's decision to build the South Mall. Long before that, he'd been wrestling with the problem of a severe shortage of office space for state government employees. And then, of course, there was his own family's precedent: Back in the thirties, Rockefeller Center in New York City had shown what could be brilliantly done to revitalize a dying urban core.

Rockefeller and his aides decided that the present site was ideal because, first, it would allow them to incorporate the Capitol Building in their plans; and second, the 98.5 acres probably could be had at a reasonable overall price. In July 1962, the project, soon to develop into one of the largest and most expensive ($2 billion) in history, began.

Rockefeller's choice for the chief architect was Wallace K. Harrison, who had been deeply involved in the creation of Rockefeller Center, the United Nations headquarters and, at the same time he was working on the South Mall, the development of Lincoln Center, all in New York City. All were pet projects of the Rockefeller family, and Harrison had been close to Nelson, in particular, for years.

On a plane from New York to Washington the governor told Harrison what he wanted, outlining his ideas on the back of a postcard. In the main area, the South Mall would consist of four small office buildings based on a skyscraper design Harrison had never yet realized but that had fascinated Rockefeller for years; the plan is distinguished by the fact that each building is "held" by a 23-story "clamp" that contains the elevator shafts and building services. There also would be a 44-story office tower, the tallest in the state outside Manhattan, a convention center, the Legislative Office and Justice buildings and the Swan Street Building—the latter structure a quarter of a mile long. (The Cultural Education Center, housing the state library, state archives and state museum, and the Performing Arts Center—The Egg— would come later.) All of these buildings would be placed on an immense platform consisting of five stories that would be a quarter of a mile long and an eighth of a mile wide, making the platform itself one of the largest structures in the world. This would serve not only as protection from Albany's notorious winters but would also contain dozens of shops and the South Mall's world-class collection of modern paintings and sculpture. It was Rockefeller, too, who wanted the eastern edge wall—the South Mall's best feature and so striking when seen from the city below; his inspiration supposedly came from the monastery walls he had been so impressed by in Tibet.

From the beginning the project was plagued with problems: delays, cost overruns, strikes … you name it. Finally, in 1978, with the completion of The Egg, the South Mall was done. Years behind schedule, true, and hundreds of millions of dollars more than the original published estimates, but there it finally sat. So what, in fact, did the state of New York get for those two billion dollars?

Aesthetically, I don't find the Mall all that interesting in its parts. The four Agency buildings, with the C-clamp configuration Rockefeller so admired, are minimally effective and then only through repetition. The office tower is banal, but it does have a free observation deck. The five-block-long Swan Street Building is not only in harsh contrast to the surrounding residential neighborhood, but totally boring in execution as well. The Egg, supposedly designed to provide an effective counterpoise to the strong verticals and horizontals of the other buildings, is, instead, lumpish and faintly threatening. There is a story that Rockefeller designed the building by placing a grapefruit half over a container of cream. It's not true, but it's also not a bad description of what he got. The Justice, Legislative Office and Cultural Education Center buildings are completely undistinguished. The Education Center is particularly irritating to me; the grand staircase leading up to it usually can't even be used to gain access to the building—the doors are kept locked. Supposedly, Harrison thought this was his best contribution to the Mall, but it's only ponderous.

Still, the South Mall has had an undeniably beneficial impact on Albany; the surrounding houses and office buildings are being carefully and beautifully restored and the Plaza itself is in constant use, providing an extremely welcome oasis in this urban setting. One nice touch—the steps in front of the Cultural Education Center may lead nowhere, but they can and do serve as bleachers for concerts and other events on the Plaza. The overall problem is that the Plaza is not a welcoming space. It's handsome enough with its trees and pools, but it's just too big and official-looking. Has it turned Albany into one of the most striking capitals, as Rockefeller envisioned? Could be. It is unique and vast and monumental and severe and striking and many other things. But it is not beautiful.

The single most interesting aspect of the Mall—and certainly a prime reason for you to explore it—is the **art collection** acquired by the state under Rockefeller's direction during construction of the Plaza in the 1960s and '70s. Originally, all the works of art included were to have been created by New York artists, and most of them still do meet this criterion. There are 92 paintings and sculptures in a collection that originally cost just under $2 million and is vastly more valuable today. The sculptures are scattered about the Plaza and on the Concourse below. The paintings are along the Concourse. Some of the legendary names you will encounter: Alexander Calder, Adolph Gottlieb, Helen Frankenthaler, Philip Guston, Isamu Noguchi, Robert Motherwell, David Smith, Louise Nevelson, Claes Oldenburg. The collection constitutes a magnificent retrospective of American art at a particularly vibrant time in its history. Tours of the art collection can be arranged on weekdays by calling a week in advance for an appointment.

Admission: Free. Phone: 518-473-7521. Free Acoustiguide tours are available from 9–3.

You should also go up to the Tower Building observation deck, from which you can see for miles. (Open: Monday–Friday 9–3:45; Saturday, Sunday and holidays 10–3:45. Closed January 1, Thanksgiving and Christmas Day. Admission: Free. Please call in advance for schedule verification. Phone: 518-474-2418.) The **New York State Museum** is fun, too, particularly for kids, and has thousands of historical and scientific objects for you to see. Three permanent displays are on view: New York Metropolis, Adirondack Wilderness and Native Peoples. The museum also offers a dozen changing exhibits each year.

The overall idea of these displays is to re-create aspects of life at different times and places in the state, and this is so beautifully accomplished that the museum has become a major tourist attraction.

In the Adirondack Wilderness section, ranging in time from 4,000 years ago to today, you hear a blue jay calling from a tree, watch old films of the great logging days and wander through exhibits covering everything from camping and fishing to Adirondack resort history to models of animals and birds in their native habitats. In the New York Metropolis exhibit, my own favorite, you can see a replica of a tenement sweatshop or explore a 1940s version of a subway car or peer at people dining in turn-of-the-century Delmonico's or study old fire engines. And the Native Peoples exhibition begins over 10,000 years ago with a life-size diorama of mastodons in the Lower Hudson Valley opposite Storm King Mountain. Other dioramas show different peoples who inhabited the region beginning in the Ice Age and continuing through the Iroquois. These exhibits are a cornucopia of life in New York State, and many of the visual displays are supplemented by award-winning films and/or narration. Three other very special sections: the first two are a nineteenth-century working carousel in the Windows on New York exhibition, and, also for kids, the museum's Discovery Place, which offers hands-on learning experience (the latter is open from 10–4:30); the third is World Trade Center: Rescue, Recovery, Response, which documents our nation's worst terrorist attack. Give yourself at least two hours to see it all.

Within the museum, too, is a book and gift shop with a collection of books on New York State.

The New York State Museum is open daily 9:30–5, except on January 1, Thanksgiving and Christmas Day. Admission: Free. Phone: 518-474-5877. Web site: nysm.nysed.gov

The State Capitol ■ If the Mall is formed of straight lines, vertical and horizontal, the Capitol is all exuberant curves, angles and disparate styles and, thankfully, very much in joyous contrast to its neighbor. It is an immense relief, after trudging through the Mall, to come upon the Capitol, quaint and cozy by comparison, and a fascinating building to visit. Nevertheless, the two complexes do have a couple of things in common; in particular, they both took forever to build (1867–99 for the Capitol) and both involved immense outlays of money. Two of the four staircases, the Great Western and the Eastern Approach, cost well over $1 million each, and the whole structure exceeded $25 million, far more than any other capitol building in the nation and twice as much as the one in Washington. By the way, it is also one of the few capitols without a dome.

The history of the building is a saga in itself. The first architect to become involved was Thomas Fuller, responsible for the Gothic parliament buildings in Ottawa. Fuller was chosen by the state to erect his winning design for an edifice that was essentially Italian Renaissance in style. He went energetically to work but, by 1876, had managed to spend a great deal more money than anyone had anticipated, and besides, somewhat belatedly, the legislature decided they didn't like his plans for the interior. Out he went.

In came Leopold Eidlitz and Henry Hobson Richardson. Here the story takes on a more Byzantine complexity. Eidlitz, an immigrant from Prague, loved anything Gothic and also had a passion for the Near Eastern approach to ornament, in particular a mélange of Moorish and Saracen elements. One of his more astounding contributions along these lines was P. T. Barnum's house in Bridgeport, Connecticut, called, aptly enough, "Iranistan." Eidlitz, not as well known now as Richardson, was extremely important to mid-nineteenth-century American architecture and is recognized as a major architectural theorist. It was his belief that a building's relationship to its purpose, both mundane function and societal symbolism, should determine its form. In addition, he was one of the founders of the American Institute of Architects (1857) and a fellow at the Royal Institute of British architects.

Richardson—who would die at age 48 in 1886, before the building's completion—was one of the great architects in American history. His masterpiece is Trinity Church in Boston, but he also built City Hall in Albany, just across the park from the Capitol. Richardson was particularly fond of the Romanesque style and adapted its forms and principles to his own highly idiosyncratic approach. Both Charles McKim and Stanford White worked with him (see page 139) and, later, Frank Lloyd Wright studied Richardson's buildings with great care.

The Great Western Staircase in the Capitol. Designed by H.H. Richardson, it offers a seeming infinity of magnificent stone carvings quite fascinating to explore.

But on with the story. By the time these two men were chosen, the first two floors of the building had been completed—in grandiose Italian Renaissance style. Not at all disconcerted, they drew up their own, totally different plans for the remaining three stories—and somehow got them approved. So what you see today is practically a short-order history of architecture in one single building. The first two floors are Italian Renaissance, as noted; the third is some kind of hybrid transitional to the fourth, which is Romanesque; and the fifth is French Renaissance. To read about it beforehand is to expect architectural anarchy, I grant you, but take a close look at it: somehow it does all come together and emerges a unified whole.

Eidlitz and Richardson divided the interior between them; Eidlitz, for instance, took the Assembly Chamber (called the "most monumental interior in the country" when it opened in 1879) and the Senate Staircase, Richardson the Senate Chamber and the Great Western Staircase, called now "the million-dollar staircase" even though it cost half again as much.

The Senate Chamber has been termed the most beautiful legislative hall in this country. That may be taking it a bit too far, but it is a remarkable tour de force and shouldn't be missed. A large sum of money was appropriated for its decoration, and Richardson was just the man to spend it. Consider his materials and colors: golden onyx from Mexico, rich brown mahogany from the Caribbean, deep red leather for the chairs and for some of the paneling, gold leaf and yellow sienna marble, red granite and pink marble and stained glass. The effect isn't dazzling—the colors are too soft—but there is a warmth and opulence and overall masculinity well suited (at the time, anyway) to the highest legislative body of the Empire State. For once the legislators got what they paid for. Richardson even designed the furniture, including the extremely handsome tall-case clock you see to the right front of the chamber. The massive fireplaces were to have been carved according to sketches by Stanford White, who was working with Richardson at that time; unfortunately, the carving on the fireplace was never executed. Even so, the chamber remains formidably impressive, especially now that it has been completely restored to its original splendor, and visiting it is an enlightening experience. Maybe it *is* the handsomest legislative chamber after all.

Other than this chamber, the most interesting parts of the interior are the Senate Staircase and the Great Western Staircase. For the Senate Staircase, Eidlitz decided to indulge his passion for the Gothic, including a rose window form set within the staircase itself. Far more interesting was another idea of Eidlitz's: to illustrate all kinds of life forms in carved stone on the arabesques that border the stairs from the bottom to the top. At the bottom are forms of sea life—no figure is repeated, by the way—and at the very top are an elephant and a camel. It works wonderfully, the carvings are extremely well done, and the progression of life forms gives the staircase a sense of "flow" it would otherwise lack.

The Great Western Staircase is another Richardson extravaganza. The stairwell measures 77 by 70 feet and from floor to skylight the distance is 119 feet. It was begun in 1884, structurally completed in 1897, but the last figures, the sumptuous work of Isaac Perry, weren't carved until 1898. As I mentioned earlier, it cost about $1.5 million to complete. So much for statistics. The fact is that you could look at it for hours on end and still not see it all because of the near fantastical number of carvings that, vine-like, decorate so much of the surfaces. Most of the heads are historical—there, for one, is James Fenimore Cooper, surrounded by characters from his *Leatherstocking Tales*, while around the corner Civil War Major General Winfield Scott Hancock looks bravely out at the world. Harriet Beecher Stowe may be smiling, but Susan B. Anthony is definitely not amused. In the "Poet's Corner" Walt Whitman barely emerges from the surrounding foliage, while William Cullen Bryant stares heavenward in a confident manner. Washington is there, of course, and Hamilton and Franklin and Lincoln and Grant. On and on it goes, a veritable national portrait gallery in stone, a delight to the eye and to the senses and a magnificent tribute to the dying art of the stone carver and, in particular, to Isaac Perry.

The stone carvers—at one time more than 600 cutters and carvers worked on the building—were given one other magnificent project, the Eastern Approach staircase on the front of the Capitol. Here the carvings are either generally symbolic (a farmer, a freed slave), or of animals and birds and flowers (an owl, a raccoon, bison, roses, clematis), or else idealized concepts—Plenty (feminine) and Progress (male) stand guard over the entrances to the porte cochere, for example, the two most elaborate carvings on the entire building. And, once again, you can spend as much time as you like exploring the staircase without ever exhausting its possibilities.

It is, yes, a unique building and very definitely worth seeing.

Guided tours weekdays, 10, 12, 2 and 3; weekend tours at 11, 1 and 3. Free Acoustiguide tour available weekdays, 9–3. Closed January 1, Thanksgiving and Christmas Day. Admission: Free. Please call in advance for schedule verification. Phone: 518-474-2418.

The Albany Institute of History & Art ■ 125 Washington Avenue. The Institute is a rarity, a brilliant, many-faceted gem of a regional museum that, since this area was extremely rich and diversified in its art of the eighteenth and nineteenth centuries, has been able to amass collections which go beyond the strictly regional to form part of the mainstream of our national cultural heritage. There is much here that's vital to any understanding of how American art developed. In particular I'm thinking of the Institute's extensive holdings in folk art, its canvases of the Hudson River School, and various exhibits of New York furnishings. There also is a surprising selection of Egyptian artifacts. If any of these interest you, a visit here is all but imperative.

Although a forerunner of the present Institute opened in 1791, making it one of the oldest museums in the country, it wasn't until 1824, with the merger of the Albany Lyceum of Natural History and the Society for the Promotion of Useful Arts, that the present organization began to take shape. Then, in 1898, the Albany Gallery of Fine Arts was added, and finally the revised and expanded society moved into its current quarters in 1907. In 1926, its present title was adopted and today, according to its bylaws, the Institute's mission is "dedicated to collecting, preserving, interpreting and promoting interest in the history, art and culture of Albany and the Upper Hudson Valley Region. The museum achieves this mission through its collections, exhibitions, education programs, library, research projects, publications and other programs offered to the general public."

The collections are on two floors, and to describe them in detail would overload you with information you don't need. Suffice it to say that the Hudson River School collection includes superb examples by Thomas Cole, Asher B. Durand, Frederic Church, John F. Kensett and Jasper Cropsey, to drop only a few names. As for the folk-art canvases from the nineteenth century, almost every one is top drawer and you'll probably come across several that seem strangely familiar—for they are often reproduced in books and on posters as prime examples of Americana.

I have certain favorites—as usual—and I particularly like the collection of early American paintings that, in its size and overall quality, is genuinely splendid.

Done, basically, between 1700 and 1750 in the Hudson River Valley, this group of canvases, mostly by anonymous artists, represents the first significant work by any group of painters in this country. To see so many of them together is overwhelming, but a description of only three should give you some idea of what to expect.

My favorite is the life-size, full-length portrait of Ariaantje Coeymans (Mrs. David Ver Planck), painted about 1717 and attributed to Nehemiah Partridge. This lady was born in Albany in 1672 to a Dutch émigré father who proceeded to make a fortune and owned a great deal of land in the area. Ariaantje married Ver Planck at the age of 51—he was only 28—and died in 1743 at what was then considered the ripe old age of 71.

In this portrait Ariaantje seems encased in her no-nonsense steel-gray dress with its black and brown trim and stiff, symmetrical folds. Her feet, large and ungainly, look more like balancing supports than part of her body, and in her outstretched hand she holds a red rose. Her face, though, is wonderful—not beautiful, but strong and filled with character and life, while her eyes and slight smile indicate a woman of high intelligence and no little humor as she looks out at the viewer, inviting him to share her pleasure. The background, an Italianate view in shades of pink, has been traced to a mezzotint of Lady Bucknell (ca. 1686) after Sir Godfrey Kneller, although here it has been greatly changed. It was not unusual at this time for artists to use mezzotints after English portraits as inspiration for their backgrounds and poses. What makes this picture so breathtaking, though, is its overall impression of great strength and honesty. Awkward it may appear, but in its straightforwardness and independence in execution from contemporary European models, this could only be an American painting.

The second canvas is completely different and is attributed to Pieter Vanderlyn (ca. 1687–1778), grandfather of John (see page 107). (Pieter came to this country from Holland via Curaçao around 1718. He first lived in Albany, then Kingston.) It is a portrait from about 1725 of Pau de Wandelaer, son of a prosperous family who lived in both Albany and New York City. The colors are subdued and soft, browns and buffs, and the boy stands in front of us with an almost mystical expression, a small bird perched on one hand, the other thrust inside his shirt. The background, one of the first depictions of the Hudson, underscores the mystical feeling with its small sloop, lying empty and at anchor. There is a dreamy quality about the whole, a sort of fading vision of a primitive, childhood Eden that the boy is losing as he approaches manhood. It is a superior example of inner psychology given outward expression.

The third portrait is of Mrs. Petrus Vas and was probably painted by Gerardus Duyckinck (1695–1746). As in the Pau de Wandelaer portrait, the colors are muted—brown, blue, gray—but the overall effect is totally different. Mrs. Vas wears a gray-white shawl that sets off her long, elegant face as in a frame and whose ends fall almost to her waist. Seated, her exquisite hands relaxed and in full view, she neither questions nor demands; there is an aura of delicacy about this portrait that borders on the chaste. A woman of great refinement and depth, this Mrs. Vas, who keeps a discreet distance between herself and the viewer yet whose eyes are so veiled with experience you keep going back to the picture to try and penetrate her secrets.

One other artist should be mentioned and that is Ezra Ames (1768–1836), whose daughter married William James, the uncle of novelist Henry James and philosopher William James. (Her portrait, done by her father, is in the Institute collection.) Known as the portrait painter of Albany, Ames was not among the greatest of his day, but when he had an interesting subject he could catch his or her characteristics with a vigorous intelligence that makes him worthy of respect.

Open: Wednesday–Saturday, 10–5; Sunday, 12–5.
Closed: Monday and major holidays. Phone: 518-463-4478.
Web site: www.albanyinstitute.org

HISTORIC HOUSES OF ALBANY

Schuyler Mansion State Historic Site ■ Of all the historic houses in Albany this is by far the most interesting and beautiful. If you have time to visit only one, the Schuyler Mansion should definitely be your choice. Philip John Schuyler, who built the house, was born on November 10, 1733, into an extremely prominent family who had first arrived in this country in 1650. He became a successful businessman himself and at one time was said to own 125,000 acres of land in the upper Hudson area. In 1755, Schuyler married Catharine Van Rensselaer of Crailo (see page 55); he began to build the present house six years later. In 1761, during a trip to England, Schuyler bought vast amounts of goods for the house. In those days, it stood on 80 acres of land at the southern end of the city, high on a ridge, and offered lovely views of the Hudson and the Catskills far to the south, while 12 acres of lawns and gardens surrounded the building itself.

As the Revolution approached, Schuyler sided with the patriots and was named a delegate to the Second Continental Congress. A close friend of George Washington he later was commissioned a major general in command of the Northern Department, an appointment that would become his grief, for he was removed—unjustly, most historians believe—just before the Battle of Saratoga (see page 33) and the major share of the glory for that victory went to General Gates. Schuyler was later exonerated completely of any wrongdoing. After the battle, the defeated General Burgoyne was Schuyler's guest for a time, and he also entertained Washington, Franklin and Lafayette, among others. In 1780, his daughter, Elizabeth, married Alexander Hamilton in this house.

Schuyler led an active public life after the war and became a U.S. senator in 1789. He also was prominent in state government, serving two terms as state senator. He died in 1804, and the mansion was sold out of the family. Finally, in 1912, the state of New York bought the house. The current restoration reflects research done over the next several decades.

Today the Schuyler Mansion remains one of the most beautiful Georgian houses in the state. Built of rose-red brick, its most striking features on the exterior are the double-hipped roof with its six dormer windows and a particularly exquisite Chinese-fret roof balustrade, and the hexagonal entrance vestibule, added ca. 1815 and giving the house a peculiar uniqueness that I enjoy, although architectural purists inevitably cringe when they see it.

Inside, the house is divided in half on each floor by a very wide and beautifully proportioned hallway, with two spacious rooms on each side. A few highlights here, just to give you a taste of the whole: The staircase, shipped from Boston, has three different balusters, beautifully carved, on each stair; the formal parlor contains a magnificently ornamented chimney piece (mantelpiece, to us modern-day Americans) with a broken-scroll pediment and Philadelphia marble facings, not to mention superb ornamental carving throughout the room. The house is undergoing interior restoration. The woodwork is painted to reflect the eighteenth-century colors of Schuyler's choice, and the restoration includes installation of flocked wallpaper of the type Schuyler purchased in England. The times I have been there, few other visitors have gone through the house with me, so it's a safe bet that you, too, will have your guided tour pretty much to yourself.

The house is at 32 Catherine Street on the south side of Albany, between Morton Avenue and Delaware Street.

It is open: Wednesday–Saturday 10–5, Sunday 1–5 from mid-April to June; open Tuesday through Sunday, June–August. In winter the mansion

is open by appointment. Phone: 518-434-0834. Closed holidays
except Memorial Day, July 4 and Labor Day. In the visitor center there
is an exhibition featuring family objects and a model of the estate.
Web site: www.nysm.nysed.gov/albany/loc/schuylermansion.html

The Ten Broeck Mansion ■ My favorite story about this house took place
in 1977. Someone happened to be exploring the old wine cellar and came
across a cache of nearly 25 cases of Burgundies and Bordeaux that had been
bottled in the 1870s and '80s. About half the bottles were intact and realized $45,000—one bottle sold for just under $3,000—at special auctions
that drew wine connoisseurs like flies to honey. The proceeds went to such
mundane projects as repairing the roof and installing a new furnace.

Like the Schuylers, the Ten Broecks were an old Albany family, the
first Ten Broeck having arrived on these shores in 1626 with Peter Minuit,
the first governor of New Netherlands and the man who bought
Manhattan for $24. One early Ten Broeck, namely Abraham, married
Elizabeth Van Rensselaer (did a Van Rensselaer ever marry a bum?), grew
increasingly prosperous, gained some renown for his leadership at the
Battle of Saratoga and eventually went on to become mayor of Albany, a
member of the State Senate and president of the city's first bank. Abraham
built this mansion in 1798 after his first house had burned to the ground.
In 1810 he died, and 38 years later the house passed from the Ten Broecks
into the hands of the Olcott family, one of whose members built the
executive mansion (see page 54). The Olcotts lived in the house that
Abraham built until 1947, when they gave it to the Albany County
Historical Association.

The house is Federal on the exterior with a Georgian plan—four
rooms to a floor—inside. Unfortunately, in 1850 some major architectural changes were made, but it does contain some choice examples of Federal
furniture and portraits, and fine nineteenth century pieces, many by local
craftsmen. Also of interest are the Greek Revival entrances and interior
doorways, which were added later, and the ca. 1850 butler's pantry with a
silver safe and, finally, the ca. 1890s bathrooms.

The house is located at 9 Ten Broeck Place and is open
May–December, Thursday–Sunday 1–4. Closed: Monday, Tuesday,
Wednesday and holidays. Phone: 518-436-9826.

Historic Cherry Hill ■ If you never thought that a house could be crazed and boring while containing some beautiful things, check out Cherry Hill. Built in 1787, the house was originally part of a 900-acre farm that belonged to Philip Van Rensselaer. A pretty frame structure in the Georgian style, but extensively remodeled inside, it remained in this branch of the family until the last member died in 1963 and left it to the group that now operates it, Historic Cherry Hill.

The house is jammed to the rafters with some good—even superb— things and a whole lot of junk: Kerosene lamp collections and old kitchen utensils and dolls vie with excellent china examples and unique textiles. You get the idea. According to their own material, there are 30,000 manuscripts "and 20,000 objects including 7,500 textiles, 1,500 pieces of ceramics, 750 pieces of furniture, 3,000 examples of silver and decorative arts, 600 paintings and other fine art, 2,500 household implements, 5,000 books, and 3,000 photographs—all associated with one family." If you are a scholar of this period, it's a gold mine. But otherwise it's a stretch.

Still, there is one fascinating event connected with Cherry Hill—a rather gruesome murder. It involved Elsie Whipple, the ward of Philip Van Rensselaer and his wife's niece, and her lover, one Jesse Strang, who had earlier feigned his own murder to escape from his family. Together, Elsie and Jesse bumped off Elsie's husband, John. Jesse swung for it, but Elsie got off scot-free thanks to her influential connections. Jesse's execution took place on the present location of the Mall and attracted more than 30,000 people who came from all over the county to watch him die.

Cherry Hill is located at 523 South Pearl Street and is open: April–June, October–December, Tuesday–Friday, tours at 10, 11, 12, 1, 2, 3; Saturday at 10, 11, 12, 1, 2, 3; Sunday at 1, 2, 3. July–September, Tuesday–Saturday, tours at 10, 11, 12, 1, 2, 3; Sunday at 1, 2, 3. Closed: January–March, Mondays, major holidays. Phone: 518-434-4791. Web site: historiccherryhill.org

The Executive Mansion ■ This building, the original part of which was built by Thomas Olcott in the 1850s (see page 53), has many of the characteristics of the Queen Anne style—clustered chimneys, lots of turrets, gables and porches and a tower—but little of the beauty. Big and rambling, without much warmth, this place is enough of an atonement for any sins the governor may commit; after all, he's got to live there throughout his term. There is, however, a very decent art collection.

The Mansion is at 138 Eagle Street, one block south of the Mall.
Tours are available, Thursdays at 10, 11, 12, 1 and 2.
Admission: Free. Reservations required two weeks in advance.
Phone: 518-473-7521.

ENVIRONS OF ALBANY

Crailo State Historic Site ■ Just across the river in Rensselaer, this house was probably built in the early eighteenth century by Hendrick Van Rensselaer and is named after the Van Rensselaer's estate in the Netherlands; in Dutch, the name means "crow's woods." After Hendrick's death in 1740, his eldest son remodeled the house in the Georgian style. In the late eighteenth century, another descendant remodeled using Federal features.

Finally, after many owners and changes in usage, in 1899 a family descendant bought the house and, in 1924, donated it to New York State to be used as a museum, which it is today, concentrating on the story of the early Dutch settlers in the Upper Hudson Valley. Both exhibition and house are pleasant, and there is an interesting story, perhaps apocryphal, that says that here, in 1758, Dr. Richard Shuckburgh, a British army surgeon, composed the verses for "Yankee Doodle" while sitting at the well in the garden. His inspiration was the arrival of the New England troops in Albany to reinforce the British in their war against the French.

Open: Mid-April–October 31, Wednesday–Sunday 11–5.
Last tour at 4. Tours are on the hour and the half hour.
Phone: 518-463-8738.
Web site: nysparks.state.ny.us/sites/info.asp?siteID=5

Rensselaerville
and Other Things to See and Do in Albany

About 27 miles southwest of Albany lies the absolutely charming and very small village of Rensselaerville, which was established in 1787. Drive out of Albany on Route 443 to Route 85, which will take you right into the village. The road itself is beautiful after you leave Albany, and as you travel south there are some wonderful views of the Catskills looming ahead. The village seems to have been plucked whole out of the eighteenth and early nineteenth centuries and is among the most delightful towns in the state. One of the primary reasons it has remained in such pristine condition is that a well-to-do local family bought and restored many of its houses and then resold them to visitors who couldn't resist their obvious charms. Today Rensselaerville is an oasis of peace, a wonderful place to take a stroll in and enjoy the perfectly cared-for homes. My particular favorite is to the left as you enter the main street down at the bottom of the hill. Known as the Conkling House and built in 1825, it's quite small, with a low roof and windows in arched openings. But best of all is the minute portico with its three slender columns that give the whole a surprisingly elegant look.

You also should take time to walk on the blocks around the **Capitol** and **Mall**. Many of the buildings have been carefully restored, and there are some pleasant shops and interesting architecture. Be sure to take a look at the **Albany Academy** (1815) in Academy Park next to the Capitol. This was designed by Philip Hooker (1766–1836), the city's greatest native-born architect, and he may have been inspired by New York City's masterful City Hall. In any case, this is a very good-looking and elegantly classical building, one of the last survivors from its period in all of Albany.

Nearby, opposite the Capitol at the head of State Street, is Henry Hobson Richardson's **City Hall** (1882) and within the adjacent **Court of Appeals** is a splendid courtroom also designed by Richardson.

I would also suggest that you stop in to see the Gothic Revival **St. Peter's Church** designed by Richard Upjohn and constructed in 1859. Upjohn's most famous masterpiece is Trinity Church, built in 1846 in Gothic Revival style, in New York City. There are handsome stained-glass windows—the Burne-Jones window, second from the rear on the east aisle, was called by Matthew Arnold "the finest piece of stained glass in

America"—and a particularly beautiful silver communion service donated by Queen Anne to the church in 1712. A second service, sent by the queen at the same time, is still used by the Mohawk Indians in Canada.

At the foot of State Street is one of my favorite buildings, **State University Plaza**, built in 1918 by a local architect named Marcus T. Reynolds and modeled after the clothmaker's Guild Hall in Ypres, Belgium. It is a particularly striking building and has a six-foot weather vane representing Henry Hudson's ship, the *Half Moon*. Once the offices of the Delaware & Hudson Railroad, it was taken over in 1978 by the State University for its central administration offices.

Last of all is the **First Church in Albany**, on North Pearl Street at Clinton Avenue, which was organized in 1642 by a missionary from the Netherlands. The present church, built in 1799, was designed by Philip Hooker and can boast that both the oldest pulpit and the oldest weather vane in America belong to it.

Tiny Rensselaerville, one of the most beautiful villages in New York State, is filled with houses that people dream of making their own.

COLUMBIA COUNTY

Hudson

Just after the Revolution, some of the most prominent whaling families in Nantucket somehow got convinced that Great Britain would never allow the permanent loss of her colonies. They knew that their island home, out there in the Atlantic, would be particularly vulnerable in any new war coming from England. So they decided to move to a safer place. Early in 1783, Seth and Tom Jenkins, two Nantucket brothers, carrying a sum of $100,000, set off to look at possible sites. They explored Long Island and even New York City, but eventually settled on a spot 100 miles up the Hudson, at a place called Claverack Landing, which was later renamed Hudson.

That fall, and throughout 1785, a number of families moved there not only from Nantucket but also from Martha's Vineyard, Providence and Newport. By 1784, they had established the present grid-pattern layout, and in 1785 the city of Hudson was incorporated.

Being pure-bred Yankees, they planned the whole operation down to the last wooden peg nail. The families moved by sea, in their whaling ships, so that they could bring their household furnishings and supplies with them—indeed, many lived aboard their vessels until the new houses were completed—and would also have, ready-made, an impressive whaling fleet. By 1786 the town had grown fast enough to boast of 1,500 people, and its industries included a sperm oil works, a shipbuilder, a distillery, and various sail- and rope-making operations.

The whalers prospered until the embargoes prior to the War of 1812 came into effect, and then the war itself destroyed what remaining trade they had been able to maintain. It was not until 1830 that whaling was revived, and gradually the city began to thrive once more. In fact, other Hudson River towns—Poughkeepsie and Newburgh, in particular—began to compete for the rich profits, but none ever really rivaled Hudson. Soon Hudson was the commercial, political and industrial center of Columbia County, a position it still holds today. (Hudson became famous for something else; until 1950 it had a notorious red-light district that gained it almost as much fame as its former whaling business. Gone forever now, and weekenders have bought up and restored the old brothel houses.

There is a fascinating book about it by Bruce Hall called *Diamond Street: The Story of the Little Town with the Big Red Light District.*)

Hudson is well worth a visit these days. Over the past few years the careful restoration of its fine old houses—many strongly influenced by the Nantucket whalers and looking slightly misplaced on the banks of the Hudson—has made the older sections of the city a treasure trove to wander through. By far the most interesting street is Warren Street, right in the heart of this little metropolis.

My particular favorite is the old **Bank of Hudson** (ca. 1809) at 116 Warren. It was built by a man named John C. Hogeboom during the middle of a depression, hardly a good time one might think to start a bank— and you'd be right, for the bank soon failed. Hogeboom, ever resourceful, turned it into his private house. In the Federal style, the brick edifice has some Adam detailing that lends it a distinction that would make it notable anywhere. I'm thinking in particular of the four elegant white Ionic

Once famous for its whaling ships, then for its notorious red-light district, Hudson has since settled into a quiet river community offering a treasure trove of old houses to weekenders seeking second homes.

pilasters—note the tiny heads between the scrolls—that march across its façade and the two marble medallions decorated with swagged draperies between the windows of the first and second floors that give what is, after all, a rather small building a look of originality and elegance.

Across the street, at number 113, is the **Robert Jenkins House** (1811). Another Federal building, its interior was entirely—and mistakenly— reorganized in the early part of this century, but the façade retains that wonderful, soothing sense of classical proportion that is a joy to look at; I'm particularly fond of the steps and railing leading up to the handsome front door.

The third house of distinction is the **Cyrus Curtiss House** (ca. 1834–37, with a wing added ca. 1870) at 32 Warren, which would look totally at home on Nantucket. Curtiss was involved in whaling and also had a profitable oil and candle works that allowed him to build this impos- ing and substantial residence. Unfortunately, Curtiss' business burned to the ground—twice, in fact—and he was forced to sell his house to one Seneca Butts, a name I can't help but pass on. This Greek Revival house with an octagonal widow's walk is severe overall but made quite beautiful by its detailing: the elaborate grillwork at the attic level and above the front door, for example, not to mention the extremely well-done porch with its two Doric columns flanking the door and two Ionic columns supporting the porch itself, all four painted stark white.

Hudson has become famous for its antique shops; there are now more than 50 in this small town of fewer than 8,000 people, and to a large extent it is their presence that keeps the town on its feet. At the same time, with all the growth in shops and so forth, a certain charm has been lost. When I first started coming here years ago, Warren Street had a raffishness and there were real finds for you to pounce on triumphantly. Today, many of the dealers can be seen buying items in the auction rooms of Christie's and Sotheby's, and the prices now frequently match those in New York City. Nevertheless, you can find almost anything from every period and conti- nent, making it great fun to go from shop to shop (except on Wednesdays, when everything is closed up tight as a drum). Here's a sampling.

Going from upper Warren Street, the furthest point away from the river, the 700 block, I would include **Vincent R. Mulford and Doyle Antiques**, both at 711. The former has some of the more unusual materi- al in all of Hudson and is great fun to browse in. The latter has eighteenth

Incredibly, this building in Hudson was built as a bank—smack in the middle of a depression. Needless to say, it immediately failed and was converted into a private dwelling.

to twentieth-century English and American pieces and decorative arts material. In the 600 block I would suggest a stop at 602, the shop of **Florence Sack, Ltd.**, an eclectic collection that ranges from the seventeenth to the twentieth century and which also offers decorative arts pieces. In the 500 block, at 548, **Theron Ware** has wonderful material, but I find the prices generally to be way out of line, although I have found some things there from time to time that were more reasonably priced. In the 400 block, at 430, **Frank Swim Antiques** has eighteenth–twentieth-century continental and American furniture, but he also has twentieth-century glass and nineteenth- and twentieth-century lighting. At the same time, at 438, I always enjoy **Arenskjold Antiques Art**. They very cleverly mix eighteenth- and nineteenth-century European paintings, antiques and decorative material—with some excursions into Asia and America—with a strong Scandinavian flavor. **(Web site: www.arenskjold.com.)**

That's only a beginning. You're sure to find something you can't live without while you're here, and if the individual Warren Street shops don't have what you want, go to **Armory Antiques** at 5th and State Street, which houses a variety of dealers. And before you die of fatigue, pay a visit to the **Carrie Haddad Gallery** at 622 Warren Street, the most interesting of the contemporary art galleries in Hudson. However, there are more than a dozen other galleries, and it's worthwhile stopping in to see what's available. You never know.

Warren Street has other offerings I must mention. One is **Rogerson's Hardware** at 615. Right out of the nineteenth century, it's fun to stop in. Another—and certainly one of my favorite stores in Hudson—is **Hedström & Judd**, at 401. They offer the best-looking stock you can imagine designed for house (need a chandelier? dishes? bird prints?) and garden (how about a fountain—or some bulbs for spring bloom? or handsome clay pots?) Glassware, china, dishtowels, cachepots ... it's just a wonderful spot. (**Web site: www.hedstrom-judd.com.**) And while we're on gardening, stop by **The Secret Gardener**, at 250, a very appealing nursery with cut flowers and containers. Finally, in recent years **Stair Galleries** at 549 (**Web site: www.stairgalleries.com**) has become one of the most interesting auction sites in the Valley.

In short, explore. It is a pleasant way to spend an afternoon while enjoying the architecture in and around Warren Street. In fact, Hudson is little changed from the nineteenth century in this particular area, something that cannot be said about too many towns, and it is well worth a walking tour whether you wish to shop or not. If you have the time, for example, walk up North Fourth Street two blocks to State Street and the **Hudson Area Library Association**. One of the most distinguished buildings in Hudson, and built of native stone in 1818, the structure has an entrance now guarded by two cast-iron lions, one sound asleep. Inside, there is a handsome blue-and-white marble floor in the central hallway, but the real reason you are there is the Historic Room on the second floor, where you can examine some of the history of Hudson in books and pictures and see for yourself how little the town has changed.

OTHER THINGS TO SEE AND DO

American Museum of Fire Fighting ■ My first few visits to Hudson I skipped this museum, thinking it would be boring. How wrong I was. It's fascinating and a wonderful place to visit. Ask any child. Located adjacent to the Firemen's Home—when you drive up you'll see the residents out enjoying the sun or strolling about—the museum boasts a collection of fire equipment and memorabilia dating back to 1725 that has to be among the most complete in the country. Wandering through it makes you feel like a kid again.

Far and away my favorite single thing in the collection is the **Statue of a Fire Chief**, originally from Coney Island of all places, and one of the best pieces of folk carving you'll ever see. Probably done about 1850, there he stands, or rather strides, his right arm flung out, huge silver trumpet to his lips, in his sky-blue coat lined with red. He's the epitome of gallantry and dash, everybody's image of the brave fireman to the rescue.

There are also some wonderful pictures to see—Currier and Ives prints, among others—and some absolutely incredible decorated fire engines from the nineteenth century. To mention only one, don't miss the **Hose Carriage, Weiner Hose Company No. 6** of Kingston, beautiful and fanciful enough to have taken Cinderella to the ball. It was never used to put out fires, only for parades, and consequently every attention was lavished to make it as stunning as possible. Item: The hose reel is encased in etched mirrors and is supported by silver-plated lions. Item: The crowning touch on the summit is a silver-plated fireman rescuing a child. Item: The wheels are an impossible 68 inches high. But then the whole museum is like that, full of surprises and treasures and fantasies, and you should allow yourself enough time to enjoy it.

Located on Harry Howard Avenue (he was one of New York City's greatest fireman heroes), the museum is open daily 9–4:30. Phone: 518-828-7695. Web site: www.fasnyfiremuseum.com

ENVIRONS OF HUDSON

Olana ■ This, the most original house on the Hudson, was built by the painter Frederic Church (1826–1900) between 1870 and 1876. Although Calvert Vaux worked on it, Church remarked, justifiably, that "as the good woman did about her mock turtle soup, 'I made it out of my own head.'" Today, nearly 300 drawings and watercolors that Church created to define his mind's vision still survive.

Of the site itself he wrote, "About one hour this side of Albany is the center of the world—I own it." He exaggerated only a little. Perching 500 feet above the Hudson it offers one of the two or three most spectacular views of the river and the Catskills, a view that Church was to paint

Olana, Frederic Church's creation, of which he said, "as the good woman did about her mock turtle soup, 'I made it out of my own head.'"

many times and in all seasons. As for the name, it is believed to have been inspired by a Persian hilltop stronghold and treasury called *Olane*. Whether or not you tour the house, you must see this spectacular panorama stretching for miles.

Church was not only the most famous landscape painter of his time, but also the most successful. He studied with Thomas Cole, one of the leading lights of the Hudson River School, even boarding with him for a few years. Church then traveled extensively and became world famous and rich from his exotic and huge South American landscapes, in particular "The Heart of the Andes," now in the Metropolitan Museum in New York City, as well as for American-inspired paintings such as "The Great Falls, Niagara," presently in Washington at the Corcoran Gallery. Church's canvas of "Icebergs," rediscovered in England in the 1970s, sold for $2.5 million in 1979, at the time the highest price ever paid for an American paint-ing. These vast pictures, with their dazzling use of light and color, have the effect of putting the viewer right into the subject matter and are on such a grand scale that one's final feeling is that of awe, creating in some a near-mystical experience.

By the time Church built Olana, he could afford to do exactly as he pleased, and what he pleased was to create a Moorish extravaganza of yel-low stone, glazed Mexican and Persian tiles, polychrome brick, wooden decoration and, on the mansard roof, colored slate.

Over the years I have developed a real fondness and respect for it. Whether or not one admires the architecture, it must be admitted that somehow it all works, and this Arabic fantasy on the Hudson does not—don't ask me to explain why—seem out of place in the Valley. In fact, it can be curiously reassuring to see the bell tower looming above the hill as one crosses the Rip Van Winkle Bridge.

Inside, for me, the paintings by Church (and a few others) are of pri-mary interest—in particular, Church's marvelous "El Khasné, Petra," with its brilliant contrast of light and shadow, which hangs over the fireplace in the sitting room. (An aside: In 1996 a group of more than 50 drawings, watercolors and oil sketches, early works by the great French Impressionist Camille Pissarro—all depicting Caribbean scenes—were found here. They had been left with Church by another artist, Fritz Melbye, while he went to China. But he never returned to Olana to claim them, and they subse-quently were not attributed to Pissarro until fairly recently. Even Olana has attic treasures.) The house, jammed to the rafters with furnishings, every inch of wall and floor crammed with yet another example of Victorian exotica, exemplifies a taste I find completely foreign. But once again, it's a fascinating exploration of one man's peculiarly exotic vision.

Don't leave without exploring the grounds, which were brilliantly designed by Church as a landscape painting. They are beautiful at every season of the year, and the glorious masses of wildflowers in June, spilling down the hill as you approach the house, are worth the trip in themselves.

Olana lies 5 miles south of the city of Hudson, on Route 9G, and is part of a 250-acre park that is open to the public for picnicking and nature walks. The house museum itself is generally open April–October, Tuesday–Sunday 10–5, while tours are limited to weekends for the remainder of the year, but it is recommended that you call first to make sure of hours and house tour availability. The visitor center and museum shop are open daily 9:30–5. The visitor center has an exhibit and audio-visual program.

Phone: 518-828-0135. Web site: www.olana.org

The grounds are open year-round from 8 until sunset—try and see a sunset over the Hudson from here. What a sight!

Clermont ■ The difference between Clermont and Olana is that between night and day. Where Olana's view is romantic drama, Clermont's is classically intimate, the Hudson almost at your feet. Olana is exploding exuberance, Clermont restrained elegance. Of the two, I prefer Clermont, both for the house, light and airy and definitely one in which I could happily settle, and for the grounds, which I love to wander through at all times of the day

Clermont, white and classically elegant, has looked upon the Hudson for more than 200 years, ever since the British burned the old structure and this was built on the same site.

and in every season, to enjoy the banks of lilies, the beds of roses, the venerable old trees and lilac bushes, the vast undulating lawn, the hushed woods and, beyond it all, the omnipresent Hudson. The times I've been there I've had the place almost to myself and have enjoyed it most early in the morning when the light is crystalline, or at sunset which, from here, is poignantly intimate, as if it were a special display put on just for me.

This estate was part of the Manor of Livingston founded by Robert Livingston (1654–1728), who was born in Scotland but spent a good part of his youth in Holland, which stood him in good stead when he came to America and then to Albany in 1674. He was successful almost from the beginning and soon allied himself to the patroon system (see page 39) through his marriage in 1679 to Alida Schuyler Van Rensselaer. In 1683, Livingston purchased 2,000 acres from the Indians, the foundation for an estate that would eventually encompass 160,000 acres— achieved, to put it gently, by hook or by crook. This became the Lordship and Manor of Livingston and secured his family's fortune. He died, leaving the manor to his eldest son, Philip, and the portion known as Clermont to Robert junior.

The family has since produced many distinguished men, but the most famous was Livingston's great-grandson, Robert R. (1746–1813), first Chancellor of New York State and the man who administered the first oath of office to George Washington in 1789. He also served in the Continental Congress, was involved in drawing up the Declaration of Independence, helped negotiate the Louisiana Purchase while minister to France under Thomas Jefferson and even introduced merino sheep into the United States, thereby vastly aiding in the development of American woolen manufacture.

During the Revolution, in October 1777, Clermont was burned to the ground by the invading British, right after they destroyed Kingston (see page 109). Undaunted, the Livingstons rebuilt it, essentially in the same Georgian manner as the old house. Later, in the 1870s, a roof "in the French style" was added, giving the house the appearance you see today.

In 1803, when Livingston was in Paris, he met Robert Fulton and became his partner in building a workable steamboat, which first appeared on the Hudson in 1807 and became known as the Clermont after the Livingston estate. (The real name of the boat was first *The Steamboat*, then it was rechristened the *North River*; *Clermont* was a name given it many years later, after the steamboat had been taken out of service and broken up.) Fulton himself married Livingston's cousin, and the two men soon gained a monopoly on steamboating on the Hudson until it was declared unconstitutional in 1824 by Chief Justice John Marshall, with Daniel Webster arguing for the antimonopolists.

The 480-acre **Clermont State Historic Site** is 16 miles south of Hudson off Route 9G—watch for signs—just on the border of Dutchess County. (For political reasons, the original Robert Livingston didn't want to have any land in Dutchess County.) There is a visitor center in the restored nine-teenth-century carriage barn that houses a small video theater, a permanent orientation exhibit, a restored stables wing and a gift shop. The grounds are open all year from 8:30 until sunset and picnic facilities are available.

The house and visitor center are open: April 1–October 31, Tuesday–Sunday 11–5 (last tour leaves at 4:30); Monday and holidays 10–5. Open weekends through mid-December 11–5. Phone: 518-537-4240. Web site: www.friendsofclermont.org

A Drive through Columbia County

In many ways Columbia is the most beautiful county on the Hudson, both in the richness of its landscape and in the diversity and quality of its architecture. Back in the early 1800s, Washington Irving depicted this region as consisting of "little retired Dutch valleys, found here and there embosomed in the great State of New York [where] population, manners, and custom remain fixed." His description still holds amaz-ingly true, and the drive that follows should give you a taste of the best Columbia has to offer. You can do it in a few hours, but to fully enjoy it, plan on a leisurely day.

Begin at Hudson, following Route 23B where it divides from 9G, following the sign for Claverack. (A reader who lived in Claverack as a child passed along some interesting information, which I will now pass along to you. Among other things, she said that Route 9G through Claverack was part of the Underground Railroad system, helping slaves flee north to Canada. She also says that at the intersection just after Hotaling's farm [see p. 70], "up the hill going east you can get a wonder-ful view of the Rip Van Winkle of the Catskill mountains—the contours

The 1767 Dutch Reformed Church in Claverack, my candidate for the loveliest house of worship in Columbia County. This wing, added about 1850, is perfectly integrated into the older building, with its long green shutters running the length of both window and door.

define a body in repose." She's absolutely right, and it's a wonderful view. As for the houses in Claverack, she points out that the courthouse "at the corner of Route 23 and Old Lane was the site where Alexander Hamilton tried cases." She notes, too, that west of the courthouse and on the north side is a house that belonged to Robert Fulton, while east of the courthouse, on the south side of the highway, "is the old stone house where it was said that Clement Moore wrote 'The Night before Christmas.' ") As you approach this little village, the first county seat, be sure to note the houses, some of which go back to the eighteenth century and lend the village considerable charm.

You soon will come to a crossroad; turn left and go north on 9H. Almost immediately, on your right, you will see a sign for the **Reformed Dutch Church**, the prettiest place of worship in the county. Turn into the drive and take a few minutes to enjoy this appealing building built in 1767. (The wings were added about 1850.) The brick has aged to a warm, rosy pink, and along the side facing the road the numerals of the year it was built have been laid into the brick above the windows. The windows themselves, beautifully proportioned, are set off by deep-green shutters that add a touch of elegance to the simplicity of the design. As you walk around the outside of the church, you will note that the wings have been perfectly integrated into the whole; for instance, at the center of each is a door surmounted by a window, and the shutters here run the length of both, balancing proportionately with the windows along the side. Inside, the pale-green walls and white ceilings are divided by a graceful balcony around the sides and back. The overall feeling is one of welcome, a place for families to gather, not a formal house of worship.

The church did have its problems, though. One of the more august Van Rensselaers was principally responsible for its being built and, staunch patroon that he was, he put in a pew for himself and his family that was not only elevated above all the other parishioners' seats but also had a canopy. This ostentation did not sit well with the rest of the congregation and eventually led to a schism. Here, too, the last minister in America required to preach in the Dutch language arrived—in the year of 1776, symbolically enough.

Continue north on 9H and within a few minutes, on your left, you'll see **Hotaling's Farm Market**, a roadside stand brimming with produce. The farm that supplies the stand, to give you an idea of its size, has 50 acres of sweet corn, 8 acres of pumpkins, grows annually 6,000 cabbages and 7,000 tomato plants, and features a pick-your-own orchard—apples, cherries, plums, apricots. They also make their own jams and jellies and fruit pies … but why go on? It's open every day from 9 to 5. (A caveat: The service here is not as pleasant as it once was, and overall I much prefer the nearby **Holmquest Farms**, which is between Claverack and Hudson, off Route 23B on Columbia County Route 29, and is operated by a wonderfully friendly family. Watch for the sign.)

Back on the road, you'll be driving through open, rolling farmland, and as you approach Kinderhook you'll see a sign for **Lindenwald** to your left. This was the home of Martin Van Buren (1782–1862), eighth president of the United States (1837–41). A Jacksonian Democrat, Van Buren is almost forgotten today (unfairly, most historians think) and failed twice (in 1840 and 1848) to get reelected. (He was so unpopular in Virginia in 1848 that he received only nine votes—which prompted one Virginian to remark, "We're still looking for that son-of-a-bitch who voted nine times.") It is thanks to him that "OK" entered the language; Van Buren used to call himself Old Kinderhook, and soon the initials took on a life of their own.

Van Buren bought Lindenwald in 1839. At the time it was a Federal-style mansion where Washington Irving had once frequently visited and was even for a short period tutor to the children of the house. (It was during this earlier time—the turn of the century—that Irving first became engrossed in the local legends and folk tales that would later appear in some of his most famous stories.)

It was Van Buren's youngest son who decided that he wanted an Italianate villa and in 1848 hired Richard Upjohn, whose most famous achievement is Trinity Church (1846) in New York City, to remodel the original Georgian house into a comfortable 36-room Italianate mansion with a four-story brick tower. It later passed out of the family—one of the

Lindenwald, home of Martin Van Buren, eighth President of the United States, and, later, home of Winston Churchill's grandfather, Leonard Jerome. This drawing does not show the elaborate front porch, a bold mixture of Romanesque and Gothic, added by architect Richard Upjohn.

owners was to be Leonard Jerome, Winston Churchill's grandfather, who won it, one story has it, while gambling with Van Buren's son; it's not true, but it's too much fun not to pass on—and was only taken over by the federal government in 1974, when it was established as a National Historic Site.

The interior of the house is spacious and bright, with well-proportioned, comfortable rooms restored to the period of the Upjohn renovation and with many of the furnishings original to the house. But, without any doubt, the single most handsome room is the wide and deep central hall, originally two rooms, with its spectacular—and original—French wallpaper

The Luykas Van Alen House, built in 1737, now is a fascinating museum of Dutch farm life in the eighteenth century.

of 51 brilliantly colored panels that depict a hunting scene. A pleasant surprise, this outwardly quirky, inwardly staid upper-middle-class home.

Open: 7 days a week from Memorial Day weekend to the end of October. Open Saturday and Sunday in November through the first week in December. The grounds are open year-round, from dawn to dusk. The visitor center is staffed from 9–4:30 on days the house is open. Access to the house is by guided tour only.
Phone: 518-758-9689. Web site: www.nps.gov/mava/Main.htm.

Just a little beyond this site, and again on your left, is the **1737 Luykas Van Alen House**, in which members of the Van Alen family lived until the 1930s. The Columbia County Historical Society has since acquired and restored the house as an example of Dutch life during the eighteenth century. It is extremely well done and shouldn't be missed. And if it looks familiar to you, maybe you recognize it from Martin Scorsese's film adaptation of Edith Wharton's *The Age of Innocence*.

You park by a little white-frame building, ca. 1850, that was moved here from its original site. Now known as the **Ichabod Crane School House**, it served as a school until the 1940s. The name, of course, is that of Washington Irving's famous schoolmaster, and in fact, the character of Ichabod Crane was modeled by Irving after a schoolmaster in this district named Jesse Merwin. Today it has been restored to the period of the 1920s.

Once you've passed a small pond, the home of a few busybody ducks, you walk up a short hill to the red-brick, one-and-a-half-story house, a rare survivor of Dutch architecture with its steeply pitched roof, parapet gables and separate outside doors for each of the rooms. It looks like a direct descendant of some medieval house in Holland—which it basically is.

The three main interior rooms have been restored with particular care and taste, and each has an open fireplace, unique to the Dutch style, with wide chimneys starting at the ceiling level. Primitive in feel, with exposed posts and beams, there also is a Dutch sturdiness that gives the house an appealing solidity, and the handsome furnishings, Delft tiles and pictures are all from the Netherlands or the Hudson Valley. The place affords a unique glimpse of the daily life of the old Dutch settlers and, because there usually aren't too many visitors, you should have the house to yourself.

Open Memorial Day–Labor Day, Thursday–Saturday 11–5, Sunday 1–5. Closed: Monday, Tuesday and Wednesday. Phone: 518-758-9265. Web site: www.cchsny.org

Now follow the signs into **Kinderhook**, a lovely village that got its name from Henry Hudson when he anchored here in 1609. The ship quite naturally aroused the curiosity of the local Mohican Indian children, who came to gaze at this strange beast, and Hudson promptly named the spot Kinderhook, or Children's Corner. By 1640 the area had been settled, and today it is a virtually unspoiled setting for eighteenth- and nineteenth-century architecture good enough to merit its inclusion on the National Register of Historic Places.

To get a feeling of the village, walk south on Route 9, which here is called Broad Street, to the **James Vanderpoel House** (also known as the House of History, ca. 1820). This exquisite example of Federal architecture, one of the most sophisticated of its type in the Valley according to some historians, was once the home of James Vanderpoel and is now owned by the Columbia County Historical Society. It is open to the public as a museum of the Federal period. One curious feature of the brick exterior is that front and back are identical, making the building not only completely symmetrical—four chimneys, four windows on two floors on each side of a central door with a fanlight and beautiful Palladian window—but "reversible." The real beauty of the exterior, though, comes from its completely realized sense of design and proportion. Once inside, the first thing you notice is the curved stairway, extremely sophisticated and graceful; the rooms, with their architectural detail and delicate ornamentation, are all lovely and furnished with some fine examples of the New York furniture of the period.

The James Vanderpoel House is open Memorial Day–Labor Day, Thursday–Saturday 11–5, Sunday 1–5. Closed: Monday, Tuesday and Wednesday. Phone: 518-758-9265. Web site: www.cchsny.org

When you leave, walk a little further south where you will see the **David Van Schaack Mansion** (1774), which is identified by a historical marker. This private house, a magnificent specimen of Georgian architecture with eight wonderful chimneys and wings added during the early part of the nineteenth century, even has a small cemetery on its grounds where one past owner buried his slaves.

During the Revolution, General Burgoyne and his captors were entertained here by the Van Schaacks after "Gentleman Johnny's" defeat at Saratoga. The Van Schaacks, loyalists in sympathy to begin with, were not helped when one of their young children proposed a toast to England's royal family in front of Burgoyne's Yankee escort. (Kinderhook was more divided in its loyalties than most towns in the Hudson Valley, particularly among the conservative landowners.)

Next, stop in at the **Columbia County Museum** at 5 Albany Avenue. Two exhibition areas offer changing exhibits illustrating Columbia County's historic and cultural heritage, and some of the paintings in the permanent collection are choice. My particular favorite is a life-size portrait of Sherman Griswold and his wife, Lydia, by James E. Johnson (ca. 1810–1858), a local artist about whose personal life little is known. Griswold was a local nabob, and there he and Lydia stand, in their best clothes, their farm in the background. Sherman is holding a round box from which a ram is feeding. Apparently it was the custom in the area for the men, after church each Sunday (which also explains the finery), to feed their sheep. Around this time, wool constituted an important industry in the county, to some extent due to the introduction of merino sheep by Robert Livingston at Clermont (see page 66). This portrait is particularly endearing; partly it's the gentle expression on the faces of the Griswolds, partly it's the way Lydia holds her husband's arm, and partly it's the sheep, one in particular who patiently awaits her turn at the salt. Sad to note, Mr. Griswold eventually lost his money and his farm through railroad speculation, and even now it's hard not to feel a twinge of sympathy for such a kindly looking man.

The museum also houses an excellent research library containing material on New York State as well as local history, genealogy and architecture.

The Columbia County Museum is open year-round. For visiting hours, phone 518-758-9265. Web site: www.cchsny.org

When you leave Kinderhook, after wandering along a few of its attractive streets, go back out on the same road you entered on until you see a sign for Chatham and Ghent, where you will turn right. (This is Columbia

County Route 21.) The winding country road will take you through scenery that approaches perfection, with distant views of the mountains to the east, and large cattle and horse farms on either side. Continue following the Chatham signs—this means a left at 21B, then turn right on 203, and left again (north) at 66, which will take you into **Chatham**.

Chatham was once a major railroad center, more than a hundred trains a day passing through, and the station, on your left as you enter the village, was built in 1887 to reflect this importance. It is now on the National Register of Historic Places.

Continue north on 66 toward **The Shaker Museum and Library** in Old Chatham. The right turn is hard to see, but it's just before a steel bridge, and there is a sign for the museum here. This road will lead you through a countryside of elegant houses and horse farms with those wonderfully sinuous wooden fences that flow across the contours of the landscape. It is one of the prettiest areas of the county, proving that money well spent has never diminished Mother Nature's natural talents. Go past the signs for the museum entrance to take a look at Old Chatham, about 1.5 miles farther. (It sometimes seems that there are an infinite number of Chathams in the county.) This little group of buildings is appealing, in particular one large old brick house with brick pillars. Then turn back and enter the road that leads to the museum.

The Shakers have a long and honorable history, much of it in the Hudson Valley where their first community was established. The movement was founded across the Atlantic by Ann Lees (much later, in America, to be called Lee) who was born in Manchester, England, in 1736. In 1758, Ann Lees joined a small group of Quakers, but Quakers with a slight difference—they would sit in silent communion, like all Quakers, but at some point during their meditations they would be taken with "a mighty shaking."

In 1762, Ann married a blacksmith named Abraham Standerin (or Stanley—the name is spelled variously) and then, in quick succession over the next few years, lost four children in infancy. Bad enough in themselves, these deaths further traumatized Ann because each delivery had been extremely difficult. She came to see her tragedy as a judgment from God and began to avoid sexual relations with her husband. When she went to bed with him, she said, she felt "as if I had been in a bed of embers," hardly surprising in view of the results. Eventually this and other factors led to a conversion—"My soul broke forth to God," she later wrote—and she went out into the world with a tiny band of six or seven followers. Several times Ann and her group were arrested for disturbing the peace. (Understandable perhaps, since she preached that the two sexes living together was the source of all the evil in the world and that men and women must be treated as equals—but exist apart.) These ideas are still considered radical enough today, so it's no wonder Ann ended up in an English jail. There she had her single most important vision—Jesus came to her and became one with her. It was the Second Coming, but this time the spirit resided in a woman.

Once out of jail she became known as Mother Ann, or Anna the Word, and was soon having visions telling her to go to America. On May 10, 1774, Mother Ann and eight members of her band (including her husband, from whom she was already separated) sailed from England, bound for New York City, where they arrived on August 6. Upon disembarking, she marched her group up to a house where a family named Cunningham was sitting on their stoop, addressed them by name—she had no way of knowing it—and announced that they were to take her and her followers in. Astoundingly enough, they did.

This little band of Shakers soon heard of some land, available cheap, located about eight miles northwest of Albany, called by the Indian name of Niskayuna (now Watervliet), and there they settled. By 1780 they were making converts and, in the eyes of Revolutionary patriots, trouble. The latter believed the Shakers were in collusion with the British, and Ann and some of her followers were thrown into jails in Albany and Poughkeepsie. It did their cause more good than harm—Americans have always been notoriously sympathetic with the underdog—and they were quickly released.

By 1781, the Shakers were established enough to undertake a mission to New England, which would eventually have highly favorable results, spreading their religion even further.

Three years later, in 1784, Mother Ann died. Luckily for the Shaker society (some might term it Divine Providence), she was succeeded by several superb leaders who would spread the faith not only throughout New England but to Indiana, Ohio and Kentucky as well. So successful were they that the United Society of Believers in Christ's Second Appearing (as they now called themselves) codified their beliefs and way of life in 1821 into the Millennial Laws (revised in 1845).

This fascinating document established the colony in the Hudson Valley at New Lebanon, New York, as "the first and leading Ministry" headed, originally, by Brother Joseph Meacham and Mother Lucy Wright. (It was Meacham who formalized a dual order of male-female leadership, based on the perfect equality of the sexes, that would prevail for the entire history of the Shaker movement.) Also, the laws organized groups of believers into "families ... in order to accommodate and provide for the different circumstances of individuals in temporal things, and ... for the advancement of spiritual travel in the work of rejuvenation, and the universal good of all the members, composing such society." (New Lebanon, for instance, at its height would have eight "families," each containing, ideally, 50 members. Over the years the Shakers would establish 19 such major communities, with anywhere from two to eight families in each, as well as several minor ones.)

Over each family were Elders and Eldresses. Their primary responsibility, of course, was "to oversee the family under their care" in all spiritual matters. Next came Deacons and Deaconesses, who were in charge of the material welfare of the family, and finally the Trustees, who were "to perform all business transactions, either with the world, or with believers in other families or societies."

Every aspect of communal life was touched on in the Millennial Laws. For instance, "The gospel of Christ's Second Appearing strictly forbids all private union between the two sexes, in any case, place, or under any circumstances, in doors or out." Also: "No members except those in the Deacon's or Trustee's order, may go from home, even off the farm, without liberty from the Elders."

On education: "Girls' school should be kept in the summer and boys' school in the winter, and they should never be schooled together." (All the same, their system of education was so highly regarded that many non-Shaker parents in the region sent their children to these schools.) You may wonder how the Shakers got their children. They were placed there either by parents or by trustees of orphans, who thereby relinquished all rights to them, and lived under caretakers' supervision. At maturity they had the right to leave or stay, as they chose.

On personal property: "No private interest or property is, or can be allowed of, in families that have come into the covenant relation of a full dedication."

And so on, down through clothing (no special pockets), the ordering of each day, how to keep dooryards and farms as neat as a pin—there are even five prescriptions "concerning locks and keys."

If all this makes the Shakers seem unnecessarily grim, well, they weren't—nor were they perceived to be so by their neighbors. After initial persecutions, they slowly but surely advanced to a position of deep respect among their fellow citizens. It wasn't only their industriousness and the quality of their produce and manufactured goods and the wonder of their farms (although these were the most beautiful in the country, many agreed) that earned them this respect. It was equally their emphasis on hospitality and charity. "Do all your work as though you had a thousand years to live and as you would if you knew you must die tomorrow." In their hymn "Simple Gifts," so well known to most of us from Aaron Copland's adaptation of it for his *Appalachian Spring* ballet score, the Shaker way of life is perfectly summed up, I think:

> 'Tis the gift to be simple,
> 'Tis the gift to be free,
> 'Tis the gift to come down
> Where we ought to be,
> And when we find ourselves
> In the place just right,
> 'Twill be in the valley
> Of love and delight.
> When true simplicity is gain'd,
> To bow and to bend we shan't be asham'd
> To turn, turn will be our delight
> Till by turning, turning we come round right.

The Society reached its apogee of about 6,000 members in the years just before the Civil War—throughout their history the Shakers had a membership total of about 17,000—and then slowly went into a decline whose last glimmerings are still with us today. They have lasted longer and gained more fame than any other idealistic community this country has yet produced. In their own time they were famous for their seeds and herbs, farm produce and leather goods, clocks and furniture, agricultural machines and implements, so much so that the terms "Shaker" and "quality" became synonymous. They were ingenious both as improvisers and improvers. It is to them that we owe the flat broom (devised by Brother Theodore Bates in 1798), the first circular saw in America and the clothespin, among other homely inventions.

But today they are perhaps most famous for the incredible beauty with which they imbued everything they made, from the most common kitchen utensil to household furniture that appears unworldly in its purity. "This strange people have fertilized the rugged hills of New England by their systematic industry," Nathaniel Hawthorne wrote in his short story "The Shaker Bridal." To say the least. It is a legacy of extraordinary beauty unique in our modern-day existence.

The Shaker Museum here in Old Chatham, one of the largest in the world dedicated to Shaker culture, is housed in a low-lying complex of barn-red buildings, and their contents are displayed to perfection. Again,

Set amidst horse farms and undulating hills, the Shaker Museum and Library is one of the more interesting regional museums in New York State.

because it's off the beaten trail, you can be fairly certain you'll have the buildings and grounds mostly to yourself.

Aside from the exhibits of furniture and tools, there is a blacksmith's shop, a gallery devoted to small crafts, textile and weaving shops, nine period rooms, and a schoolroom. The entire place is fascinating and deeply moving in its simplicity. For me, two objects in particular symbolize the whole. The first lies just beyond the entrance, a large circular wooden foundry pattern hung high against a stark white wall beside three steps leading up into another exhibit space. So simple and evocative of an inner stillness are those bent, radiating spokes that one is oddly moved, reminded once again of the aesthetic perfection that resides in a circle. The second object is a high chair in the dining room on the first floor full of such chairs and rockers. Exquisitely conceived, its lines are so delicate and graceful that it seems to float in its space, timeless, weightless as a feather. Such love went into making this piece. When I first saw it, in a special exhibit on the second floor, there was above it a reproduction of a letter written in the 1940s from a Shaker sister to a nonmember of the sect when that particular community was coming to an end. In it she said that they could not repair a certain chair since the sister who would normally do it could no longer use her hands, crippled now from many years of such work. The whole museum is like this: a nostalgic—even heartrending—glimpse of a pure and devoted people.

The museum also has a gift shop that offers, among other things, superb herbs, still grown in the tiny Shaker community of Sabbathday Lake, Maine, kits for making Shaker furniture, a wide selection of books on the group and even records of their music.

Open May–October 10–5, closed Tuesday. Phone: 518-794-9100. Web site: www.shakermuseumandlibrary.org.

There also is a wonderful Shaker setting in New Lebanon, a Shaker settlement called **Mount Lebanon Shaker Village**. It now is home to the Darrow School, where, each summer, a series of six to seven concerts is presented in the old (1834) tannery, which is blessed with especially good acoustics. Named, logically enough, **Tannery Pond Concerts**, this is one of the most charming settings imaginable, and the artists are world class. Because it only seats 290 people, the feeling of intimacy and participation is wonderful, and wandering about the grounds is a joy. Get there early to enjoy it. Phone: 888-820-9441. **Web site: www.tannerypondconcerts.org**.

Art Omi ■ This is one other place in Columbia Country you should consider visiting. Basically, Art Omi is a residency program for international visiting visual artists, writers and musicians whose home is 300 acres of farmland, and more than 400 residents from 50 countries have stayed here. But the reason you would come here is The Fields Sculpture Park, a 90-acre section devoted to more than 80 pieces of contemporary sculpture, which you visit by a path that follows the edge of a natural pond. (Each year they plan to add another ten sculptures to the collection.) Some of the artists represented: Donald Lipski, Beverly Pepper, Grace Knowlton, Peter Stempel and Jene Highstein. There also are temporary exhibitions in this beautiful landscape. For complete information and directions to the site, go to their web site: **www.artomi.org**.

Greene County

Located on the west bank of the Hudson opposite Columbia County, this small county has one site that it is imperative to see. I'm not exaggerating when I say that it offers a view the peer of any in the Northeast.

The Catskill Mountain House Site ▮ There is a place in this Valley so lovely that it transcends mere description to become a symbol of the profoundest yearnings within the soul of the beholder. James Fenimore Cooper called it "the greatest wonder of all creation" and, in his novel *The Pioneers* (1823), had Natty Bumppo remark that from here he could survey "all creation," the Hudson "in sight for seventy miles under my feet, looking like a curled shaving, though it [is] only eight long miles to its banks." The English writer Harriet Martineau, notorious for her outspokenly pro-abolitionist work, Society in America (1837), wrote that it was "the noblest wonder of the Hudson Valley" and that from it she could see the Green Mountains of Vermont (true) and the Atlantic Ocean (false). The view for her, she implied, was so awe-inspiring as to give a new meaning to the act of Creation. Thomas Cole, founding father of the Hudson River School, who lived in nearby Catskill, observed that "all Nature here is new to art" and philosophized that this "grand diorama" was far too sublime for him to paint. A lesser-known visitor termed it "one of the most glorious prospects ever given by the Creator to man's imagination." Even Frances Trollope, Anthony's mother and author of a book deeply critical of just about everything that America represented, was forced to admit her delight in it. What they were all talking and writing about was the view from the then world-famous Catskill Mountain House, perhaps the most beloved hotel in nineteenth-century America.

It all began in 1823 when Erastus Beach, a stagecoach operator, built a small inn of a dozen rooms on a rock ledge, the Wall of Manitou, 2,500 feet above the floor of the Hudson Valley. It commanded a view of a good 50 miles (*pace*, Natty Bumppo) up and down the Hudson. In 1845 Erastus' son Charles took over the hotel and would continue running it for the rest of the century. He also expanded it. In its final form it became a magnificent structure, Greek Revival in style, with 13 handsome white pillars, their Corinthian capitals brilliantly gilded, marching across a deep piazza framed by extensive wings on either side and providing 300 rooms for its distinguished guests. Everyone—and I mean everyone—stayed here. Consider this partial but representative list: Henry James, Jenny Lind, Winslow Homer, Oscar Wilde, Ulysses S. Grant, Alexander Graham Bell, Mark Twain, Thomas Cole and virtually every other artist of the Hudson River School (but not, thank God, all at the same time), Washington Irving and President Chester A. Arthur, whom I mention because his daughter was such a horrifying brat she gave "acute discomfort to other children."

The Mountain House was the first great mountain resort in the United States but, far more important, it became a symbol of the new nation's wealth and recently discovered cultural ambitions. The epitome of American aspirations in the nineteenth century, it was even credited by some as providing the singular atmosphere necessary for the foundation of the American Romantic movement. Who knows? Perhaps it did. It's certainly true that it exercised an authority over its visitors that no hotel before or since in this country has ever done.

The Mountain House lasted well into the twentieth century, falling into a slow decline that paralleled the rising national boredom with all things romantic. Finally, in 1942, the last guest left. By 1963 the state had taken it over, including its 3,000 acres of land, and because the by-now ramshackle building was deemed dangerous, they burned it to the ground on January 25, 1963, at 6 in the morning. Gone forever was that "drift of snow that had not melted in the spring," as one traveler described seeing it from the Valley.

Well, knowing all that, how could I not go and see the site for myself? But, with one thing or another, I didn't. Not for years. Perhaps it was because I was afraid nothing could live up to that kind of advance billing. Or maybe it was plain old inertia. Finally I decided it was time—but how, exactly, did one get there? All I knew was that it was near the town of Catskill. After several phone calls I did get a route: Exit from the New York State Thruway at Saugerties and then get on Route 32 to Palenville. Once there, follow 23A to Haines Falls, and then take a right turn on County Route 18, where there is a sign for North Lake State Campsite, and at North Lake they will give you a map to the Mountain House site.

The drive turned out to be a beautiful surprise, for a good part of it is through the Catskill State Park region. Once in the park, you can immediately understand why painters have loved it so; at the same time, you get the eerie impression that you are moving through some kind of time-space continuum, for the feeling is entirely of another era. Completely unspoiled, with rushing streams, a ravishing waterfall, steep mountain slopes and dark precipitous drops at the road's edge, this is certainly "the forest primeval."

From the entrance booth to North Lake the drive grows more prosaic, pretty woods with carefully marked trails, all rather uneventful. North Lake, a small, sky-blue mountain tarn fringed with wooded slopes, has a parking lot and beach, and from there it's a short walk to the Mountain House site, upon which now rests merely a commemorative marker. As you approach the escarpment you still have no idea of what this view will really be like until, all of a sudden ... Incredible! ... There it is—the world at your feet! No other place in the Northeast has this kind of infinite glory, and while there are sites in other areas of the nation that are as splendid— the Grand Canyon, for one—none is more moving. It has to be one of the great natural sights in this world.

Straight ahead, you look east to the Taconic and Berkshire ranges, the Hudson a silky blue ribbon laid down the Valley. Clouds cast their plump shadows over the landscape, and here and there tiny little buildings add thumbprints of color to a landscape of greens and blues and browns and dove-gray. (I've read accounts of guests at the hotel who, while watching thunderstorms in the Valley, bathed, themselves, in brightest sunshine.) Over all reigns a deep peace and quiet. It is no wonder that so many people have invoked the Creator while gazing out upon this view, for it awakens intimations not only of immortality but of omnipotence. To be more prosaic, it's like having in front of you a stupendous HO scale model of a good section of the Earth, and you almost believe you can reach out and pluck up that red barn 8 miles or so away and make it more effective by moving it, say, 5 miles farther north. As it happens, I have a terrible fear of heights, yet here I wasn't affected in the slightest by my phobia. Perhaps because I was so high in such a vast panorama that fear could no longer comprehend it. I stayed for more than half an hour, moving back and forth along the escarpment to enjoy the different vistas and to watch the changes in the shifting light patterns. Then I began to note the reactions of other visitors. Almost everyone did the same thing: As they approached they'd be chatting and then, when the full force of the prospect before them hit, they'd fall silent, even drift apart, and just look. It was a rare and thrilling experience, now a memory I shall always keep with me. I'm not even sure I'll go back. Could it ever be quite the same as that first time?

On leaving, I turned left at the first road beyond the entrance booth and followed the road to its end. Then I walked down a narrow dirt path and came out at the head of the **Kaaterskill Falls**, another great favorite of the Romantics—Washington Irving called them "wild, lovely and shagged"—whose glories have been depicted by several of the more famous members of the Hudson River School, my particular favorite being an introspective study by Asher B. Durand now in the collection of The New-York Historical Society in New York City. Unfortunately, I couldn't see much. Given what I've already told you, to say that the drop down is longer than Niagara's explains why I didn't go anywhere near the edge. Next time I'll find out how—and if—one can approach it from the bottom. And anyway, in life there should always be one more thing to look forward to ... or so I keep telling myself. (A correspondent wrote me that, "the way to see the falls is to hike in from the hairpin curve on 23A, from which you can see Bastion Falls. The hike is about 25 minutes, a gentle meander up a wooded glen following the creek, with a steeper climb at the end to view the falls.")

WHAT TO SEE IN THE ENVIRONS

Bronck Museum ■ In 1663, Pieter Bronck became the first builder on this land. (One of his relatives, Jones, had a 500-acre "bouwerie" in New York City that later became the Bronx.) Today there stands on Pieter's property a little complex of buildings dating from 1663, 1685 and 1738 as well as various barns—Dutch, Victorian and a famous one that's 13-sided.

It's a nice find and well worth your while if you're nearby. In the museum proper, there are paintings by John Frederick Kensett, Ammi Phillips and Nehemiah Partridge (see page 49), among others. There also are some excellent pieces of furniture and good examples of china and glass. In the barns fascinating local memorabilia are preserved, including a few of the famous capitals and other artifacts recovered from the Catskill Mountain House and a large-scale model of that famous resort. All in all, a kind of grandmother's-attic treasure trove of history—you'll enjoy your visit here, I promise.

The museum is about 4 miles south of Coxsackie, just off Route 9W on Pieter Bronck Road. Watch carefully—the sign for it is small and easily missed.

Open: Memorial Day weekend to October 15, Wednesday–Friday, 12–4; Saturday 10–4; Sunday, 1–4; Monday, holidays, 10–4. Closed: non-holiday Mondays and all Tuesdays. Phone: 518-731-6490 or 731-8862. Web site: www.gchistory.org.

Cedar Grove, The Thomas Cole National Historic Site ▆ Cedar Grove was the home of Thomas Cole (1801–1848) from the 1830s to his death in 1848. In 1998, it was a wreck. That same year the Greene County Historical Society bought the property, in 1999 it was declared a National Historic Site, and in 2001—appropriately enough the 200th birthday of Cole—it opened to the public as a handsomely restored, mostly Federal building with a lovely second-story piazza from which there is a view of the Catskills that, with a little bit of judicious editing, is unchanged from Cole's day. Today it is operated jointly with the National Park Service.

Not much is left in the house from Cole's residency—some china, a top hat and initialed trunk, his paint box (with a charming Italian scene on the inner surface of the lid), traveling easel and chair—but the furnishings have been done with care and thought and are perfectly appropriate to the period he lived in. And—in an aside—note the very handsome, elegantly carved tiger maple banister.

Most interesting in the house is an inspiration that adds a great deal to the visit. Each year, in two largish rooms, small exhibitions are held for the summer and early fall months that are related to Cole and the Hudson River School experience. It adds immeasurably to the visit and is an exceptionally intelligent solution to a problem other sites also face—what to do with that unimportant-in-itself space?

The tour begins and ends in the barn. The front, now the visitor's center, offers relevant books and prints as well as wall placards that give a summation of Cole's life and material on other residences in the Valley. Plans are now in development that will result in a film based on Cole's life and work and, in fact, the whole site is very much a work in progress. But it is the back of the barn, where the tour ends, that is my favorite spot. It was Cole's studio, again appropriately furnished and containing some of his material, but what I found quite beautiful are the walls, the handsome beams of which have been in-filled with a salmony-pinkish-gray brick that gives the whole room—modest in itself—a great feeling of warmth and charm and, for me, it is the one place where you truly feel Cole's presence.

A visit here is pleasant and rewarding, and combining it with a visit to Olana—which is nearby—would make a perfect day excursion. After all, Cole was Church's teacher, and it's interesting to juxtapose the way the two men lived, one the father of a school, the other perhaps its most famous practitioner.

Before you leave be sure to pick up "The Hudson River School Art Trail" brochure that Cedar Grove has published. It gives you information on seven nearby sites well worth visiting, and the directions are excellent. The Art Trail ends near North–South Lake campground in Haines Falls where you'll also find the Hudson River School Art Trail Interpretive Center at the Mountain Top Historical Society campus (www.mths.org). The Center houses interpretive panels combining biographical profiles and historical paintings of artists Thomas Cole, Asher B. Durand, Frederic Church and others with contemporary photographs of those same views.

Cedar Grove is located at 218 Spring Street in Catskill. It is almost on top of the western entrance to the Rip Van Winkle Bridge. The main house and studio are open from the first weekend in May through the last week-end in October on Friday, Saturday and Sunday from 10–4. Tours are given on the hour and are offered at other times by appointment. The house also is open Memorial Day, Labor Day, Columbus Day and Independence Day, 1–4.

Phone: 518-943-7465. Web site: www.thomascole.org.

WHERE TO STAY AND EAT

Saratoga Springs
Area Code: 518

WHERE TO STAY

For current rates, check the websites.

There is something to suit every taste. And remember—if you wish to be there in August, you must reserve as far in advance as possible and, in comparison to off-season, be prepared to pay through the nose.

HOTELS

The Adelphi ■ 365 Broadway, Saratoga Springs 12866.
Phone: 587-4688. Web site: www.adelphiahotel.com.
Rates vary according to the time of year you plan to be there, whether you wish to stay during the week or on weekends, etc. Closed in winter.

Built in 1877, this is the last whisper of Saratoga's great resort-hotel days with its handsome, columned piazza and Victorian decoration. It has been restored and now has turn-of-the-century furnishings and ornamentation. Some readers recommend it for its Victorian charm and friendly staff. Others find the decor overdone.

The Gideon Putnam Resort and Spa ■ Box 476, Saratoga Springs 12866.
Phone: 584-3000, 800-732-1560. Web site: wwwgideonputnam.com.

A favorite, because it is right in the heart of the Saratoga Spa State Park, which means that all events at the Saratoga Performing Arts Center are within walking distance. The rooms are comfortable and newly redecorated, the service efficient.

The Inn at Saratoga ■ 231 Broadway, Saratoga Springs 12866.
Phone: 583-1890, 800-274-3573. Web site: www.theinnatsaratoga.com.

This attractive 38-room inn dates from the 1880s and has been restored to that period. It gets high marks from people who live in Saratoga, some of whom recommend it above any of the others.

The Saratoga ■ 534 Broadway, Saratoga Springs 12866-2252.
Phone: 584-4000. Web site: www.primehotelsandresorts.com.

A comfortable hotel with such amenities as a pool and health club.

BED & BREAKFAST INNS (in order of preference)

Saratoga Arms ■ 495–497 Broadway, Saratoga Springs 12866.
Phone: 584-1775. Web site: www.saratogaarms.com.

Built in 1869 by Gideon Putnam's grandson, this very attractive 16-room inn with six rooms that have fireplaces is at the top of my list of recommendations, particularly if you want to be in town. There's also a wonderful porch from which you can watch the world go by—and in August, it does. No expense has been spared to bring this wonderful old building back into shape, and the results repay all the work. I'm sure you'll be happy here.

The Mansion Inn ■ 10 minutes west of Saratoga on Route 29,
Rock City Falls 12863. Phone: 885-1607.
Web site:www.themansioninnsaratoga.com. No credit cards.

This 1866 five-bedroom Victorian mansion was named one of America's top 12 inns by *Country Inns—Bed & Breakfast Magazine* in 1990. A full breakfast is served, the rooms are comfortable, the owners friendly without being intrusive. Very pleasant indeed, and the Victorian furnishings—including a Herter Bros. mantlepiece—and original lighting fixtures as well as splendidly preserved details will warm the heart of anyone interested in the period. There is also a carriage house with two suites, and the public rooms are inviting and comfortable.

Saratoga Bed & Breakfast ■ 434 Church Street, Saratoga Springs 12866.
Phone: 584-0920. Web site: www.saratogabedandbreakfast.com.

The Farmhouse (1860) is an old-fashioned B & B with cozy, well-furnished rooms, some with fireplaces, and a feeling of welcome and hope-you-all-get-along-together. This is a real find.

Union Gables Bed & Breakfast ■ 55 Union Avenue, Saratoga Springs 12866. Phone: 584-1558, 800-398-1558. Web site: www.uniongables.com.

A wonderful 1901 Queen Anne mansion with a tower and a vast, comfortable porch. The rooms (two have their own porches) are spacious and comfortable if, in a few cases, a bit overdone. The owners have done a splendid job of restoration, and this is a nice place to stay. A full continental breakfast is served.

Batcheller Mansion Inn ■ 20 Circular Street, Saratoga Springs 12866. Phone: 584-7012, 800-616-7012. Web site: www.batchellermansion.com.

Yet another—but fabulous looking—Victorian mansion, this one with nine bedrooms that are, again, spacious and comfortable. On the exterior, this is one of the most memorable buildings in Saratoga, and again, if you're interested in the period, you'll enjoy staying here. A full breakfast is served on the weekends and every day during the racing season, a continental breakfast at other times.

WHERE TO EAT (in order of preference)

Chez Sophie Bistro ■ 4 1/2 miles south of Saratoga on Route 9, Malta. Phone: 583-3538. Web site: chezsophie.com.

Sophie Parker was the brilliant chef who made this restaurant. Sadly, she died in 2001. Her son, Paul, has taken over and maintains her high standards. This is the best restaurant in Saratoga, and the wine list is wonderfully well chosen. The food is bistro style—duck, fish, poultry—meaning not fancy but made with the freshest ingredients and cooked with elegance and loving care: imagination without pretension. The restaurant itself is fun/attractive, for it is housed in an old diner with café curtains at the windows and comfortable booths and tables. This was my favorite restaurant here when I first wrote this book. It's wonderful that it's back and thriving. It is moderately expensive, and reservations are essential. Open: Tuesday–Saturday 5:30 during the off season. During the racing season it is open six nights that can vary; call for the nights. Closed from the Saturday following New Year's Eve to February 14.

Sperry's ■ 30 1/2 Caroline Street. Phone: 584-9618. Web site: www.saratoga.org/membersites/sperrys.

Don't be fooled by this unpretentious-bordering-on-homely restaurant. The food here is delicious, there's a well-chosen selection of wines, and the prices are reasonable. Open for both lunch and dinner, you can have everything from a sandwich at lunch to excellent entrées, well prepared and served by an especially friendly staff. Desserts and pastries are homemade, too, and very good.

Mrs. London's ■ 464 Broadway. Phone: 581-1834.
Web site: www.mrslondons.com.

This was a wonderful bakery and café many years ago, and now it's back and just as good if not better. Located in an extremely attractive space, the breads, pastries, coffees, desserts and savories cannot be beat. This is the place to go for a delicious breakfast. It's also perfect in the afternoon or evening for a gourmet snack. Don't miss it.

Gaffney's Off Broadway ■ 16 Caroline Street. Phone: 587-7359.
Web site: www.gaffneysrestaurant.com.

This is a very attractive restaurant with good—not great—food, and service that can range from extremely pleasant to cold. My complaint is that the food is too much. By that I mean, for example, that you can't just have a simple dish, oh no—you have to have several other things on the plate to make it all look like a tower to gluttony. The entrée by itself is fine, so why add another roomful of unwanted food? This is my gripe about a lot of cooking today. You may agree or not. If you don't, you'll be very happy here. If you do, you'll think it's okay. It's also expensive.

Hattie's ■ 45 Phila Street. Phone: 584-4790.
Web site: www.hattiesrestaurant.com.

This is a Saratoga classic with the "best fried chicken north of the Mason-Dixon line," one writer enthuses. Well, I don't know if I'd go that far, but it is good. Hattie's also is the perfect place to watch the Saratoga scene pass by. Best of all, the price truly is moderate, particularly considering the quality of the food. And it has a full bar.

BURGERS, SANDWICHES, SALADS

A zillion of these, as you would expect. The best of the lot is **The Olde Bryan Inn** (123 Maple Avenue, phone: 587-2990, web site: www.olde-bryaninn.com), which is in a 1773 building that is inviting on the outside, cozy on the inside. It has good enough food (sandwiches, pasta, seafood, steak, etc.), and pleasant service.

Albany
Area Code: 518

WHERE TO STAY

The Crowne Plaza Albany Hotel ■ State and Lodge streets, Albany 12210. Phone: 462-6611, 800-2CROWNE. Web site: www.cpalbany.com.

For many years, downtown Albany had no decent hotel. When this hotel was the Albany Hilton and the Omni Albany, it was awful. As a Crowne Plaza hotel it's somewhat better, and the rooms have wonderful views of the Capitol and Mall or of the Hudson. And let's face it—this is the only halfway decent hotel. As for the food and service … well, they will do … barely.

There are two Bed & Breakfasts that I can recommend as alternatives to the Crowne Plaza. The first is the **Mansion Hill Inn** (115 Philip Street at Park Avenue, Albany 12202. Phone: 888-299-0455 or 465-2038. Web site: www.mansionhill.com). Actually a small compound of buildings, this 8-room B & B is conveniently located, clean and comfortable. There is also a good restaurant (see below). The other recommendation is The **Morgan State House** (393 State Street, Albany 12210. Phone: 888-427-6063. Web site: www.statehouse.com). An attractive, comfortable, well-restored B & B that will be of interest to those interested in late (1888) Victorian buildings. This is my first choice in Albany.

WHERE TO EAT

Aubergine ■ Hillsdale. Phone: 325-3412.
Web site: www.aubergine.com.

About a 45-minute drive from Albany. (See page 98.)

Daniel's at Ogdens ■ 42 Howard Street. Phone: 694-5320.

This is pretty good and is in a century-old building that has been handsomely restored. It also has an inviting outdoor space for summer dining. The food is fairly standard steak and seafood, but it's well prepared … and expensive.

Jack's Oyster House ■ 42 State Street. Phone: 465-8854.
Web site: www.jacksoysterhouse.com.

This is right out of the late nineteenth century, with wonderful old photos, no frills but an inviting decor, excellent service and a large, no-nonsense menu that features, in particular, the biggest selection of seafood for miles around as well as steaks and chops. It's always crowded at lunch, so you should reserve. But—and it's a big "but"—I feel that in recent years it has fallen off in terms of quality. Still, it's one of the better restaurants in downtown Albany, and it's moderately priced, too.

McGuire's ■ 353 State Street. 463-2100.

Fairly new on the Albany scene, the chef likes to create elaborate dishes that combine unusual ingredients. He does have good, fresh fish, but then it can disappear in all the other things he throws in. The setting is very pleasant—a brownstone with attractive dining rooms—but to my taste it all gets too busy. On the other hand, it's very popular, so what do I know?

Nicole's Bistro ■ 633 Broadway (Broadway and Clinton).
Phone: 465-1111. Web site: www.nicolesbistro.com.

The Quackenbush House, the oldest residence in Albany, is now reincarnated as Nicole's Bistro. Outside, it is a very attractive eighteenth-century brick building. Inside the restaurant, neither the upstairs nor the downstairs seems to have retained much from the original. The walls as you come in are lined with pictures of Nicole with various celebs and Albany pols, and there's a cozy bar. Chef Daniel E. Smith was the head chef at the Beekman Arms in Rhinebeck and then had his own restaurant, The Thymes, in Kingston. Even the best restaurant in Albany doesn't merit a special visit here to sample the food, but if you do come you'll have a good meal, well prepared and served, and although the prices are moderately expensive, there is a prix fixe dinner that is well within a budget.

Mansion Hill Restaurant ■ 115 Philip Street at Park Avenue.
Phone: 465-2038. Web site: www.mansionhill.com/restaurant.html.

Small and cozy, the restaurant serves basically simple, well-prepared food. One reader notes that "for once, it really is like eating a good, home-made meal." Dinner: Thursday–Saturday, 5 on.

None of the remaining restaurants in Albany are all that special. However, if you like rubbing shoulders with politicians, you might try **Lombardo's**, 121 Madison Avenue. (Phone: 462-9180) Friendly old-fashioned waitresses—"What'll yours be, dear?"—wonderful murals, reasonable prices and huge portions help make up for the lackluster food. Open Monday–Friday 11–11, Saturday 3–11.

The only French restaurant of any note is **La Serre**, 14 Green Street. (Phone: 463-6056.) It's pretty, but the food is soon forgotten. Still, it seems popular, so perhaps I'm missing something.

Columbia and Greene Counties
Area code: 518

WHERE TO STAY

When I first wrote this book, there were few places to recommend in Columbia County and nothing in Greene County. Today there is a pleasant place to stay in Greene (**The Greenville Arms**—see page 96), as well as several attractive Bed & Breakfasts in Columbia, including Hudson, which are spotted throughout the county, allowing you to pretty much choose exactly where you would like to be. If these are booked, you may wish to consider **The Beekman Arms** (see page 171), within a comfortable driving distance of about 30 minutes from Hudson. Here are my recommendations.

446 Warren Street ■ 446 Warren Street, Hudson 12534. Phone: 828-0526. Web site: www.446warrenst.com.

There is only one suite available in this attractive Federal (ca.1790) house on Hudson's main street. It's very attractive, with a working fireplace, full eat-in kitchen and bedroom and living room.

Aubergine ■ Box 387, Hillsdale 12529. Phone: 325-3412. Web site: www.aubergine.com.

Four rooms, two with private bath, two with private bath in the hall. The food here is very good (see page 98), but the rooms are simple. Well, you can't have everything. Some solve the problem by eating a long, wonderful dinner and enjoying the wines and then staying overnight.

The Greenville Arms ▥ P.O. Box 659, Greenville 12803. There are 15 rooms, all well furnished. Phone: 888-665-0041.
Web site: www.greenvillearms.com.

Kim and Mark LaPolla are the innkeepers and owners of this Queen Anne home built by William Vanderbilt in 1889. Right in the attractive little village of Greenville, this comfortably rambling house sits on 6 landscaped acres that include a swimming pool. The dining room serves dinner evenings with advance reservations, for inn guests only. The LaPollas also sponsor the Hudson River Valley Art Workshops for the study of art for painters and quilters. They have indoor facilities for studio classes and a roster of well-known artists. You can write to the above address for a descriptive brochure.

The Inn at Green River ▥ 9 Nobletown Road (junction of Route 22 and Route 71), Hillsdale 12529. Phone: 325-7248.
Web site: www.innatgreenriver.com. Seven rooms, some with fireplaces. Full breakfast included.

The word to describe this 1830 house near the Massachusetts border in the Berkshire foothills is cozy. It also is very pretty. And comfortable. The hostess, Deborah Bowen, is friendly, the setting, near the Green River, is sylvan and relaxing (there's even an old cemetery behind the house), the furnishings are handsome and the photographs and pictures, some by Deborah's grandfather, make the setting homelike enough that you will feel like a weekend guest rather than a paying customer. I can happily recommend it.

The Inn at Hudson ▥ 317 Allen Street, Hudson 12534.
Phone: 822-9322. Web site: www.theinnathudson.com.

This is a rather extraordinary brick and stone Dutch/Jacobean house designed by Marcus Reynolds and completed in 1906. If the owners can restore it to its original splendor, it will be one of the most interesting B&Bs in the Valley, for the interior has spectacular woodwork, stained glass, amazing plasterwork, a central beamed ceiling with stained glass panels … on and on it goes. If you're at all interested in architecture and design, you should definitely consider staying in one of the three available bedrooms. Also, it's right in the middle of Hudson on the nicest street, and most of the furnishings are for sale.

The Inn at Shaker Mill Farm ■ Canaan 12029. Phone: 800-365-9345 or 794-9345. Web site: shakermillfarminn.com.

This inn (24 rooms), not far from the Massachusetts border, is, indeed, a converted Shaker mill. Simply decorated, informally run, it may be a bit too Spartan for some. Yet guests here tend to mingle and many return, so it obviously has a dedicated following. During the summer and fall they serve dinner. On the plus side: Nearby cross-country skiing, a pond and pleasant walks in summer. On the (possibly) debit side: You'd better be friendly and love the communal approach to life.

The Inn at Silver Maple Farm ■ Route 295, Canaan 12029. Phone: 781-3600. Web site: www.silvermaplefarm.com.

Picturesque best describes this inn. Very attractive, on ten acres of pretty land and with eleven guest rooms. I find the great room and library particularly appealing. More formal than the Inn at Shaker Mill Farm, and also less chummy.

Mount Merino Manor ■ 4317 Route 23, Hudson 12534. Phone: 828-5583. Web site:www.mountmerinomanor.com.

This handsome Victorian just outside Hudson and situated on a 100-acre property adjacent to Olana State Historic Site (see page 63), was built by Mrs. Frederic Church's doctor and is now owned and operated by Rita and Patrick Birmingham, who have made every effort to make this as comfortable and inviting as possible. Wonderful bathrooms, in particular—most tubs have jets, and the showers have comfortable chairs. The views are lovely and there are walking trails.

The Sedgwick Inn ■ 17971 Route 22, Berlin 12022. Phone: 658-2334. Web site: www.sedgwickinn.com.

Cozy. Lots of antiques. Also has a restaurant. All in all, a good choice, but it is pretty far north in Columbia County, making it not as convenient as some of the other places to stay. But there's a lot of good hiking in the area.

Spencertown Country House ■ County Route 9, Spencertown 12165.
Phone: 392-5292, 888-727-9980. Web site: www.spencertowncntryhouse.com.

This attractive B&B is in the foothills of the Berkshires and is conveniently located for events in the Berkshires as well as all that goes on in Columbia County. There are five guest rooms in the nineteenth-century main building and another four in the Carriage Barn. Very comfortable, nice fireplace in the parlor, attractively furnished, and a good breakfast—not to mention location. Can't ask for much more than that.

Swiss Hutte ■ Hillsdale 12529. Phone: 325-3333.
Web site: www.swisshutte.com.

Fine for general comfort and overall appeal, this inn sits practically on top of the Massachusetts border in the middle of the Catamount ski area. It offers two rooms in the main inn and motel-style rooms. There also is a swimming pool. It also has a very good dining room (see page 100).

WHERE TO EAT

The dining scene in Columbia and Greene counties is becoming increasingly interesting and varied. The restaurants listed below are far and away the best in their categories.

Aubergine ■ Hillsdale. Phone: 325-3412.
Web site: www.aubergine.com.

This used to be L'Hostellerie Bressane, one of the best restaurants in the Upper Hudson, and when Chef Jean Morel retired and sold the restaurant to Chef David Lawson, there was a certain amount of nervous trepidation among the regulars. Not to worry. Lawson has maintained Morel's standards of excellence and brought a fresh point of view to the dining rooms in this handsome old house that sits on top of a hill in the center of Hillsdale. The food is delicious and thoughtfully prepared, the service is excellent, and there still is the extraordinary selection of cognacs, Armagnacs and Calvados. Open: Wednesday–Sunday 5:30. Closed last week in March.

Baba Louie's ■ 517 Warren Street, Hudson. Phone: 751-2155.

This is a good find for a quick lunch—particularly if you like pizza. They have really good ones, with a sourdough crust, and also panini, regular sandwiches, and salads. It's popular and gets filled up fast, but you can eat at the bar if worse comes to worst. The restaurant, by the way, is attractive, with nice seating and a lovely tin ceiling. They also have good wines by the glass.

Blue Plate ■ 1 Kinderhook Street (on Central Square), Chatham. Phone: 392-7711. Web site: www.chathamblueplate.net.

Finding a good restaurant in Chatham used to be like looking for the proverbial needle, but this restaurant has filled that niche. Good, seasonal ingredients make for good food, and that's what you get—all in a non-pretentious, friendly atmosphere … and it's very reasonably priced.

Ca' Mea ■ 333 Warren Street, Hudson. Phone: 822-0005.

Things are looking up food-wise in Hudson. This restaurant has a very nice northern Italian menu and a good wine list. I also find that the specials are numerous and very good, and I usually go for one of them. There's an attractive garden area for summer dining, and while service can be slow it's always cheerful, and that makes up for a lot.

Carolina House ■ 59 Broad Street, Kinderhook. Phone: 758-1669.

This log-cabin restaurant attracts those among us who particularly favor prime rib and baby-back ribs as well as seafood and chicken, all cooked with a Southern bias. Not great dining, but hearty food at moderate prices. Open: Monday, Wednesday, Thursday 5–9:30, Friday and Saturday 5–10:30, Sunday 4–9:30.

Nola Bakery and Café ■ 454 Warren Street, Hudson. Phone 828-4905.

This unprepossessing spot is perfect if you're in a hurry and need to eat on the run, and the little outside terrace is great in summer for people watching. Very good breakfast and luncheon food.

Red Dot Bar & Restaurant ■ 321 Warren Street, Hudson. Phone: 828-3657.

If you like mussels and Belgian pomme frites, you'll be in heaven here. This funky bar and restaurant is definitely informal and definitely a Hudson favorite. Simple, well-prepared food, and there's also a garden.

Serevan ▓ Route 44, just outside Amenia. Phone: 845-373-9800.
Web site: www.serevan.com.

Located in a nice old house, with a small dining room, the service is warm and welcoming, the menu changing with the seasons and the chef's whims. I like it. It's one of those places with good food that is reasonably priced (including the wine list) and without pretensions.

Stissing House ▓ corner of Route 199 and Route 82, Pine Plains.
Phone: 398-8800.

Stissing House has had its ups and downs. Mostly downs, as far as I'm concerned. But now things are looking up in its most recent incarnation as what I would describe to be a Franco-American bistro, with everything from mussels and pizza to steaks and fish. For me, it's the rooms that are the most appealing—two have fireplaces, and the bar is welcoming and relaxed.

Swiss Hutte ▓ Hillsdale. Phone: 325-3333. Web site: www.swisshutte.com.

Gert and Cindy Alper have owned this inn since 1986, and Gert is the chef. Not hard to believe that there are Swiss specialties, but he also serves continental and American selections, and I think the food is consistently good. And consistency is, in my book, a real virtue. Nice fireplace in the winter, outside dining in the summer.

Swoon Kitchenbar ▓ 340 Warren Street, Hudson. Phone: 822-8938.
Web site: www.swoonkitchenbar.com.

This is my favorite restaurant in Hudson. The décor is mildly kinky-chic—pressed tin ceilings, lots of plants and paintings—a generally homey hodgepodge. The service is excellent, the wine list is original and thought-ful. Excellent food (do start with the charcuterie—it's wonderful) and really good desserts. I like sitting in the front room and watching Hudson life pass by. Go for lunch or dinner. You can't lose.

THE
MIDDLE HUDSON

Ulster and Dutchess Counties

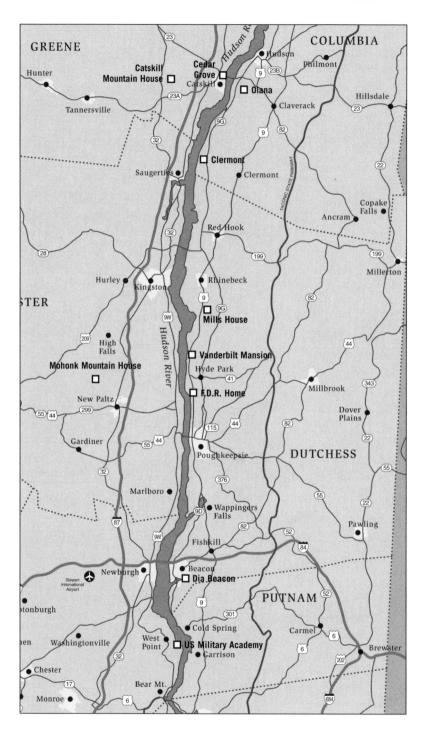

THE SWANS ARE BACK And they've chosen this, the soul of the Valley, as the spot in which to build their nests, right in the dark green vegetation where Rondout Creek at Kingston joins the Hudson. To me it's exactly right that they should be here, dead center in the most beautiful and tranquil section of the river, where it flows through Dutchess and Ulster counties.

No other place in America is quite like the Middle Hudson. As in certain parts of Europe, past, present and future merge here in a seamless flow; a spirit of equality rather than of struggle. It gives the area a timeless stability that lifts you out of yourself; you've finally and truly gotten away from it all.

At the same time, this region is extraordinarily rich in its diversity: Ancient (by American standards) families struggling in genteel poverty to preserve a heritage handed down for more than three hundred years while living cheek by jowl with IBM … River views unchanged and unchanging since Henry Hudson first arrived … The old port of Rondout, its ugly contemporary bridge swooping over—but not quite able to hide—the exciting renovation and revitalization slowly but steadily under way … Exquisite country roads, twisting and turning through woods and mountains, past wineries and thoroughbred horse farms, orchards and fields filled with corn.

Then there is the faintly pot-scented aroma of Woodstock (especially on Saturday nights), the all-American moneyed village perfection of Rhinebeck, the beautiful, lived-in restoration of old Kingston, the elephantine estates, the simple, unique-to-the-Hudson Dutch stone houses. Not to mention a vast nineteenth-century resort (Mohonk Mountain House), tiny Bed & Breakfast hostelries, the oldest inn in America in continuous operation (The Beekman Arms) and many excellent restaurants. And over all, there is the light—that light so beloved by the Hudson River artists who lived and worked here, a light that gives the green of the Valley its special depth and richness and clarity. The time you spend here will be richly rewarded.

Ulster County

Kingston

Kingston is one of the undiscovered treasures of the Hudson. A small city of about 25,000 people that lies 90 miles north of New York City, it retains—perhaps more than any other town on the Hudson—its centuries-old, balanced relationship with the river. Possessing that increasingly rare quality of honest charm, it's nevertheless sophisticated enough to support a four-star restaurant (within 20 minutes' driving distance) and offers a boat ride through scenery that can only be described as achingly beautiful. There also are more than 20 of those handsome seventeenth- and eighteenth-century Dutch stone houses and a church that Calvert Vaux, codesigner of Central Park in New York City, described as "ideally perfect."

HISTORY

Kingston was first settled in 1652 by the Dutch, who called it Wiltwyck, a name that stuck until the English took over. As the settlers began moving out into the surrounding areas, the local Esopus Indians, members of the Algonquin tribe, grew restless enough to go on the warpath. They were promptly crushed, but Peter Stuyvesant, Dutch governor of New York from 1647 until 1664, when the English ousted him, was upset enough to order a simple stockade built in 1658 that would surround the settlement and protect the area. A good thing he did, too; the Indians attacked twice more, first in 1660 and then in June 1663, when they massacred a few settlers and burned everything in sight. (Why, by the way, are the Indians always referred to as "massacring" while the whites are only "defending" themselves as they walk off with all the real estate?) This did not amuse Stuyvesant, who got on his silver-encrusted wooden leg and undertook a full-scale summer campaign that proved so successful, the Indians' sway in the Valley was broken forever.

Along the main street of old Kingston, the covering gallerias offer a fanciful touch that makes it a most attractive place down which to stroll.

WHAT TO SEE AND DO: *A Perfect Day with Two Endings*

Today what is called the Stockade District forms the oldest and most interesting section of the town, an area of several blocks that was once the heart of old Kingston. It is where I always head, first thing in the morning, whenever I visit Kingston, driving past the **Old Dutch Church** at the corner of Main and Wall streets and, a few buildings further on, just by the County Court House, leaving my car in the very convenient municipal parking lot. It's a short walk back to the church.

The original church on this site was built in 1661, but the present bluestone Renaissance Revival building dates from 1852, based on designs by Minard Lafever. (One of the most sought-after architects of the period, Lafever [1797–1854] was most famous for his Gothic Revival churches, but he also designed other kinds of buildings and in other styles. Aside from this church his finest works, I feel, are St. Anne's [1847] in Brooklyn

Heights in Gothic Revival style and with the earliest—and very spectacular—stained glass windows in America, and the glorious Greek Revival central building of Sailors' Snug Harbor, built in 1831, on Staten Island.) The Old Dutch Church here in Kingston is a masterpiece. As Vaux said, "I cannot change a thing without impairing the exquisite unity."

To me the most perfect part of the church is its steeple, so ideally proportioned that it seems weightless, ready to float gently but purposefully upward, taking your heart right along with it. Then you look down once again at the church itself, and realize how comfortably it's situated, like the solid Dutch citizens it represents.

Given such a pretty spot, people are always about, sitting or strolling in the tree-filled churchyard, watching the birds and listening for the bells, and it's quite pleasant to wander a few minutes here, reading the old gravestones that date back to 1710 and enjoying the different perspectives the building offers. If you're lucky, you'll hear the bells play—"Onward, Christian Soldiers" is what I usually get.

Inside, the building seems so totally without pretension that it takes a moment to realize just how good is the whole, both as a structure and in what it represents. It's the cumulative effect: the handsome Tiffany window (1891) behind the pulpit; a framed letter from George Washington to "the Minister, elders and deacons" in which his fervent prayer is "that you may be enabled to hand down your Religion pure and undefiled to a Posterity worthy of their ancestors"; the elegantly vaulted ceiling, the commemorative plaques throughout, the faded Civil War flags.

Leave the church through the office to the left at the back and you're out again on Wall Street with enough time before lunch for a short stroll. Turn right and, after a block or so, both sides of the street become arcades covered by one-story white wooden galleries topped with balconies. The buildings themselves, mostly nineteenth century, are painted in complementary pastels and along the sidewalks are well-spaced trees and judiciously placed tubs of flowers. For some, the effect may smack too much of a stage set—but it's not; it's an inviting, very pretty, unified setting.

The shops are the usual things you'd expect to find in a major town, but here there's still an aura of nineteenth-century friendliness and relaxation.

Now wander off through the **Stockade District**, exploring any street that looks interesting (almost all are). Study some of the stone houses. The nice thing is that they're still used, some as private residences, others as offices, and so they don't have that glazed, restored-to-perfection look. This is a town, remember, not a museum, with pleasant gardens and yards to delight in, half-open Dutch doors to peek through, historical plaques to read and, every now and then, a friendly dog with a perpetual-motion tail, trying to cadge a pat or two.

Once you feel you've seen enough, turn back toward Wall Street, go again to the end, turn right and walk up to Clinton Street. You're now at the **Senate House State Historic Site** and its neighboring **Museum**.

For information on current hours, programs and exhibits, phone 845-338-2786. Web site: www.cr.nps.gov/nr/travel/kingston/k2.htm

I suggest you visit the museum first. It houses an extensive collection of paintings by John Vanderlyn (1775–1852), a Kingston native who is recognized primarily as one of the first American-born landscape artists, but who was also a portraitist of some distinction. According to John Howat's *The Hudson River and Its Painters*, "Vanderlyn's ambition was to be a great painter of history in the tradition of Jacques-Louis David." Howat also quotes from a letter of introduction Vanderlyn's patron, Aaron Burr, wrote in 1801 in which he states that Vanderlyn "is pronounced to be the first painter that now is or ever has been in America."

Indeed, Vanderlyn's paintings are good, particularly his portraits. True, there is a certain stiffness in some of the latter, despite his six years of study in Paris, but there are some very nice touches, too. A gently mysterious portrait of a young girl (Mrs. John R. Livingston) turned away from a mirror, yet with her profile reflected back to the viewer, is quite haunting. He's a nice "find" and the collection on display is large enough for you to get a thorough appreciation of his work. (By the way, the Metropolitan Museum in New York City now has on permanent display in its American wing Vanderlyn's enormous—and great fun—view of the palace and gardens at Versailles.)

It's also interesting to know that Vanderlyn's grandfather Pieter (see page 50), who lived in Kingston part of his life, was one of the leading folk artists of his time and a member of the first cohesive group of American portraitists, all of whom were centered in the Hudson Valley. The collection here includes two early portraits by Pieter Vanderlyn as well as works by John Vanderlyn, Jr., the nephew of the better-known John Vanderlyn.

Upstairs, the museum displays temporary shows and a few things from its own collection. The small shows are usually quite imaginatively presented. One that I particularly remember was devoted to Ammi Phillips (1788–1865), who lived and worked in the Valley for many years and is considered one of the finest folk artists of the nineteenth century. This exhibit was introduced by a marvelous quote made in 1829 by John Neal, a long-forgotten American author (*Keep Cool* is one of his titles), that aptly sums up a more jaundiced approach to American folk art: "You could hardly open the door of a best-room anywhere without surprising, or being surprised by, the picture of somebody, plastered to the wall and staring at you with both eyes." Works by Ammi Phillips, James Bard and others in the fairly extensive collection are sometimes exhibited in the Loughran House, an 1873 Italianate mansion, also part of the site, located behind the museum at 296 Fair Street.

The Senate House, which you should visit next, is a small gem. Here you will see the kitchen, bedroom and parlor where the first official New

Built in 1676, the Senate House now looks so ancient it seems to have sprung from the earth like the flowers in its hedged garden.

York State Senate met. Actually, the house was the private residence of the Van Gaasbeek family, but when Kingston became the first capital of New York as the legislators fled here to escape the British, the Van Gaasbeeks let their home be used by the Senate. On April 20, 1777, the lawmakers adopted the state's first constitution, and George Clinton was chosen as governor two months later. While this building was being used by the Senate, the State Assembly met in a nearby tavern, and Ulster County Courthouse served as both the capitol and the home of the Supreme Court. By October 1777, however, the British threatened again, and the government took off to nearby Hurley just before the redcoats, under Major General John Vaughan, burned Kingston to the ground. Vaughan later explained his action by writing that the city was a "nursery for almost every villain in the country," a wild exaggeration since the legislators had left, and that upon "[our] entering the town they fired from their houses, which induced me to reduce the place to ashes, not leaving a house." Well, he was almost right. Other British and American accounts describe the entire destruction of the city except for a single house that was spared from the flames, reducing Kingston, then the third largest city in New York, to a smoldering pile of stone and ashes.

Now, one more stop in the Stockade District. Go back to Wall Street and, opposite the churchyard, at 63 Main Street you will have arrived at the **Fred J. Johnston Museum**. Fred Johnston was an old friend and extremely helpful when I was first writing about the Hudson River Valley. He also had one of the finest antique shops in the Northeast and a national reputation as a dealer; the Metropolitan Museum, the White House and many other famous institutions have pieces that were originally in his shop. Today the shop houses museum activities. When Fred died in 1993, he left a trust fund for the Friends of Historic Kingston to maintain his house as a museum. The collection in the house is well worth a visit to see his superb furnishings from the early eighteenth to the early nineteenth centuries, with an emphasis on the Federal period, his greatest love.

Fred Johnston himself was a fascinating man with an incredible knowledge of the area's history. He worked closely with Henry du Pont when the latter created Winterthur, that splendid house-museum outside Wilmington, Delaware, containing the greatest assemblage of American decorative arts in the world; and, in truth, Johnston's house here in Kingston could pass for a miniature version of Winterthur. He also was largely responsible for the preservation of Kingston, and his love for the Valley amounted to a fierce passion. "This river has a more diverse history than any but the Nile," he used to say, and though one is tempted to point out that the Tiber, Seine and Thames also have a story or two, the more you think about it the more you realize that Johnston had a point.

The museum is open May–October, Saturday and Sunday 1–4. Phone: 845-339-0720. Web site: www.cr.nps.gov/nr/travel/kingston/k9.htm

Back to your car, out to Broadway, and follow it to the end, which will take you to **Rondout Creek**, the scene of the action when Kingston was one of the state's most important river ports in the nineteenth century. It was here that the 108-mile-long Delaware & Hudson Canal, completed in 1828, ended, just a short distance from where the creek joins the Hudson. (One of the canal's engineers was John Roebling, later of Brooklyn Bridge fame.) Carrying anthracite coal from Honesdale in northeastern Pennsylvania, the barges would unload here, and the coal would be transferred to other boats and then shipped south to New York City.

This, in turn, helped establish **Rondout** as home base for the steamship and towboat lines, and the city of Kingston prospered. Today the old port is only a shadow of what it once was. A good deal of it was torn down by urban renewal fanatics, but there's a movement underway to restore and revitalize what is left. One definitely senses a feeling of life flowing back.

The **Hudson River Maritime Museum**, located here, exhibits a wonderful old tug, now run aground and rechristened the *William O. Benson*, in honor of Kingston's most famous old river man. The late Captain Benson, a one-time tugboat skipper and extremely talented folk artist, creator of many delightful reproductions of Hudson River steamboats, was also a wonderful person to talk to if you wanted to learn more about the old days of Rondout and life on the river in general. Short and round, pipe always in hand, he used to love to reminisce.

"Twenty-four hours a day you heard steamboat whistles and paddle-wheels," he would say. "I got in the business … well, my father and brother were in it, and around Kingston in those days there was only about three ways you could make a decent livin', unless your people were well-to-do and sent you to college or somethin'. There was the shipyards. That was

This wonderful old tug has found a permanent home at the Hudson River Maritime Center in Kingston and tries desperately to maintain a modicum of dignity under rather trying circumstances.

hard work. There was the brickyards. That was hard work. And there was the steamboats and the nightboats and the Central Hudson Steamboat Company. And their main terminals was Kingston and New York City.

"Every afternoon at three-thirty, we'd hear that big *Benjamin B. Odell* blow three whistles, or the *Homer Ramsdell* on the way out. You'd see the *Martin* and others come in. You'd see the ferry running between Kingston and Rhinecliff. And then there was tugboats towin' coal boats and scows in and out of the creek all day long.

"At one time it was a very busy place. You never had to go uptown to buy anythin', clothes, hardware, anythin'. There was four or five restaurants, a hotel, newsstands with all the papers and magazines you could want. And there was a railroad station in case you wanted to go up to Oneonta, trolley cars—the Colonial Line and the Broadway Line—and Kingston Point, where the pleasure park was. And, of course, there was always some kind of excursion trip goin' outa Kingston.

"You know, I was born the week the *Benjamin B. Odell* made her maiden voyage out of Rondout Crik. My mother liked the lines of the boat so she gave me the middle name of *Odell*. So I'm prejudiced, but I think she was the most beautiful boat on the Hudson. I remember she'd be leavin' the crik here at eleven on a Saturday mornin'. And just as she got to the mouth, a big Albany nightboat would be deadheadin' back to New York City to bring the crowd out that night and they'd be goin' full speed. So the *Odell* would fall a little behind. I'd stand on a hill to watch her, and when they'd both get to Esopus Light, three miles down the river, where they turned, and just before they went outa sight, well, what do you know, the Odell would be goin' out in front, always, the black smoke comin' out of her stacks. Oh, it was a beautiful sight!"

Web site: www.hrmm.org

The trolley lines Captain Benson talked about are the reason for the **Trolley Museum**, which provides a pleasant jaunt along Rondout Creek. (Do note the sign "No Parking Trolley Traffic.")

Open: Saturday, Sundays, Holidays, Memorial Weekend–Columbus Day. Phone: 845-331-3399. Web site: www.TMNY.org

But the real reason to be here is **one of the best river cruises on the Hudson,** aboard the *Rip Van Winkle*. (Hudson River Cruises, phone: 800-843-7472; operates May–October. For complete information, go to the web site: www.hudsonrivercruises.com.) It is absolutely not to be missed. This is a family-operated business, and they make you feel at home immediately. Climb aboard. A lovely deep blast on the boat's whistle and you're moving out into the creek, past the spot where the swans nest and the Rondout Light, and then you're on the Hudson.

No matter how often I take this trip my heart always leaps at this moment. The river is so vast. Off to the left, before you turn downstream, the Kingston-Rhinecliff Bridge, so prosaic when you're on it, seems now the slenderest of filaments connecting the two shores. Downstream the tree-covered banks look uninhabited, and the Catskills, gray-blue in the distance, appear almost protective, the natural guardian of the river. (But don't be fooled. Storms can sweep down from these mountains in minutes.) The water is so opaque that it looks solid, only the great undulations of the river giving a hint of its power. The commentary is genuinely interesting and mercifully unobtrusive on what you're seeing.

Really, though, all you need is the experience itself. You can sense the tension being drained from your body, leaving you profoundly relaxed. I've taken many friends, with quite different interests and personalities, along on this trip, and all of them have felt this same letting go.

There is little conversation; the scenery is so majestic that talk seems out of place, except when you see something that you don't want the others to miss, like the Esopus Light on its tiny rocky island—now restored and decorated with witty trompe l'oeil paintings of curtains and pots of geraniums and even a cat in the window—or else glimpses of the great

My favorite lighthouse is this one south of Kingston, the Esopus Light, with its trompe l'oeil paintings in the windows, including one of a very worldly cat.

mansions, their dark roofs looming over the trees, their well-kept lawns sweeping down to the water. Sailboats, motorboats, tugs, even freighters seem miles away, the river is so wide, and every few feet the view changes, something new springs into sight, or the light on the water suddenly shifts its patterns as a cloud passes over.

The vistas justify, for once, the word "magnificent." You can't help but think of Henry Hudson arriving here almost 400 years ago, looking out upon what one of his officers described as "a very good land to fall with and a pleasant land to see" and then remember that you, basically, are viewing the very same thing. No other great river in the world that runs through such highly developed country has remained in such a pristine state as the Hudson right here. It's very moving. "I always think the country is never as interesting as the city," one passenger said to me, "but this is the exception."

That, as I remember, was spoken as the sun was setting behind the Catskills, which someone once said, "heave from the valley of the Hudson like the subsiding billows of the ocean after a storm." No wonder the Hudson River School of painters was the first group of American landscape artists. When you see the Valley from this kind of vantage point, there can be no question that the scenery is as beautiful as any in the world. And it is our great good fortune that this particular stretch has escaped almost all exploitation and development—so far. If you do only one thing in the Hudson Valley, this, then, should be it. For unless you actually get out on the river you will never understand what it has meant—and still means—to so many people.

The other perfect ending for this day would be dinner at John Novi's **DePuy Canal House** (phone: 845-687-7700; web site: www.depuycanal-house.net) in High Falls, to which the late Craig Claiborne, world-famous food authority and food writer for *The New York Times*, awarded four stars, and which another famous food critic calls "one of the most entertainingly bizarre dining places in New York State." She also notes that owner John Novi can "justly be dubbed the father of new American cooking" and, like Craig Claiborne, thinks much of the menu is "outstanding." Certainly, it is the most creative restaurant in the Valley (see page 170).

The handsome stone inn was originally built by Simeon DePuy in 1797, and its fortunes as a hostelry were fully assured when the Delaware & Hudson Canal went into operation in 1828, for the waterway passed

The DePuy Canal House. Should you look through one of these windows, you might see diners enjoying some of the best food in the Hudson Valley.

within a few yards of the building. Today one of the most romantic features of the setting is the restored lock by the restaurant. When the canal died in 1899 because other means of transportation proved cheaper and quicker and because oil was becoming more and more important, so did the tavern. Then, happily, John Novi bought and restored it, reopening it as a restaurant in 1969. Now the place is divided up into small, intimate dining rooms with, at the main entrance, an attractive bar. Guests are also welcome to drop in to the spectacular kitchen and visit with John and his sous-chefs as they work their marvels.

There are five dining rooms. The main one, right behind the bar, seats 18 and has a working fireplace. A slightly smaller room beyond it, once the lockkeeper's quarters, seats 10 and also has a fireplace. Upstairs, there are three more dining rooms, one with a view of the lock, that can take up any overflow or serve as the perfect setting for a private party. Guests are free to wander through all of the rooms, which contributes to the informal, at-home atmosphere.

But there's nothing at home about the food. I remember one dinner in particular. I was coming up from New York City on one of those hot, humid August days that make you feel as if you're trying to breathe and move in damp cotton balls. I had called ahead to John, by now a friend, and warned him I didn't know what time I'd get there. "Don't worry," he replied. "If you miss the regular dinner I'll throw together a soup and salad or you can have some leftovers."

As it happened, we got there just after sunset, and the outdoor lighting made the building an oasis of pleasure. John, a good-looking man with a gentle, friendly manner, came out to say hello, mumbled something about our dinner, and disappeared back into the kitchen after I asked him to decide on the menu for us. A few minutes later a small plate of hors d'oeuvres arrived. Delicious. Next the soup, a light-as-air, beautifully chilled coconut confection with just-picked raspberries. Out of this world. The entrée was fresh shiitake mushrooms in Stone's Ginger Wine Sauce, so subtly right it was part and parcel of the mushrooms, with a piece of grilled beef and fresh-from-the-garden buttered vegetables cooked not an instant beyond perfection. For dessert I had more raspberries, my companion an exquisite pastry.

But every meal there is an experience, whether it be Smoked Salmon Ricotta in Pasta with Basil Cream (John does his own smoking) or Quail with Sausage Stuffing on Wild Rice with Plum Sauce or Lobster Bouillabaisse with Saffron Leek Sauce. To take advantage of seasonal ingredients, the menu is constantly changing, but whatever you order you can rest assured that it will be beautiful to look at, delightful to taste and, oh, so easy to love. Some people find the food a little bit too "original," but when John Novi is at his best, this restaurant is hard to beat.

Now the DePuy Canal House has a more casual restaurant downstairs in what was the old wine cellar. Called Chefs on Fire, it has a stone oven for baking gourmet pizzas and artisan breads, and there is a bistro-style menu that changes seasonally and features European-style sandwiches, pastas, salads, desserts, gourmet coffees, wine and beers, both local and imported.

That's not all. Next door to the restaurant, John has opened The New York Store. It offers freshly baked breads, croissants, muffins and scones along with gourmet coffees and teas, desserts, and a large selection of New York-made food products ranging from jams and jellies to pickled beets and chutneys. Caviars, smoked meats, New York cheeses … the list goes on and on.

New Paltz

New Paltz is, after Kingston, the most interesting town on the west bank, yet when you drive into it, it's rather disappointing at first glance. Perhaps it's because there's a State University branch here, and somehow I always expect it to look more razzle-dazzle collegiate than it does. And then, too, you can drive straight through the village on Main Street in what seems like two minutes flat without seeing one thing that would make you want to stop. Nevertheless, don't be fooled; New Paltz has much to offer and, including lunch, you can spend a very pleasant half-day here.

WHAT TO SEE AND DO

The single most interesting spot is **Huguenot Street**, with its six restored stone houses dating from 1692 to 1890 and allowing the proud and accurate boast that this is "the oldest street in America with its original houses." It's easy to find. Just drive down Main Street, which is also Route 299, toward the Wallkill River. Turn right on Huguenot Street, just before the bridge, follow the road to where it divides, go left and you're there.

I would suggest that you call ahead to the tour office to arrange your tour.

Huguenot Street Tour. Available early May to late October, Tuesday–Sunday 9–4. Phone: 845-255-1660 in season. Web site: wwwhhs-newpaltz.org

As the tour can take as long as two hours, more time than many of us have, I would also suggest that you request yours last no more than an hour. That way you could begin your tour at 11, before many tourists arrive, and then have lunch. Get there a little early, look for the sign for Deyo Hall (it's on your right, and the tour starts there), park your car and then walk back to Huguenot Street. It is indeed a charmer, and this way you'll orient yourself before starting. There is, by the way, a small, rainbow-hued, old-fashioned country garden that you'll see almost immediately. It's a memorial to one of the benefactors of the street.

As for background, you should know that this land was first settled by 12 Huguenot families in the spring of 1678 and that, by 1792, the street looked basically the same as it does today. (The Reformed Church, dead center on the street, was built in 1839, with additions made later.) The Huguenot families named the settlement New Paltz after Die Pfalz, the Rhenish Palatinate region in Germany that served as their refuge from French persecution. The houses are now protected and owned by The Huguenot Historical Society, whose membership includes dozens of descendants of the original families, presently scattered all over the country.

If you're really pressed for time I would ask to see just two buildings, the French Huguenot Church, still used on special occasions, and the Jean Hasbrouck House. **The French Church** is actually a reconstruction, completed in 1972, of the original built in 1717. It is a small, square, stone building with a steeply canted roof topped by a cupola from which a horn or giant conch shell was blown to summon the worshippers. The whole is quite unlike anything you might see in New England or other parts of New York State. Inside it is extremely simple and very appealing with wide pine-plank flooring, an old French Provincial communion table and elegantly proportioned pews.

The old French Huguenot Church, built in 1717. Worshippers were called to service by a giant conch shell blown from the tower.

One thing about the Huguenots—they knew how to build a solid house and chimney. These two look forward with confidence to their fourth century.

The Jean Hasbrouck House (open on weekends all year) is, in my opinion, the best on the street. (Hasbrouck is one of the oldest names in the area, and the local phone book is filled with them.) Not only are the rooms in general better furnished than in any of the other residences, but also the attic has a most spectacular brick chimney that rises about two stories over your head and is supported by a stone wall at the back of the structure and balanced by a frontal beam. It seems odd to rave about a chimney, but this is the only original one in the country, and it makes a powerful impression.

For lunch, continue on for a minute or two down Huguenot Street until you see a sign for the **Locust Tree Restaurant** on your left. The inn is actually a restaurant set in a stone-and-frame house, the stone part built in 1759, with the frame section added in the early nineteenth century. This restaurant has been through several owners since I first wrote this book, but the current ones are far and away the best. Lunch and dinner is a pleasure, the food being French, Italian, German … inventive and very good. I like the menu and the service, and both food and wine are reasonable. You really must go there if you are in or near New Paltz.

ENVIRONS OF NEW PALTZ

From here, drive back to Main Street, turn left, go to South Manheim Boulevard (Route 32 South), turn right, and after about 4 miles you'll see a sign for **Locust Lawn**, a good-looking white-frame Federal mansion built in 1814 by Colonel Josiah Hasbrouck, who fought in the American Revolution. One thing about the Hasbroucks, they never threw anything away, and this house not only harbors superb examples of Duncan Phyfe and Sheraton furniture but also retains all the original documentation for them, such as bills and correspondence, indicating cost and manufacturer. Hasbrouck was rich—real estate was the basis for his fortune—and he was not afraid to spend his money. For me, the single most impressive thing is the group of four portraits of family members by Ammi Phillips—and particularly so since the furniture depicted in the paintings can still be seen in the house. John Vanderlyn and Alden Weir are also represented, as well as some of the more mediocre Hudson River School painters, and the house is filled with mementos of the Hasbrouck family, clothes and dolls and books, that give it a very personal quality. It's an excellent documentation of how an upper-middle-class family lived in the early nineteenth century.

Open: early May through late October, weekends or by appointment only. Phone: 845-255-1660. Web site; wwwhhs-newpaltz.org

The property also contains a smallish **Wildlife Sanctuary**, pleasant for a leisurely walk along the nature trails. And there's a slaughterhouse, smokehouse and carriage house, where you can wander amid coaches, farm implements and other tools. Far more interesting to me is the tiny, typically Dutch, stone **Terwilliger House**, built in 1738 and across the lawn from the Hasbrouck mansion. Inside there's not all that much to see, although the house itself is a charmer, but at the back of the central hallway there's a window looking out upon a small stream … and all of a sudden you're transported back to the eighteenth century. Nothing has changed; the beauty and the wonder remain.

A Drive through Ulster County

In any season, Ulster County presents some of the loveliest scenery in a valley famous for its beauty. Always there is, of course, the river, but the pleasure of this particular drive is the countryside: changing views of the Catskills, vast panoramas from the mountains, lovely old farms with great sweeps of cultivated fields, woods and streams, handsome old houses and small, sleepy villages. If you don't stop anywhere, you could do the circuit in about two hours, but to fully enjoy it I would suggest you plan to make a day of it.

I usually begin from the Kingston-Rhinecliff Bridge, taking Route 209 south toward Ellenville. (If you're coming off the New York State Thruway, take exit 19, then 28W, which also puts you on 209S.) I first like to stop in **Hurley**, a right turn off 209. This wonderful little village was founded in 1662, promptly burned by the Esopus Indians a year later and, finally, resettled in 1669.

Today, what gives Hurley its great charm is the more than dozen eighteenth-century stone houses, all privately owned and lovingly maintained, and the fact that there is practically nothing here that dates from after 1900. The result is a village from the past that has survived intact, and it's pleasant to walk along Main Street looking at the old houses, some with walls as thick as 18 inches. (One, the 1735 Crispell House, just down from School House Lane, has iron spikes in the chimney to catch witches who might decide to enter that way.)

Each year, in early July, Hurley celebrates "Stone House Day," with a tour of about a dozen of the stone houses and the Hurley Reformed Church, as well as the **Hurley Patentee Manor**, originally built in 1696 and then vastly expanded in 1745.

Open: mid-July–Labor Day, daily except Monday, the rest of the year by appointment only. Phone: 845-331-5414.

There are also a country fair, an antiques show and good, homemade food the same day.

Drive back to 209 and continue south to the village of **Stone Ridge**. There's no one thing in particular to see here, but the village has some lovely buildings, and almost any road off 209 is worth at least a brief excursion to look at the stunning houses and rich, beautifully cared-for land. The area has become a favorite for weekenders who buy houses and summer visitors who rent, bringing in enough money to maintain a heritage that probably never had it so good.

As you leave Stone Ridge, watch for a sign on your left for Rosendale and turn here (213E) to go on to **High Falls**. This is the home of the DePuy Canal House (see page 170), but the tiny village—really a hamlet—has a great deal to offer as well.

Right next to the Canal House is Lock 16, part of the old Delaware & Hudson Canal system, a handsome, monumental tribute to the past. Barges loaded with coal were lowered here, and you can see the six-inch-deep grooves in the Canal House where the ropes burned their way through.

Why does an ancient cemetery, lonely and abandoned, still exercise a romantic tug at our hearts and impel us to walk among its crumbling stones?

Next, take a look at the falls that gave the town its name, then walk back toward the Canal House, pass it, and turn right when you see a sign for the Mohonk Mountain House. A little farther on, to your left, you will come to the **D & H Canal Museum.** They have a brochure that gives you a plan for a walking tour (about 45 minutes) of the 5 locks in the area, which are now listed as National Historic Landmarks. In addition, you can see the John Roebling (of Brooklyn Bridge fame) abutments for the old aqueduct as well as some lovely falls. On a nice day, this can be a very pleasant visit. As for the tiny museum, it displays canal boat models, photographs and other items from the great days of the D & H; very informal but well done.

**Open: May–October, Thursday–Monday 11–5, Sunday 1–5.
Phone: 845-687-9311. Web site: www.canalmuseum.org**

Once you're ready to leave, turn right at the Mohonk Mountain House sign. (By the way, from 1945 to 1954 the great painter Marc Chagall had a studio on Mohonk Road, and it became a spot dear to his heart.) Now you begin the most beautiful section of the drive. Very quickly you're in "real" country, with only a few scattered houses, mostly fields and woods. After a few miles you will come upon a large meadow and, looking up ahead, will see that the road makes a hairpin turn as it begins to climb the mountain. Slow down as you approach the turn and you'll notice a spot where you can pull off the road. Stop, get out, and look back. The view from here is completely unspoiled, with the Catskills for a backdrop, and it's as lovely and tranquil as anyone could ask for; I'd give a lot to have a house right here and watch the changing seasons. Once, in early autumn, I frightened a covey of pheasant here, the perfect finishing touch as I watched their brilliant colors flash away across the meadow.

At the top of the mountain is the entrance to the **Mohonk Mountain House** (see page 166), the last great survivor from the nineteenth-century era of Hudson River Valley resort hotels. Then, on down the mountain, follow the road to its end just outside New Paltz.

Here you will turn right on 299, with the Shawangunk Ridge off to the west. (The tower that you see on the ridge as you drive along is at Mohonk and was erected to honor the memory of Albert Smiley, who built the hotel with his twin brother Alfred.) The scenery is completely different here, a valley with great broad vistas and filled with farms, all surrounded by mountains.

At the end of 299, turn right on Routes 44 and 55, and once again you begin climbing. (Note all the parked cars. They belong to people who are rock climbing.) Soon you will come to areas where you can stop and look back for miles out over the Valley and, during warm weather, you will see dozens of cars pulled off on either side of the road, their owners gone to explore the woods and enjoy the loveliness of their surroundings. This is the setting, too, for Lake Minnewaska, a public center for swimming and skiing and allied sports, whose entrance gate you will see on the left.

A typical late eighteenth-century Dutch stone farmhouse.

Farther on, just as you begin your descent, there are two areas where you can again pull off the road to enjoy a vista that extends for 50 miles, both favorite spots of mine. No wonder the father of the Hudson River School, Thomas Cole, on his return from Europe, told people the Alps couldn't hold a candle to the Catskills. Of its kind, this is one of the loveliest views in the East.

Now you should watch, on the right, for a sign for the Granit Hotel, and—once you see it—turn right, following the directions for the hotel but passing its entrance. Once again you're in backcountry. Follow the road to the first stop sign, in Accord, and turn right again. At the sign for Alligerville, New Paltz and Mohonk, bear left. (It was in Alligerville, by the way, that the peanut-butter sandwich is said to have been invented, based on a recipe brought back from the Caribbean. Who added jelly, I don't know.)

This entire road is lovely, but I do have two favorite spots. One is a stretch bordered on both sides with fragrant pines and a woodland stream on your right that has several tempting swimming holes. The other is a field that ends at the base of the Shawangunk Ridge. Look up and there is the Mohonk Mountain House brooding over the landscape like some fairy castle out of Grimm. At the next stop sign bear right, and you're on Ulster County Route 6. (If you have time, explore one or two of the fascinating side roads.) Once at the end of this road, you will see a sign showing High Falls to the left, New Paltz to the right. You are back on the road you originally took from High Falls.

Woodstock

It's sad to say, but the charm of Woodstock, though it still remains an arts center with serious pretensions, has been almost obliterated by the tourists who now flock there. The Woodstock Playhouse has reopened after a fire, and there are other endeavors worthy of note—the Woodstock Artists Association, for example, with its changing exhibits of works by local artists, is always worth a visit. But I would strongly suggest that you see or do any of these things during the week; the weekends attract too many people into too small a town, and the result is not pleasant.

The artist tradition goes back to 1902, when Ralph Radcliffe Whitehead, an Englishman out of California with the quintessentially nineteenth-century ideal of founding a center that would work toward the betterment of mankind, chose a spot just north of the town to establish his arts and crafts colony. Then, a few years later, the Art Students League of New York City opened a summer school, and soon musicians, novelists, painters, poets, dancers and the like discovered the considerable charms of the area and began settling in. But along with real talent came, in increasing numbers, the would-be talents and hangers-on, and then, in 1969, the famous—or infamous— Woodstock Festival put the village on the world map and has since caused people to stream into the town who don't know Picasso from Rembrandt and think the only Humperdinck ever is alive and well and singing in Las Vegas. (Oddly enough, the festival was actually held in Bethel, more than 60 miles away, but it was Woodstock that received the curse of fame.)

Since then, the village has tried hard to refurbish its image, and it still attracts many interesting people who live outside the town. It still has, too, a pretty setting, an excellent bookstore, some pleasant shops. But the old Woodstock is gone forever, and a weekend night here in summer can be more like Sheridan Square in Greenwich Village than the civilized sylvan retreat it once was.

ENVIRONS OF WOODSTOCK AND KINGSTON

Maverick Concerts ■ This is a splendid Woodstock institution that originated in 1916. It is a summer series of chamber music concerts, presented by top-flight artists, in a wonderfully rural setting and performed in a barn built by the founder of the Maverick Concerts, poet-novelist Hervey White. He named the concerts after the arts colony he had already established on his farm. The intimacy of the setting is just what is needed for chamber music. What's particularly appealing is that the series juxtaposes relatively unfamiliar and/or contemporary work with the standard repertory. Their season generally begins in late June and runs to early September. It is a delight.

The site is located on Maverick Road between Route 28 and 375, West Hurley. Phone: 845-679-8217. Web site: www.maverickconcerts.org.

Opus 40 ■ It seems that every time you turn around in Ulster County, there's another poster or brochure for Opus 40, with a picture of some section of this vast, environmental sculpture by the late Harvey Fite. Admittedly, it's a very curious work.

What Fite did was to create his sculpture on the 6-acre site of an abandoned bluestone quarry. (Quarries such as these provided the stone to pave the sidewalks of New York City.) Fite worked on it for 37 years and it was still unfinished when he died in the 1970s. Pathways lead up, down and around pools and trees, and the summit is dominated by a 9-ton monolith.

Quite frankly, I find the whole depressing, an interesting idea gone crazy, but some of the parts do come off. I'm thinking particularly of a section with birch and pine trees that is very beautiful in its contemplative, faintly Japanese way. On the other hand, the somber pools, dark and primeval, definitely do not appeal to me. "A great place for snakes," I overheard one visitor say to another as they peered down into one of them, and that described it perfectly.

There also is a small **Quarryman's Museum** containing Fite's collection of old quarrymen's tools and furnishings. Opus 40 is near Woodstock and Kingston. It can be hard to find, and should you decide on a visit, I'd suggest you call for directions.

**Open: This can vary, so double-check by phone: 845-246-3400.
Web site: www.opus40.org**

Dutchess County:

America's Loire Valley

THE GREAT HOUSES OF THE VALLEY: An Overview

The Hudson Valley estates are unique. Nothing in the country can equal the variety of these chateaus here, farther north and in the lower Valley. Virginia, it is true, has more than its fair share of important houses, and New England is a historical gold mine of domestic architecture. But the sheer number, size, concentration and periods represented in the Valley give the whole an importance that cannot be rivaled.

The riverfront estates in the northern part of Dutchess County and the adjacent town of Clermont in Columbia County (see page 66) now form part of a National Historic Landmark District, promulgated by the United States Secretary of the Interior in December 1990. Encompassing some 10,000 acres and 2,000 buildings, it is said to be the largest such district in the nation. The principal properties have been described by the Preservation League of New York State as being "architecturally and historically among the most magnificent estates in America." Incredibly enough, many are still in private hands, but 6—Franklin Delano Roosevelt's Springwood in Hyde Park, the Frederick Vanderbilt Mansion, the Staatsburgh State Historic Site (formerly the Ogden Mills Mansion), Wilderstein, Montgomery Place and the Livingston Mansion at Clermont—are now open to the public. The rest have become semipublic institutions. (The Reverend Sun Myung Moon owns one of the latter, and I asked one old Hudson Valley denizen what he thought of the Unification Church as a neighbor. "They've proved to be— after a shakedown period—tolerable," he said.)

I've subtitled this section "America's Loire Valley" because that's exactly what it is, a section of the country where our aristocracy and nouveau riche—Vanderbilts, Livingstons, Astors, Roosevelts, among others—established great country seats on hundreds of acres and upon which they lavished millions in today's dollars in landscaping, architecture, works of art and furnishings. This extravaganza could never be repeated today.

I've also long been fascinated by how this area has been preserved to such an extraordinary extent (it's almost un-American!) against what must have been intense pressures to sell and develop—and thereby destroy. So I began looking around for someone who could answer my questions, and soon enough found Winthrop Aldrich, a pleasant man with wire-rimmed glasses who looks like a successful cross between an authentic country squire and an Ivy League professor. All his life he has been a passionate advocate for preserving both the natural and historic resources of the Valley. Among other achievements, he was a major factor in establishing the Hudson River National Historic Landmark District mentioned above.

Winthrop, his brother Richard and sister own Rokeby, a house originally built in 1815 for their ancestors General John Armstrong and his wife, Alida Livingston, on Livingston land and one of many nineteenth-century Livingston estates here along the Hudson. John and Alida's daughter Margaret married William B. Astor, son of John Jacob, who is said to have bought the house for the young couple as a wedding present, and enlarged it to its present 45 rooms. Margaret, obviously of a romantic nature, named it Rokeby after a poem by Sir Walter Scott, and the house has remained in the family ever since, the only major change coming in 1895 when Stanford White remodeled part of it.

White with dark-green shutters, an elegant hexagonal tower tucked into one side, the house is large by anyone's standards but also looks homey and lived in, though sadly down at the heels. His mission in life has been to preserve this and other places in the state as a national trust, maintaining them for a mixture of private, public and semipublic uses that would fix for all time what is a centuries-old and unique national heritage. It would be an understatement to say that Mr. Aldrich goes about his task with a near-messianic zeal that combines intelligence, wit and good sense.

And it's not easy. The family money is pretty much gone and the Aldriches can't be sure that they'll win. Still, they—and other remaining families like them throughout the Valley—have a sense of noblesse oblige that helps keep them going, taking it one day at a time. So far, at least, if they haven't won, they haven't lost, either.

The day I met with Mr. Aldrich he was just ending a discussion with his brother about fixing the porch, whose primary decoration consisted of a pram containing an enormous teddy bear. Once we went inside, though, with the warm sunlight desperately trying to bring back the coloring to an ancient Aubusson rug, the various neglected toys lying in a corner and all the family portraits and old books lent to the interior an oddly timeless aura, perfectly suited to the subject of our conversation.

"This is all I've ever known," Winthrop Aldrich started out saying. "I've lived here and my family's lived here ... well, in 1988 we started our fourth century of ownership. It's in my blood, the feeling for the land, the feeling for the landscape, the view, the heritage of the region. All of that makes this place very special for me, and by extension the properties next-door and the properties beyond that as well.

"You see, all of the properties along a twenty-mile strip that begins two miles north of Clermont [see page 66] and ends one mile south of the Mills Mansion [see page 142] all stem historically from the marriage of my ancestress Margaret Beekman, who married Judge Robert Livingston, the heir of Clermont, in the 1740s and had ten children. She inherited the Beekman lands in Dutchess and Ulster counties and parceled them out to her nine youngest sons and daughters. Her tenth and eldest child, Chancellor Robert Livingston, inherited Clermont and what eventually became the seven properties north of that. And, even today, there is this *cousinage* of Livingston-Beekman descendants, the so-called cadet branch of the family, who settled along the riverbank from Clermont to the south from the 1780s onward.

"It all remained in family hands through the Civil War period and was developed into country seats, beginning in the late eighteenth century, to which the family was enormously attached and on which, through their ten-ant farms, they depended for their incomes. Then it began to change. Some of the land went out of the family, but always the character of the landscape and, to a large degree, the character of the architecture has been respected."

What Mr. Aldrich and his ancestors and his uncles and his cousins and his aunts—to paraphrase Gilbert and Sullivan—have done then is to cre-ate—over several hundred years—a 20-mile stretch of riverfront that serves as a kind of ongoing laboratory that illustrates the evolution of landscape design, agriculture, domestic architecture and interior design by reason of the varying uses to which these estates and farm lands have been put as some of the family domains have changed hands or have gradually become converted into public or institutional properties. All this coupled with eco-logically significant tidal coves, virgin woods and romantic ravines and waterfalls—not to mention the splendid views of the Hudson and the Catskill Mountains. It remains unique in the nation.

"Fortunately so far, the new people buying here respect this tradition," Aldrich continued. "The ones who are buying the big estates and investing a lot of money in them seem to be looking for privacy and even to put down roots. That's what we want. (By 'we' I mean all of us involved in the conservation of the Valley.) We don't want the jet set or fad purchaser because they won't stay. We're not geared to meet their needs. Nor do we want the speculators.

"Places like these require continuous care—and a continuous presence, really. So we want people who will get it into their blood, because it's a very big commitment. And they do come. Perhaps it's serendipity.

"You really should see **Wilderstein**, the Suckley place. It's a good example of what we're trying to do—very exciting, a high-style Victorian frame building with a J. B. Tiffany interior and Calvert Vaux landscaping of the grounds. It needs attention, of course, but experts have told us that this property is perhaps the most important of all to save.

"Miss Suckley turned it over to one of our nonprofit organizations but retained the right to live there. She was a wonderful person, a distant cousin of FDR, and it was she who raised and gave him Fala, his favorite dog. In any case, she was one of those people who, quietly over the years, realized that what her father and grandfather had created was important, and that if she could live long enough and hold on to it (she was not wealthy), public opinion would finally come around to appreciating it. And she was right. And that's how many of us feel."

(I did go to see Miss Suckley—that afternoon, in fact—and extraordinary is a word that could have been coined to describe this tiny, wiry old lady who looked thirty years younger than she was and walked with a cane only because a broken leg was still mending. There she was, living in this very large, rather looming brown frame Queen Anne house consisting of 35 rooms encased in a three-story, multi-gabled building with a circular tower overlooking the Hudson. The landscape surrounding the house, by the way, was designed by Calvert Vaux. But as she showed me through the ground-floor rooms, the furniture shrouded and the wallpaper faded even in the golden glow from the Tiffany windows—not Louis Comfort but a cousin, Joseph Burr Tiffany—her belief in its ultimate value, her excitement in the fact that its future was now assured, her memories and her wonderful sense of humor made the house alive and vibrant. Of particular interest was her relationship mentioned above to Franklin D. Roosevelt, her sixth cousin and near neighbor. She was a dear companion, and they grew very close. She even was with him when he died. When she herself died, a suitcase full of letters and diaries that she exchanged with FDR revealed the surprising extent of their relationship. The story has been written up in a book entitled *Closet Companion*, edited by Geoffrey C. Ward. She died in July 1991, at the age of 99. Wilderstein and its surrounding acres are now open to the public from the first weekend in May to the last weekend in October, Thursday–Sunday noon–4.

Phone: 845-876-4818. Web site: www.wilderstein.org

Aldrich and I next talked of Olana, Frederic Church's house, which he had also helped to save in 1965 (see page 63). "People said to me, 'Do you really want to save *that*?' Well, the group did just that, and now, I believe, it's the most popular state-owned historic site. It's phenomenal. They have waiting lines to get in! And I don't think it's just because it's so exotic, or because it's high on a hill with a spectacular view. It's because it offers a very special message and now people are ready for it.

"I think we all have an obligation to look particularly carefully at buildings that are seventy-five to a hundred years old and not very popular, figure out which are the best, and try to preserve and save them. It's commonly held that if a property can survive one hundred and ten years— that is, survive to be appreciated by the great-grandchildren—then its prospect is greatly improved.

"You know, aside from the fact that tastes change, we're all a bit parochial. It's hard to believe that something you've grown up with and are accustomed to seeing in your own backyard is of national importance. So it becomes a matter of education. We gradually hear from the art-museum curators and the writers and scholars, and then we, the local people, begin to realize that this chair or that view or this landscape arrangement is *unique*, that there's nothing like it in the world, and slowly our own values change to reflect this.

"My point, of course, is that the whole is greater than the sum of its parts; that the whole twenty miles must be protected and must be stabilized. It also has to be recycled in an intelligent fashion or there'll be some disastrous episode of development. If a speculator gets a hold on one of these places and proves that he can make a windfall profit it will tend to increase the assessed value of all of the other properties—and make it that much harder for the rest of us to hang on and even harder for new people to come in and still pay reasonable prices.

"I like the idea of the area being a mixture of the meticulously restored property open to the public, like Clermont and Olana, and, nearby, some private property where they're getting along, somehow, as we are here at Rokeby, by fixing only the porch this summer, the tower next, and then still others like Wilderstein, which is a nonprofit venture, involving a lot of fund-raising.

"Overall, I'm optimistic. Years ago, when my grandmother died here, my brother and I thought it really was a rearguard action we were taking by remaining. We supposed these places would be swept away. We were not then, and aren't now, financially equipped to carry the burden, but this is more important to us than anything else, certainly more than our own personal convenience, or taking the long chance that some other family who bought it or some commercial company that took it over would respect it as we've tried to.

"We assumed that if we were lucky, we'd be able to hold on to it for, say, another generation, and if we were doubly lucky, the same would hold true for the owners of the properties on either side of us. Now, those years have passed and, in effect, the whole fabric of twenty miles has held because of incremental solutions to problems. We've lost some buildings, but we haven't really lost any landscape. One fantastic place, for instance— Wyndclyffe, near Rhinecliff, where Edith Wharton spent some of her childhood—has now become so dangerous you can't even approach it. It's probably too expensive to stabilize, even as a picturesque ruin."

(Edith Wharton herself had a slightly different perspective on Wyndclyffe, which she called Rhinecliff and which belonged to her father's unmarried sister, Elizabeth: "I can still remember hating everything at Rhinecliff," she wrote in *A Backward Glance*, her posthumously published autobiography, "which, as I saw, on rediscovering it some years later, was an expensive but dour specimen of Hudson River Gothic, and from the first I was obscurely conscious of a queer resemblance between the granite exterior of Aunt Elizabeth and her grimly comfortable home, between her battlemented caps and the turrets of Rhinecliff.")

After I left Rokeby, I thought: How admirable these people, here and in other parts of the country, who are fighting to keep something for the rest of us that they know to be important. In many ways, they're pioneering spirits looking to the future, staking out vital parts of our national heritage to save and develop for our descendants. "A nation can be a victim of amnesia. It can lose the memories of what it was, and thereby lose the sense of what it is or what it wants to be." That's from a historic preservation report prepared in 1966—and that's exactly what the Winthrop Aldriches of this country won't allow to happen.

HOUSES TO VISIT

The Home of Franklin D. Roosevelt (Springwood) in Hyde Park ▪ The most famous house in the Valley, this is also the most intensely personal, as if the Roosevelts were expected back at any moment. And that makes it all the more touching. In fact, going through it is a deeply moving experience regardless of one's age or politics. No other presidential house comes off quite so well or as revealingly. Its actual name is Springwood, and it is in Hyde Park.

Eleanor Roosevelt published a small booklet on Springwood after the house and grounds were turned over to the U.S. government. In it she reminisces about her life there and also includes some fragments that FDR wrote, just before he died, as the prelude to a more elaborate account of the estate.

"The Hudson River Valley was in my husband's blood," Mrs. Roosevelt states. "Franklin Delano Roosevelt's family owned land in and around Poughkeepsie and along the banks of the Hudson River for four generations, but even before that his Roosevelt ancestors lived just a bit further down the Hudson River … The river in all of its aspects and the countryside as a whole were familiar and deeply rooted in my husband's consciousness."

Roosevelt's father bought the house in 1867—the original structure was built about 1800—after the original family home burned down. This, a typical Hudson Valley house, FDR writes, "was remodeled by my mother and myself in 1915. The central square is substantially the same except that what was known as the south parlor was cut in half. The eastern half being what my mother called 'the snuggery' and the western half is the passage way from the main hall down four or five steps to the big library, occupying the stone addition.

"The architect who redesigned the house in 1915 was Francis W. Hoppin of New York and the contractor was Elliott Brown, who had built many country houses. He was called 'Tiny' Brown and was center of the Princeton Football Team and weighed about 250 pounds.

"The room in which I was born is the southeast corner of the original tower—the one directly over the snuggery. It also has been cut in half—the eastern half with the fireplace being still a bedroom and the western half part of the hallway going into the new south wing. The furniture in this room is the same as it was before. Until after my mother's death, this furniture had been moved into her room—the southeast corner of the new wing. She moved it out in 1915 and we moved it back at her request after her death."

For Franklin D. Roosevelt, Hyde Park and the Valley were always his real home, and his wife writes that "in the 1930s, Franklin became conscious of the fact that no private home could ever hold, or should ever hold, the interesting collections of various kinds which had come to him while he was the President, in addition to the things which he had personally collected. The war made him realize that one should not put things of historical interest, and papers of value historically, all in one place. Modern war could, with one bomb, destroy the Congressional Library with all the records of the past generations. He wanted his own papers and those of this period to be available to historians and evolved the idea of giving a piece of land at Hyde Park on which a library could be erected, which could be given to the government of the United States. This was done, and then my husband told me he had decided to leave the house, and the land immediately around it, to the United States government. Of course, he left us the option of living there until our children died, or until we ourselves gave it to the government.

"The place he looked upon as the most beautiful was the rose garden, in which his mother always, up to the last few years of her life, picked her own roses, and this was where he wished to be buried."

Mrs. Roosevelt ends by pointing out how particularly pleased she was that "we were able to leave the rooms exactly as they had been," and that "the front porch has memories of a very particular kind, for this is where my husband always stood with his mother to greet important guests. It is where she always met him when he arrived for a visit, and on this porch he stood when his friends and neighbors came to congratulate him after each nomination and on every election night."

Both the Roosevelts are now buried in the rose garden, and the Colonial Revival house would be impressive even if it had not been the president's home. No one thing stands out, but the whole is very moving and representative of a certain manner of living, and of a simpler, less panoplied presidential era, that strikes very close to the roots of this nation's history.

Nearby is the **Library**, a low, handsome, shuttered stone building crammed with gifts, mementos and personal items of the president and Mrs. Roosevelt, as well as their personal papers and the president's private collection on the history of Dutchess County and the Hudson Valley. It is a treasure trove for scholars, a fascinating excursion into one of the most important periods in our history for the rest of us. No one should miss it.

There is one more building on the estate that is worth visiting, Top Cottage, which sits on top of Dutchess Hill and offered Roosevelt splendid views of the Catskill and Shawangunk mountains off to the west. (The original name of the cottage was Hilltop Cottage, which very quickly was abbreviated to Top Cottage.) It was here that FDR, during his second term, built his cottage in the style he loved best, Dutch colonial with a fieldstone façade taken from old walls in the neighborhood. It's quite simple, and when you visit, the most interesting features are the large living room and the porch with its lovely view. It was here that the Roosevelts gave the famous hot dog picnic for the king and queen of England.

Val-Kill ■ lies 2 miles to the east of Springwood. It is the first National Historic Site devoted to a First Lady. It also is the only home that ever belonged to Eleanor Roosevelt. The stone house, built in Dutch colonial style, was constructed in 1925 and originally was shared by Eleanor and two friends, Nancy Cook and Marion Dickerman. "The peace of it is divine," she wrote Franklin. Two years later she built the nearby furniture factory that for a time produced authentic copies of early American furniture and whose purpose was to give the local farmers a means of earning some money during the long winter months. The factory closed in 1936, and a little later Mrs. Roosevelt turned the building into a home for herself.

After the president's death in 1945, Mrs. Roosevelt bought Val-Kill and about 825 acres of farmlands, woods and buildings from the president's estate, and she lived in the renovated factory for 17 years, entertaining heads of state from Winston Churchill to Nikita Khrushchev and John F. Kennedy.

St. James Church, where millionaires and farmers, Roosevelts and Hudson Valley merchants, worshipped in harmony. Even King George VI of England, staying at Hyde Park in 1939, attended.

The house is simple in the extreme, with many photos of her friends and admirers, and furniture produced by the factory. It is totally unpretentious—just like the woman herself. As for the stone cottage, it is not open to the public, but you can peek in the windows, and take a stroll on the grounds. In addition, there is a film biography of Mrs. Roosevelt. My favorite touch at Val-Kill—at the top of the stair hall, right at eye level, is a Herblock cartoon, in a dime store frame, showing an immigrant mother and her daughter on a ship in New York Harbor passing the Statue of Liberty. "Of course I know," says the girl to her mother. "It's Mrs. Roosevelt."

The point of both Val-Kill and Top Cottage is not their beauty—neither qualifies on that score—but to see how natural and unpretentious these two people were. As I wrote about Springwood, there is something very touching—even moving—about the two sites. They are representative of a bygone era, of an America that no longer exists, and we're the poorer for its passing.

And wait! Before you leave Springwood there's a surprise—a lovely garden designed in 1912 by Beatrix Farrand, one of this country's greatest landscape designers. It's at the Newbold House, which you see on your left as you come up the entrance road toward the parking area at Springwood. When you leave the reception center, go out by the north door, turn right, and walk over the lawn to the stone wall attached to the Newbold house. Open the door in the wall and enjoy the garden. It's open daily, but no one seems to know about it, so the chances are you'll have it to yourself.

Springwood is in the town of Hyde Park, on Route 9. The house and library are open seven days a week, 9–5, all year. Closed Thanksgiving, Christmas and New Year's Day. Top Cottage is open May–October. Guided tours are from the visitor center by shuttle bus only. Private vehicles are not permitted. Tour times: 11, 1, 3. Call to make sure those times are still operative.

Telephone: 845-229-9115. Web site: www.nps.gov/hofr

Val-Kill is open from 9–5 daily from May–October, and Thursday–Monday from November–April. Closed Thanksgiving, Christmas and New Year's Day. The grounds are open daily year-round until sunset. Last tour at 4:30. The grounds are free.

Telephone 845-229-9115. Web site: www.nps.gov/elro

The Vanderbilt Mansion ▨ The Vanderbilts loved to build. And build. No place was safe from their mania: New York City, Newport, Hyde Park, Asheville, Long Island ... if Julius Caesar came, saw and conquered, the Vanderbilts came, saw and threw down palatial houses in a profusion no other family in this country has ever dreamed of, let alone undertaken.

This one was erected by Frederick William Vanderbilt (1856–1938), grandson of Cornelius Vanderbilt (also fondly known as "The Pirate") who made his initial fortune by dominating the steamboat traffic on the Hudson and then went on to found the New York Central Railroad.

The 54-room, Beaux Arts structure, almost tiny by Vanderbilt standards, was not the first edifice here; the history of the estate goes back to

1705. In 1764, the first house on this site was built, but more important, it was then that the grounds began to be developed by their then-owner, Dr. John Bard, a process that would continue throughout the nineteenth and well into the twentieth century, eventually making them one of the most beautiful sites in the country. In 1840, John Jacob Astor bought the estate for his daughter, Dorothea Langdon; 55 years later her son Walter sold the property to the Vanderbilts.

The Vanderbilts wanted only the best and called in the greatest architectural firm of the time—perhaps in our history—McKim, Mead & White. From 1879 to 1915 this firm designed hundreds of buildings of all types including such masterpieces as the Boston Public Library (probably their greatest creation) and, all in New York City, the master plan for Columbia University (including the Low Library), the Pierpont Morgan Library and the Villard Houses, now incorporated into the New York Palace Hotel.

William R. Mead was the catalyst that held the partnership together. Charles F. McKim, probably the greatest of the three and whose sister married the American writer William Dean Howells, also was instrumental in founding the highly prestigious American Academy in Rome and became its first president. But it is Stanford White who people remember today because he got himself murdered in a particularly lurid way. White, a red-headed bon vivant and general connoisseur of the arts and of women was also, as J. P. Morgan noted, "always crazy." At one time he had an affair with a very beautiful and very young musical comedy starlet named Evelyn Nesbit. The lady later married Harry K. Thaw, a rich, unbalanced (some said he was a drug addict), pathologically jealous man who was obsessed with the idea that White had done him wrong. On June 25, 1906, Thaw went to the Garden Roof theater of the old Madison Square Garden, a building White had designed, and shot White as he was watching a terrible operetta, *Mamzelle Champagne*, which managed to run for 59 more performances thanks to the ensuing scandal. There's a 1955 movie, *The Girl in the Red Velvet Swing*, about the whole affair that shows up from time to time on late-night television. Don't take it too seriously, but it's an hour or two that's fun, and stars Ray Milland as White, Farley Granger as Thaw and Joan Collins as Evelyn Nesbit.

But back to the Vanderbilts. McKim, Mead & White soon discovered the Langdon mansion could not be remodeled because of structural problems and that, instead, the building had to be razed.

Down it came, and by 1899 the new house was ready, at a cost of just under $3 million and requiring a full-time staff of 20 for the house and 60 for the entire estate. (The interior design, by the way, was partially done by Ogden Codman who, with Edith Wharton, had written *The Decoration of Houses* [1897]. Among other things, their book established the principle that architecture and design cannot be separated, with the logical corollary that ornament is not to be used for its own sake but only as a part of the architectural whole; in essence, this meant that careful consideration of proportion, symmetry, order and harmony are vital to the success of any room. Wharton and Codman's primary role models were taken from French architecture and furnishings of the eighteenth century. From the day of its publication the book became an instant classic, so important that it radically changed American taste in decoration and has indeed shaped general concepts of interior design up to the present.)

Frederick Vanderbilt occupied the mansion until his death in 1938, but only from Easter to the beginning of July, and then again in the fall. The Vanderbilts were not alone in this ritual; most of the great estate holders followed the same pattern of staying in New York City for the late fall and winter season and then, in the summer, either moving on to Newport or another resort or else traveling to Europe.

Completed in 1899, the Vanderbilt Mansion cost about $3 million and the estate employed a full-time staff of 60. The grounds here are especially beautiful, and you can stroll down to the river itself to enjoy some splendid views.

Today, the house is perfectly maintained and appears generally the way it was when the Vanderbilts lived there. It's very beautiful, but so formal that it seems more like a public building to receive in than a home. In many ways, of course, that's exactly what it was. (Something that particularly fascinates me is that there are several tapestries bearing the coat of arms of the Medicis. Did Frederick Vanderbilt wish to imply a family resemblance?)

The most perfect room is Mrs. Vanderbilt's bedroom, for which Codman is responsible and which is exquisite despite one element, the bed, that to me is so naïvely pretentious it's almost touching. The general plan was to re-create a French queen's bedroom of the eighteenth century. The offending bed, huge and canopied, is surrounded by a rail before which, in France, the courtiers would have gathered for the queen's levee. I would bet none of Mrs. Vanderbilt's guests ever saw *her* en deshabille. Still, the room is extremely elegant, a model of what Codman and Wharton preached in their book, with its French furniture, wood-paneled walls with inset paintings, and superb detailing such as the brocade covering the wall at the head of the bed.

The estate grounds, developed over almost two centuries since the time of Dr. Samuel Bard back in 1795, are just as interesting as the house. For instance, there are about 40 species and varieties of trees (most are marked), including a gargantuan gingko, one of the largest in the country. And, along the north drive on the way out of the estate, there is a view of the Hudson, the Shawangunk Mountains (to the west) and the Catskills (to the north) that is among the most beautiful in the Valley. In addition, the gardens are undergoing extensive renovation and are very pretty.

Still, my favorite spot is down by the river itself. As you leave on the north drive, there is a road off to the left that takes you down the hill, over the railroad tracks, and out to the site where the Vanderbilt yachts once docked. Wander along the shore here. The vista, constantly changing as you move from place to place, is always breathtaking, and, once again, there's that special feeling of serenity and peace that only this river can create to such haunting effect.

The Vanderbilt Mansion lies north of Hyde Park on Route 9.

Open seven days, 9–5, all year. Phone: 845-229-9115.
Web site:www.nps.gov/vama/home.htm

Staatsburgh State Historic Site (formerly the Mills Mansion) ▨ Yet another Livingston estate, this one served as the model for the Trenors' estate, Bellomont, in Edith Wharton's masterpiece, *The House of Mirth*. (I wonder how the Millses liked her description of their library: "A few family portraits of lantern-jawed gentlemen in tie-wigs, and ladies with large head-dresses and small bodies, hung between the shelves buried with pleasantly shabby books: books mostly contemporaneous with the ancestors in question, and to which the subsequent Trenors had made no perceptible additions. The library at Bellomont was in fact never used for reading." They would have been more pleased, I suspect, with her description of the grounds in all their "opulent undulations.") The estate goes back to 1792 and a sister of Chancellor Robert Livingston (see page 67), Gertrude by

The back of the Mills Mansion, designed by McKim, Mead & White. The dining room is one of the great private rooms from the late nineteenth century.

name. She was married to Morgan Lewis, a prominent New Yorker who had been General Horatio Gates' chief of staff at the Battle of Saratoga and would later go on to become chief justice of the New York Supreme Court (1801–4) and governor of the state (1804–7). The Lewises' first home burned to the ground in 1832, but they promptly built a new one in the Greek Revival style. (It's odd that Greek Revival lasted only a short time in domestic architecture yet continued well into the twentieth century for our public buildings.)

This structure is the core of the present French Renaissance–inspired building designed by McKim, Mead & White (see page 139) at the request of Ogden and Ruth Livingston Mills and completed in 1896. (Mills' parent had made a fortune in California in banking; Ogden enjoyed the fruits of his father's labors.) The house remained in the family until 1937 when the only son, Ogden Livingston Mills, one-time Secretary of the Treasury, died, and his sister decided to give the house and its surrounding 192 acres to the state.

This mansion is larger than the Vanderbilt's—65 rooms—and in many ways far more interesting. First of all, the core of the old house gives a nicely unbalanced feeling to the whole; you immediately sense that there may be some surprises awaiting you instead of the usual matching rooms, north and south, leading leadenly off a central hall. And there are. The most beautiful of these is the dining room, long and splendid with large, framed tapestries set off against gray-green marble, its western windows overlooking the Hudson and the mountains. It has to be one of the great formal rooms of its period. Now the state of New York has begun restoration work, which will continue for many years. This house may not be a must-see, perhaps, but it's very rewarding if you're at all interested in nineteenth-century architecture and decoration.

Staatsburgh State Historic Site is north of Hyde Park and the Vanderbilt Mansion and about 5 minutes off Route 9 (there's a sign) in Staatsburg.

The mansion is open from April 1 through October 31, Tuesday–Saturday 10–5, Sunday 12–5. The grounds are open daily, sunrise to sunset. During December the site sponsors "A Gilded Age Christmas." There also is a museum shop. Phone: 845-889-8851. Web site: www.staatsburgh.org

Most of the estate is now part of the **Mills-Norrie State Park**, which has a marina, tent-trailer sites, cabins, fishing, golf and picnicking facilities as well as nature and hiking trails through the park and along designated sections of the Hudson River Greenway. Phone: 845-889-4646.

Montgomery Place ■ This is not only one of the most pleasant estates in the Valley but also, to my taste, the grounds are the most beautiful of all. House and grounds are owned and operated by Historic Hudson Valley.

A little history. Montgomery Place, now a 434-acre estate, was founded in 1802 by Janet Livingston Montgomery (1743–1828). She was the eldest daughter of Robert R. Livingston and grew up at Clermont (see page 66). She married Richard Montgomery, who died at the Battle of Quebec in 1775. (It is he who is the subject of one of the earlier and more famous American masterpieces by the painter John Trumbull, "The Death of General Montgomery at Quebec," which now hangs in the Yale University Art Gallery.) Childless, she left the estate to her younger brother, Edward Livingston (1764–1836), who, among other things, was Secretary of State under Andrew Jackson and United States Minister to France.

It was his daughter, Cora Livingston (1806–73), and her husband, Thomas Pennant Barton (1803–69), who transformed the Federal structure Janet built into the 23-room mansion we see today. The person responsible for the changes: the great American architect Alexander Jackson Davis (see page 231). In particular, Davis added the north pavilion, east portico, west veranda and south wing, transforming a rather severe building into a country seat of elegance and great charm. The north portico in itself is one of the most inviting creations of the architecture of the time. Indeed, it has been referred to as "the earliest outdoor room in America."

The buildings are closed for restoration, probably until 2009, but it is the exterior architecture that is the most interesting in any case, and it is the grounds that make visiting such a memorable experience. Andrew Jackson Downing (1815–52) was America's first great landscape architect and a leading writer on landscape gardening, cottages and country houses. It was he who brought Calvert Vaux to this country (Vaux would become Frederick Law Olmsted's partner and collaborate with him on Central Park in New York City), and he also worked closely with Alexander Jackson Davis. Downing died at a tragically young age, drowning in a steamboat accident on the Hudson.

Downing was a great friend of Cora Livingston and Thomas Barton and wrote an important article on Montgomery Place that was published in 1847. In it he said that the estate was second "to no seat in America for its combination of attractions." He continued: "As a foreground, imagine a large lawn waving in undulations of soft verdure, varied with fine groups, and margined with rich belts of foliage. Its base is washed by the river, which is here a broad sheet of water lying like a long lake beneath the eye. Wooded banks stretch along its margin. Its bosom is studded with islands, which are set like emeralds on its pale blue bosom. On the opposite shores, more than a mile distant, is seen a rich mingling of woods and cornfields. But the crowning glory of the landscape is the background of mountains. The Kaatskills, as seen from this part of the Hudson, are, it seems to us, more beautiful than any mountain scenery in the middle States." Today, almost 150 years later, the description still suits.

Several splendid walks through this exquisite landscape are available, and all were laid out by the family. A descriptive brochure is available at the Visitor Center, but my favorite is the walk to the cataracts. Down you go, through silent woods filled with ferns, the sound of the cataracts—what a lovely, primordial thing—slowly increasing until you come out on the

From the terrace of Montgomery Place the view is over the Hudson to the unspoiled greenery of the west bank.

Saw Kill River. Look upstream, and there are the cataracts, white-water spume tumbling down, a Hudson River painting come to life. Go back up the trail, and now take the West Lawn Trail, which offers lovely views of the river and house and takes you by the lake you already have seen from the house. At its end, explore the exquisite little rock garden and then relax in the perennial garden. There is no more delightful way to spend an afternoon.

Montgomery Place is open on weekends from May through October, 10–5, for self-guided tours of the grounds, gardens, and nature trails. Picnickers are welcome.

The Visitor Center and Museum Shop are open on weekends. Phone: 845-758-5461. Web site: www.hudsonvalley.org

Montgomery Place is north of Rhinebeck. For an especially rewarding drive, turn off Route 9 at the light in Rhinebeck and go toward Rhinecliff. (This is a right if you are going south, a left if you are going north.) Go to Route 103, River Road, turn right and take that north, passing through lovely countryside and by the entrances to many Hudson River estates. You will eventually cross over Route 199, which leads to the Kingston–Rhinecliff Bridge. Continue north, and first stop at Poets' Walk. This romantic 120-acre park, 1/2 mile from where you crossed over Route 199, was originally created in 1849 by a landscape architect named Hans Jacob Ehlers. He took an existing work road that had been used to haul building materials from the river and designed a charming path that was enjoyed by Washington Irving and Fitz-Greene Halleck, among others. Hence the name of Poets' Walk. In 1993, Scenic Hudson acquired the property and immediately began restoration, opening up vistas of the Hudson and re-creating the romantic original, including a summerhouse and rustic cedar pavilions. The absolutely delightful 2 miles of trails take you through open fields and woods and along a bluff overlooking the river. On crossing the first field you arrive at Overlook Pavilion, which gives you a sweeping view of the river and the Kingston–Rhinebeck Bridge. From there I particularly like the walk to the summerhouse, where you cross pretty bridges and arrive at a more intimate view of the river and can sit and enjoy it. From there go to Flagpole Lot, where you will see a river dock and a footbridge over the railroad that was built at the beginning of the twentieth century and, yet again, a wonderful river view.

An hour later you will leave totally relaxed. Poets' Walk is open from 9 to dusk and admission is free, but before I leave here I would like to tell you something about Scenic Hudson, Inc., whose first victory was saving Storm King Mountain from excavation. Today the organization is a major factor in the Valley's renaissance and is responsible for protecting and developing 18 sites for public enjoyment from Coxsackie in Greene County to as far south as New City in Rockland County.

For further information and a full list of sites, including Poets' Walk, write Scenic Hudson, One Civic Center Plaza, Suite 200, Poughkeepsie 12601. Phone: 845-473-4440. Web site: www.scenichudson.org

A Drive through Dutchess County

Once you get off Route 9, the scenery in Dutchess County can be very beautiful, mostly rolling land covered with rural property and, in particular, horse farms. For various reasons—mainly tax incentives—the entire Valley has become a major horse-breeding area with more than a hundred horse farms, fifty of them in Dutchess County alone. At the same time, horse-raising has turned into such a big business that it's listed among the larger industrial contributors to New York's tax base. Fortunately, you don't have to know a thing about taxes or horses to appreciate the beauty of these farms with their seemingly endless brown or white fences streaking the landscape.

Wine making, too, is important here, and the vineyards on the hillsides seem to be almost as common a sight as the apple orchards or cornfields surrounding the small towns and villages that dot the county.

This drive is designed to take you through a little bit of everything so that you can get a feel for the region. Depending on the time you wish to spend, you could do it in two or three hours or you can make a day of it.

Begin in Rhinebeck (see page 154), right in the heart of the village where Route 308 meets Route 9, almost directly across from the Beekman Arms (see page 171). Follow 308 (it's also East Market Street here) and take it to the sign for 9G South, enjoying in the meantime the vintage houses, dating from pre-Revolution to late Victorian, most of them kept in prime condition.

After a mile or so on 9G you will see a sign, on your left, for Slate Quarry Mill and Stanfordville. Turn off and follow this road to the sign for Schultzville and Clinton Hollow, where you will turn right. Go through Schultzville, which seems to consist of a small, pretty clapboard nineteenth-century grange and, on a triangle, a country store and a couple of houses. You will then climb a small hill, and just over the brow will be a sign on your left for Schultzville Road. Part dirt, part paved, this wonderful road will take you through a lovely wooded section, full of deer and other wild animals, that is country primeval.

After 5 or 10 minutes you'll come upon a sign for **Clinton Vineyards**, a small winery that produces the best white wine (a seyval blanc) on this side of the Hudson. Ben Feder, proprietor of the vineyard, is a transplanted New York City graphics designer who first started raising cattle, quickly got bored with that and decided to take a gamble on a vineyard. (Oddly enough, one of the best vineyards on the west bank, Benmarl, is also owned by an ex-graphics designer, Mark Miller.) That was back in 1977,

By American standards, the Valley is ancient in its history—hence this Greek Revival church now standing alone in the middle of the woods.

and Feder's venture has paid off handsomely, his first major break coming when a *New York Times* critic wrote that his was an unusually good wine. (He also makes a sparkling seyval in the time-honored *méthode-Champenoise* tradition.) Within no time Clinton Vineyards was sold out of its stock, its reputation firmly established, and today it is served at such New York City establishments as The Four Seasons (noted for its excellent selection of American wines). Ben Feder, a friendly, gregarious man, welcomes guests, but this is a small operation, and you must call ahead to set up an appointment.

Phone: 845-266-5372; web site: www.clintonvineyards.com

From here, go to the end of Schultzville Road and turn right. Almost immediately you're in Clinton Corners, a sleepy little village where you will, for a short time, get on the Taconic Parkway going south. Get off at the Millbrook exit (U.S. 44), and follow 44 into **Millbrook**.

Once in the village, 44 becomes a main street, Franklin Avenue. Park your car anywhere along here. The minute you start examining the stores along this street, you'll discover that you've lit on a swarm of antique shops. Dozens of dealers are represented in the different buildings or antique malls on either side of the street, and you can easily spend an hour or two walking through and just looking at the merchandise; it covers every conceivable interest and taste, from furniture to porcelains to paintings to old clothes to bric-a-brac, with a wide range of prices beginning at only a few dollars. If you collect, or are looking for any one thing in particular, just ask. There's bound to be at least one of whatever it is. And don't be afraid to bargain. In all these malls the prices often are 10 to 20 percent higher than they'll actually take, I've found. (After the first edition of this book appeared, all the dealers denied it was true. But it is.)

There are two very special antique shops in Millbrook. **Yellow Church Antiques**, which is just outside the town, is one mile west of the Taconic Parkway at 2545 Route 44. It specializes in fine eighteenth- and nineteenth-century English and continental furniture. Wonderful examples and prices to match the quality. (Phone: 845-677-6779. Web site: www.yellowchurch.com.) **Red Coral Ltd.**, at 3276 Franklin Avenue, right in the heart of Millbrook, has a small, eclectic collection, but every piece is first rate. (Phone: 845-677-9111.)

Millbrook has two special and unusual places to visit, the **Institute of Eco Systems** at the **Mary Flagler Cary Arboretum and Innisfree Garden.**

Mary Flagler Cary Arboretum ■ is property that once belonged to Melbert and Mary Flagler Cary. Mrs. Cary grew up in Millbrook, and in the 1920s she and her husband decided to come here and establish a retreat from New York City. They slowly accumulated farms and other property, and by the time Mrs. Cary died in 1967, the property consisted of 1,924 acres. In 1971, the property was deeded to The New York Botanical Garden by the Mary Flagler Cary Charitable Trust. Then, in 1983, the Institute of Ecosystem Studies was formed here to do ecological education and research locally, regionally and globally. The institute became an independent facility in 1993.

For the casual visitor, the exquisite pleasure comes from wandering the various trails and roads, enjoying the greenhouse, the Perennial Garden, with one of the largest collections of perennials in this country, the Howard Taylor Lilac Collection, the Fern Glen with its collection of native wildflowers and ferns, the Gifford Garden and, a particular favorite of mine, the Wappinger Creek Trail, a short (slightly over a mile) trail that takes you through fields and forests as well as streams. It never looks the same twice and is eminently rewarding. Finally, before you leave, be sure to visit the IES Ecology Shop and Plant Room at the Gifford House Visitor and Education Center. No gardener worth his or her salt can walk away from here empty-handed.

The Institute is off Route 44. About 2 miles after you exit the Taconic, traveling east toward Millbrook, you will see a sign and will turn left on Route 44A. One mile north, and you will see the red-brick Gifford House.

Phone 845-677-5359 for information on the status of the roads. The hours change seasonally. Check the web site: www.ecostudies.org

Innisfree ■ It had been some time since I had visited Innisfree, surely one of the most unusual—and beautiful—gardens not only in the Valley but in the country, and centered on a 40-acre glacial lake.

When I arrived I saw that the lotuses were in bloom. So was the pickerel rush, a lovely blue against the softer lotus, and the Joe Pye Weed was full and about to burst. There's so much there. Lichens and sedums, grasses and ferns, splendid trees, clematis, climbing hydrangea, magnificent plantings of peonies and day lilies and sweet peas, I could go on and on. From May to October this garden is downright splendid. The beautifully placed rocks inspired by Chinese garden rocks, the waterfalls and fountains and lawns ... every inch has been planned and thought out to perfection. You will need several hours—the garden encompasses 150 acres—and there's a very pleasant picnic area should you be so inclined. And you will want to return again and again to see the garden in all its many moods and aspects.

The original inspiration for Innisfree was as the private gardens of Walter and Marion Beck from 1930 to 1960. Walter Beck had long been fascinated by Eastern calligraphy and painting and saw in his designs for the gardens an opportunity for bringing a new creative and aesthetic vision to the American garden, a three-dimensional art work in which the stroller moves from one "picture" to another. Beck coined the term "cup garden" to describe this version of what was originally a Chinese garden design concept, and in particular he was influenced by the Chinese poet, painter, and garden builder Wang Wei (A.D 699–A.D. 759). As the "Innisfree Garden" brochure points out, "The cup garden draws attention to something rare or beautiful by establishing around it the suggestion of enclosure so that it can be enjoyed without distraction. A cup garden may be an enframed meadow, a lotus pool, or a single rock covered with lichens and sedums." It goes on to say that "Although the cup garden idea came from China, Innisfree is unequivocally an American garden."

In 1960 the Innisfree Foundation, under the stewardship of Lester Collins, a friend of Beck's and a former Dean of Harvard's Department of Landscape Architecture, opened the garden to the public. Collins, who also wrote *Innisfree: An American Garden*, brought the garden to the level of perfection we see today and doubled its size. It was he who had the vision to bring the series of cup gardens together as part of a total landscape with the lake at its center. He saw the lake, surrounding hills and the three cliffs as one large cup, with the smaller cups integrated into the overall cup, and he designed his own cup gardens as part of this seamless whole and brought the older cups into the schema as well. But as he wrote, "The traditional Chinese garden is usually designed so that a view of the whole is impossible. The Chinese garden requires a stroll over serpentine, seemingly aimless, garden arteries."

There are so many wonderful things that it's difficult to choose what to tell you about. First, of course, is the overall impression when you arrive. After you park, go over to the picnic area for a view of the lake. Then down to the shore where you begin following the trail around the lake, the basic path, from which you can detour into wonderful cups. Very shortly you come across the Mist Waterfall. Then the terraces, filled with plantings, where the Beck's house once stood, and just above them is a very beautiful water sculpture; two columns attached at the top from which sprays of water lift into the air, all framed by columnar ginkgos. And so it goes, all around the lake, experience after experience, and, towards the end and after the meadow, take special note of the dream-like smoke trees and the specimen maples with branches only eight inches long. It is a wonderful experience.

Innisfree Garden is 1 3/4 miles from the Taconic Parkway on Route 44. Turn right on Tyrell Road, and you will come to the entrance after 1 mile. Innisfree Garden is open May to October 20, Wednesday, Thursday and Friday, 10–4. Saturday, Sunday and legal holidays 11–5. Closed Monday and Tuesday *except* legal holidays.

Phone: 845-677-8000. Web site: www.innisfreegarden.org

Millbrook has one other claim to your attention. It was here that Peter Piper picked a peck of pickled peppers. James Kirke Paulding, the creator of that deathless line, was Secretary of the Navy under fellow New Yorker Martin Van Buren. Aside from this immortal series of p's, Paulding is primarily remembered for defending sail against steamships. Fortunately, we were not at war at the time.

Once you're ready to go on, retrace your drive back to the sign for Route 82, and go north on this to relax and just enjoy the scenery. For a good part of the way, it is carefully tended farm country with some handsome old houses and cornfields stretching out toward the mountain range to the west. It's very rural, very pleasant, and hasn't changed much since the 1800s.

When you enter Pine Plains, and before going left on Route 199 to continue your drive, take a short detour and turn right. One mile east of the village, at the bottom of a hill, you will see a sign for **Hammertown Barn** (web site: www.hammertownbarn.com), certainly one of the most delightful shops in the Hudson Valley, set amid flowers and trees.

Furniture, nineteenth-century English and American antiques, pictures, candles, soaps and soap dishes, rugs, fabrics, reproduction lighting, Simon Pearce glassware and pottery, candles, placemats and napkins, books, Mitchell Gold furniture and bedding … and much, much more, all in glorious profusion in the barn and the next-door gatehouse. You can stay here for at least an hour exploring, and I will bet you right now that you won't walk away empty-handed. There also is a branch in Rhinebeck and another in Great Barrington, but I prefer the original. Once you've put your loot in the car, head back through Pine Plains on Route 199. In Pine Plains stop at the **Chisholm Gallery**, 3 Factory Lane, which specializes in sporting art but also has good examples of Tibetan furniture and other interesting material. (Phone: 518-398-1246. www.chisholmgallery.com.) When you leave Pine Plains the scenery shifts to woods and small ponds and, as you proceed, pretty views down into the valleys. In Rock City, which makes Schultzville look like a metropolis, bear left on Route 308; in about 15 minutes you'll be back in Rhinebeck.

The star of Schultzville, this charming clapboard grange is right out of a Norman Rockwell cover for the Saturday Evening Post.

I should tell you one other thing. There are lots of dirt roads in this area, particularly around Schultzville, all great fun to explore. Don't hesitate to go off on one of them. Get lost, even. In its own quiet way this can prove quite rewarding; you're bound to come across something of great beauty, a landscape or a building or a view, that will stay forever in your memory.

Other Places to Visit in Dutchess County

Rhinebeck ■ This small village of just over 2,500 people was founded by the Dutch in 1686 but received its present name around 1713 from a group of German settlers, refugees, in remembrance of their homeland river (*beck* means cliffs).

These settlers, part of a much larger group that had dispersed to other parts of the Valley and further south to New York City and New Jersey, had a particularly tragic background. Crushed by centuries of wars and taxes, the peasants of the Rhine Valley were all too ready to listen to English agents who raved to them about the wonders of America. Within the years between 1707 to 1709, more than 11,000 of them had arrived in England, waiting to be sent on to the New World. Eventually about 2,800 embarked, the largest single migration during the colonial period, on a voyage that would take them months. When they arrived in New York, 1,800 were dispatched 100 miles upriver to produce naval stores, particularly tar, for the English. Unfortunately, the whole project collapsed after several extremely difficult years, and the settlers were abandoned by the English to get on as best they could. (One of them, by the way, was John Peter Zenger [1697–1746], founder of the New York *Weekly Journal*, a newspaper highly critical of the British colonial government. In 1734, Zenger was arrested and tried for libel. Defended by Andrew Hamilton, a Philadelphia lawyer, he was finally acquitted—on the then-revolutionary defense that truth was no libel. Thanks to Zenger—and to Hamilton, of course—freedom of the press became a fundamental right, one more step toward breaking the dominion of Mother England over the colonies.)

For a village so small, it's something of a surprise to discover that Rhinebeck has a railroad station, on the river and 2 miles west, in Rhinecliff. All becomes clear, however, when you learn that so many private railroad cars began coming up here after the Civil War, bearing the heavy freight of wealth headed for the mansions north and south of the village, that Colonel John Jacob Astor IV and his cronies insisted upon having a convenient place to disembark.

These same people had magnificent gardens and greenhouses, and as the mansions went into their long, gentle decline in the twentieth century, the gardeners once employed by the wealthy began operating their own commercial greenhouses. They soon found that violets did particularly well here, and before long, there were acres and acres of them—the largest violet market in America, with Rhinebeck becoming known as "Violet Town." But then violets grew unfashionable in the 1920s and '30s; so these days it's anemones that are raised here for the commercial markets.

In many ways, this series of failures has been nothing but good news for Rhinebeck since it's meant that there was no call to tear down the old buildings to throw up bigger, more commercial ones for expanding needs. So today what you see is an intact, charming nineteenth-century village—with a few even older buildings—and because Rhinebeck remains prosperous and concerned about its heritage, it is very well maintained as a National Historic District.

The whole village is worth touring—on foot since it's so small—but five particular buildings I'm very fond of perhaps sum up the special quality that gives the town its distinction.

For suggested walking tours go to:
www.rhinebeckchamber.com/history/walktour.asp

The Delamater House (1844), just up Montgomery Street (Route 9) from the village's only stoplight, is the quintessential example of an American Gothic house and is so fanciful that it looks like a toy. It was designed by Alexander Jackson Davis, the country's most famous architect of domestic Gothic and whose masterpiece is Lyndhurst (see page 231). It has everything—a wonderful central gable, gingerbread woodwork so exuberant it seems more important than the house, diamond-paned windows, over-tall chimney stacks, projecting bay windows. And, best of all, you can stay there, as it is now owned by the Beekman Arms (see page 171).

Across from the Delamater House, at 47 Montgomery Street, is the 1896 Episcopal **Church of the Messiah**, a very handsome English-influenced stone building designed by Stanford White and containing some Tiffany windows.

The Dutch Reformed Church (1809), on Route 9 and South Street, is a successful hodgepodge of styles (the windows are Georgian on the front, Gothic on the sides, for instance) and materials (brick and stone was a compromise between the rich and poor parishioners: the rich could afford brick, the poor only stone).

At 2 South Street, right across from the church is an absolutely wonderful ca.1860 Gothic Revival cottage known as the **Fifteen Gables House**. It looks like an illustration for a delightful children's book and now is a Bed & Breakfast with three guest rooms. (Phone: 845-876-7577.)

Finally, there's a high-style **Victorian mansion** on West Market Street, about two blocks from the traffic light, that has been so beautifully restored it could serve as the model for a Christmas card. It's perfect of its kind, a wonderful turret with an oeil-de-boeuf window, widow's walk, mansard roof and a splendid arched door. When *New Yorker* cartoonist Charles Addams saw it, he said, "Why, that's my family house. That's what I've been drawing all these years."

Old Rhinebeck Aerodrome ■ Just a few miles north of Rhinebeck, off Route 9 on Stone Church Road, the Aerodrome can be a lot of fun. Although it attracts large crowds, the last time I was there it was empty, and as I got out of my car the first thing I heard was a trumpet going crazy, a bit bizarre at ten in the morning. The site is wired for sound, and the music is of World War I vintage. From here it's not a long way to Tipperary.

You enter across a covered bridge decorated with photos of pilots, "Germans" and "Americans," who go up in the air each Saturday and Sunday and hold mock air fights to delight the spectators. Along the grass landing strip is an extraordinary lineup of antique planes, and on the other side are prop houses (the Germans have "Das Badz Boys," the French the "Hotel de Paree") that are used in the shows. You also can take a wonderful jaunt in an open-cockpit plane, "high or low, fast or slow, any way you want to go" as the barker will tell you, over the Hudson Valley.

On the ground there also are four museum buildings that hold some 55 models of antique planes that date from the end of the nineteenth century to 1935, making this one of the largest collections of antique planes in the world. The buildings also house vintage cars, motorcycles and bicycles.

The Delamater House, with its fanciful gingerbread spreading across and around and up and down. A confectioner's delight, good enough to break off a piece to munch on as you continue your walk down the street.

When you leave and are about to turn onto Route 9, do note the Lutheran church directly opposite. It was built in 1786 by German Palatinate refugees.

The museum buildings are open: 10–5 daily from mid-May to late October. Museum hours: 10–5 from mid-May to late October. Air shows are at 2 Saturdays and Sundays from mid-June to mid-October. No air shows on weekdays. Tickets for plane rides—maximum of four people in the plane—can be bought before the weekend shows on a first-come, first-served basis. During the week reservations are necessary.

Phone: 845-752-3200. Web site: www.oldrhinebeck.org

Wethersfield ■ A visit here includes the house, the carriage house and the gardens; the gardens alone are worth the trip. The house—with spectacular vistas out over Dutchess County that by themselves are almost worth a visit—was designed by Bancel LaFarge for Chauncey Stillman (1907–1989), an investor and philanthropist, in the late 1930s with a later addition from 1973. It is a brick Georgian-style residence of comfortable proportions and totally unmemorable. Inside there are some nice examples of French and English furniture and excellent paintings by Toulouse-Lautrec, Mary Cassatt and Murillo, among others. There is also a great deal of fresco work by Pietro Annigoni, a twentieth-century Italian artist of moderate ability. What *isn't* here is a magnificent portrait, known as the "Halberdier" (ca. 1527), by the Italian Mannerist Jacopo Pontormo (1494–1557), which Mr. Stillman for many years lent to the Frick Museum in New York. On his death it was sold to the Getty Museum in Los Angeles. This sale supplied the funds that now maintain the estate. As for what you'll see in the carriage house, over the years Chauncey Stillman collected and restored 22 carriages, both formal and sporting.

This Lutheran church near Rhinebeck was built in 1786 by German refugees from the Palatinate. Now it stands opposite the entrance to the Rhinebeck Aerodrome.

For me the real interest here is the truly magnificent gardens, all 10 acres of them. The original landscape architect was Bryan J. Lynch, who designed the gardens surrounding the house in 1940. Then, from the early 1950s through the mid-1970s, Evelyn N. Poehler developed and expanded the gardens into what you see today. Overall they are hallmarked by an exquisitely subtle simplicity that makes them far more memorable than many more formal gardens. They are definitely worth a detour. And don't forget to take a stroll down Peacock Walk, where, sitting down and minding my own business, I was scared out of my wits by the screech of a hitherto unseen roosting peacock, its tail feathers indolently drooping down from an overhead branch.

Wethersfield is 7 miles northeast of Millbrook, in Amenia.

Open: June through September, Wednesday, Friday and Saturday noon–5. The house and carriage house can be seen by advance appointment only. Telephone 845-373-8037 for directions, information and reservations.

Bard College ■ About 20 minutes north of Rhinebeck on Route 9G, this small liberal-arts college founded in the mid-nineteenth century has a charming 600-acre campus that is, in large part, made up of former Hudson River estates. It also has some interesting examples of contemporary architecture and each summer presents the Bard Music Festival. The festival takes place over two consecutive weekends and is devoted to the work of a single composer.

Phone: 845-758-7410; Web site; www.bard.edu/bmf

As you enter the campus, look for the tiny white hexagonal building, which once served as the gatehouse to an estate called Blithewood. This originally belonged to John Bard, founder of the college. It was the creation of architect Alexander Jackson Davis (see page 231) and was built in either the 1830s or '40s (dates vary). Go past the Davis building and you will eventually come to Blithewood House.

Farther on, to your right, is the **Center for Curatorial Studies and Art in Contemporary Culture**, completed in 1992 and designed by the Chicago architects Jim Goettsch and Nada Andric, which offers changing exhibits of contemporary art in well-planned gallery spaces. In addition, there are advanced collection storage facilities, classrooms, a library and offices. The Center most recently has expanded to include a gallery wing dedicated to exhibitions drawn from the Marieluise Hessel Collection of almost 2,000 paintings, sculptures, photographs, works on paper, artists' books, videos, and video installations from the mid-1950s to the present. The collection is international in scope and is constantly expanding.

Open all year, Wednesday–Sunday 1–5. Phone: 845-758-7598. Web site: www.bard.edu/ccs/. Closed Tuesday.

Continue on the same road and you'll see a large, very striking neo-classic mansion that replaced the original Blithewood House about 1900 and now houses the Levy Economics Institute. It's nice to get out here and wander, catching glimpses of the Hudson. If you should then decide to explore the main part of the campus, be sure to note the library, built for the college in 1893 in the form of a classic Greek temple and with an addition by Robert Venturi.

Finally, there is the **Richard B. Fisher Center for the Performing Arts** located in a building designed by Frank Gehry. (Tours of the 110,000-square-foot building, containing two theaters, four rehearsal studios, and support facilities are given every day at 2. No reservations necessary.) The Center also is the home of the Bard Music Festival and Bard SummerScape, a festival of opera, theater and dance that has become one of the premier cultural events not only in the Valley but also on the East Coast. For complete information and to be put on the mailing list, go to the web site at: www.fishercenter.bard.edu.

Vassar College—The Frances Lehman Loeb Art Center ▪ on Raymond Avenue in Poughkeepsie, has an extensive and major art collection, in particular a superb group of Hudson River School paintings and a very strong collection of works on paper. In the past, there was only enough space to show a tantalizing but minute portion of the collection. Now, however, all that has changed with the opening of the Frances Lehman Loeb Art Center, an absolutely beautiful 36,400-square-foot building and renovation designed by Cesar Pelli, with its echoes of the

Renaissance and charming glass entrance pavilion. There also is a small sculpture garden adjacent to the building, designed by landscape architect Diana Balmori, Pelli's wife. The Center is located just inside the main entrance to the campus.

Vassar College was founded by Matthew Vassar in 1861, who also started the college's art holdings through the purchase of the Elias Lyman Magoon collection of roughly 400 paintings and watercolors by the artists of his time, as well as almost 3,000 engravings and drawings. Today the collection has grown to include over 15,000 works—about 500 are on permanent display—ranging from ancient Egyptian sculpture and Chinese ceramics to Mark Rothko, Philip Guston and Ross Bleckner. The galleries are arranged in a chronological and clockwise system and are filled with light that comes through the clerestory windows. Three small galleries have been set aside for the display of works on paper from the permanent collection.

The collection on view is small but impressive, and I particularly like the twentieth-century works—including an exquisite Alexander Calder mobile from 1934 called "The Circle," so delicately balanced that the slightest movement of air puts it in motion. There's also a spectacular, I think, Francis Bacon, "Study for Portrait IV" (1953) from his variations on Velazquez's portrait of Pope Innocent X, and "Indian Composition" (1914–15) by Marsden Hartley, one of his best works. From the nineteenth century American collection, the Hudson River paintings are one of the great strengths of the museum and are, I think, perfectly hung. But I also very much like a painting by Charles Courtney Curran called "Shadow Decoration" (1887) of a washerwoman hanging her laundry. This everyday subject has been transformed by his use of sunlight casting shadows on the laundry creating an effect that is at once Japanese, mystical and timeless.

These are only a very few highlights—there are some very good Asian pieces and medieval and Renaissance work, not to mention interesting nineteenth-century European paintings and a good photography collection—but I must tell you of one more painting because I find it so amusing. It's by Salomon de Braij (1597–1664) and the subject is "Odysseus and Circe" (ca. 1650). It's worth the visit to see the two swine-transformed sailors, one looking adoringly at Odysseus, who, in turn, looks like nothing more than a not-too-intelligent Dutch burgher.

This is a splendid collection, very strong in drawings, housed in an equally splendid building. Certainly, it ranks at the very top among museums in the Valley.

Open: Tuesday–Saturday 10–5, Sunday 1–5. Phone: 845-437-5235. Web site: www.fllac.vassar.edu

Locust Grove ■ This is the former home of Samuel F. B. Morse, an artist who ended up being more famous for inventing the telegraph than for any of his paintings. Morse bought it in 1847 and created, with the help of Alexander Jackson Davis (see page 231), the Tuscan villa you see today. Sold in 1901 to the Young family, it was a descendant of this family who, in 1975, established a generous endowment to maintain the house and grounds as a historic site. There are pleasant hiking trails through the woods and an attractive garden.

But I find the interior of the house to be something of a hodgepodge of good to mediocre furniture, porcelain, prints, and paintings. In fairness, though, it is an excellent way to see how people lived in the late nineteenth century, and there are some treasures. In addition, the Visitor Center is very well done, with an excellent short video on Morse, several Morse paintings, and telegraph models and memorabilia. The interesting exhibitions here range from science to art and popular culture.

Locust Grove is open daily from May 1 through November 30, 10–3. The Visitor Center is open 10–5. For December hours, please call 845-454-4500. It lies about 2 miles south of the Mid-Hudson Bridge in Poughkeepsie on Route 9. Web site: www.morsehistoricsite.org

Revolutionary War Sites ■ The area south of Poughkeepsie is rich in Revolutionary War sites and there are at least three, each within a few minutes' drive of the others, that might interest some of you: the 1709 **Madam Brett Homestead** (open: April–December, the second Saturday of each month, 1–4; private tours by appointment); the 1732 **Van Wyck Homestead Museum** (Open: June–October, Saturday and Sunday, 1–4; private tours by appointment); and **Mount Gulian** (1730–40), also known as the Verplanck Homestead (Open: mid-April–December, Wednesday– Sunday, 1–5; private tours by appointment). All three are in or near

Beacon, which is south of Poughkeepsie. Although they aren't exactly dull, none is worth a detour unless you are a real Revolutionary War buff.

Of the three, I found the most interesting to be the Madam Brett Homestead. (In Beacon at 50 Van Nydeck Avenue. Phone: 845-831-6533.) During the Revolution, the house held commissary supplies for the American Army and was visited by Washington and Lafayette. It's a good example of Dutch architecture from the early eighteenth century and has some interesting furnishings and a pretty garden.

The Van Wyck Museum Homestead served as part of an enormous supply depot for the Americans and now has changing exhibits based on the colonial period. (At the junction of Route 9 and I-84 just south of Fishkill. Phone: 845-896-9560.)

The present Mount Gulian is a reconstruction of the original 1740 building in which General Friedrich von Steuben of the American Army forces had his Hudson Valley headquarters. Perhaps the most interesting event associated with Mount Gulian is that the Society of the Cincinnati was founded here. This fraternal group of American officers from the Revolution who had served for at least three years with the Continental

Mt. Gulian, Baron von Steuben's headquarters during the Revolution and the birthplace of the Society, whose first president was George Washington.

Army included a host of notables, and George Washington was its first president. (Off Route 9D, near I-84, in Fishkill. Phone: 845-831-8172.)

Dia:Beacon ■ In a nutshell, Dia:Beacon is the museum for the Dia Art Foundation's collection that covers the years from the 1960s to the present. For anyone interested in this period, the museum is a must, but whether you are interested or not, the museum should be seen if only for the building itself.

A little background. The name "Dia" is taken from the Greek word meaning "through" and was, according to their material, "chosen to suggest the institution's role in enabling extraordinary artistic projects that might not otherwise be realized." It was founded as a nonprofit institution in 1974 and has become one of the most influential contemporary arts institutions in this country and abroad. Today Dia continues to fulfill its original mission through commissioning, supporting and presenting site-specific installations and exhibitions by the generation represented by such seminal artists as Agnes Martin, Donald Judd, Joseph Beuys, Cy Twombly, Gerhard Richter, Andy Warhol, and Dan Flavin, as well as by younger artists whose work reflects the achievements of the older generation. (The foundation also supports Dia:Chelsea in New York City, whose exhibition programs are principally built around single artist projects, and long-term, site-specific projects in the western United States.) Dia:Beacon, converted from a former printing plant built in 1929, was created to house the permanent collection and has 240,000 square feet of exhibition space—all illuminated by natural light. Each gallery in the museum was specifically designed for the work of the artist it contains, and some of the artists actually were involved in developing their spaces.

So much for the facts. The result is one stupendous space that must be seen. The lighting is natural, the walls an elegant white, the space extraordinary. You can wander from gallery to gallery in an atmosphere at once coolly elegant and intellectually fiery. It is revelatory of the art of the time, which rarely can be seen in such perfect conditions. Richard Serra's three monumental sculptures from the Torqued Ellipses series, for example, are ideally proportioned for their gallery, while in another gallery Agnes Martin's paintings, spaced and hung to perfection, emanate a geometrically balanced radiance that both draws the viewer in and surrounds him. Upstairs you can see some splendid work by Louise Bourgeois, including one of her huge Spiders, its body covering a cage with an armchair at its center, a vision from our worst dreams. And downstairs, a darkish space supported by column/piers with lotus-like capitals that remind me of Egypt, there is a fascinating video installation by Bruce Nauman entitled "Mapping the Studio I (Fat Chance John Cage)."

Being here can only be called a unique experience. The intelligence—even daring—exhibited in the transformation from printing plant to world-class museum and the perfection of the installations make Dia:Beacon a must see.

Open: Summer, mid-April to mid-October, Thursday–Monday, 11–6. Winter, mid-October to mid-April, 11–4. Closed: Thanksgiving Day, Christmas Eve day, Christmas Day, New Year's Eve Day, New Year's Day. The museum has a small café that opens at 10:30 and an excellent and extensive bookshop. There also is a gourmet hot dog stand (open 12–5 Friday–Sunday, mid-May to mid-September) on a patio overlooking the west garden, and there are accompanying relishes and condiments. Okay for a quickie.

Phone: 845-440-0100. Web site: www.diabeacon.org

Where to Stay and Eat

Ulster County
Area Code: 845

WHERE TO STAY

Mohonk Mountain House ■ 1000 Mountain Rest Road, New Paltz
12561. Phone: 255-1000. Web site: www.mohonk.com

Open all year. Reserve well in advance.

In the nineteenth century, the Valley was famous for its enormous and splendid resort hotels, many with extraordinary views of the river, all set amid great natural beauty. Visitors from around the world would travel to them, write about them, paint them, praise them—and sometimes condemn them.

Today only Mohonk, which opened in 1870, remains, an enormous Victorian pile at the end of an exquisite blue-black lake that's 1,200 feet above the Valley. Founded by twin brothers Albert and Alfred Smiley, the hotel still is owned by the family, and now has just over 300 rooms.

The grounds are spectacular—all 7,500 acres of them. The gardens are mature and grand, specimen trees dot the lawns, 30 miles of bridle trails take you through the general magnificence and, what's more, you can see five states from Mohonk's tower. Golf, tennis, hiking, skating, skiing, swimming, riding, concerts … you name it, they've got it. And now they have opened a spa. Some people consider this one of the most beautiful hotel sites on Earth, and I would agree.

So why can't I warm up to it? Probably because it makes me feel as though I'm in a carefully regulated prep school where I'm treated well but watched too closely to see that I don't misbehave or shame my family. You enter Mohonk through a lodge gate from which a staff member calls to confirm that you are indeed a guest, not a crasher. Then you drive along a carefully maintained road, liberally dotted with "Slowly and Quietly, Please" signs until, after five minutes or so, the hotel heaves in sight. Attendants sweep you off to the parking area, gently but firmly. Gentle and firm is the rule here, a remnant, no doubt, of the Quaker background of the Smiley family.

The dining room offers panoramic views, but guests at tables by the windows often pull down the shades against the setting sun. The food has improved somewhat from earlier visits, but I still find it dull and uninteresting. Rooms are old-fashioned, reasonably comfortable if rather homely, but they do look out on breathtaking scenery.

Maybe I'm being overly harsh, although I'm not alone in my feelings. Still, many people love it, and it certainly is worth seeing. I would suggest that you first go there for a meal or as a day guest (there's an admission fee). That way you can enjoy some of the hotel's real attractions while deciding for yourself. I should also add that it's a wonderful place to bring children because there are so many planned and supervised activities for them. The resort also has special programs throughout the year—a tennis week, a garden week, music weeks, a mystery fans week (might be fun, that), and so forth—some of which may interest you. If so, write and ask for their special brochures.

Buttermilk Falls Inn & Spa ■ 220 North Road, Milton 12547
Phone: 877-746-6772 or 845-795-1310. Web site: buttermilkfallsinn.com

On a 70-acre eighteenth-century estate, this inn and spa has 13 guest rooms, each with its own fireplace. Attractively furnished and excellent service. Lovely walks and the spa is well equipped and run. It's also conveniently located for Dia:Beacon and Storm King Art Center. Expensive but worth it, and with enough to offer that you never need leave the inn.

Emerson Resort & Spa ■ 5340 Route 28, Mount Tremper 12457
Phone: 688-2451 x10. Web site: www.emersonplace.com

Located in the Catskill Mountains and not far from Woodstock, this wonderful inn and spa has gained new life after a disastrous fire. There now are five properties: the Inn, the Spa, the Lodge, the Silk Road Restaurant, and the Country Store with the World's Largest Kaleidoscope. The Inn, more upscale than the Lodge, has 24 guest suites, the Lodge 27 rooms. I have not stayed here following the rebuilding, but I'm sure it will rank, once again, as among the best in the region.

BED & BREAKFAST INNS

1712 House ■ 93 Mill Dam Road, Stone Ridge 12484.
Phone: 687-7167. Web site: www.1712house.com

This very attractive spot, although built in the style of the eighteenth century, is really very new. It features custom-made furniture in the style of the eighteenth century, wide floorboards, hand-hewn beams, fireplace, and so forth. One very nice touch: all the guest rooms have a table and chairs for having breakfast in your room. As for the rates, they're not bad considering what you get.

Audrey's Farmhouse ■ 2188 Brunswyck Road, Wallkill 12589.
Phone: 895-3440.

If you want to get away from it all, this may be your choice. The 1740 farmhouse with the big sweeping 30-acre backyard is most appealing, and the house has become a favorite spot for weddings, with the local judge officiating and a splendid view of the Shawangunk Mountains in the background. All five rooms have feather beds and there's a well-stocked library and swimming pool. Complete breakfast included. No children under 8, but you can bring your dog.

Beaverkill Valley Inn ■ Lew Beach 12753. Phone: 439-4844.
Web site: www.beaverkillvalleyinn.com

The Beaverkill, one of the great fishing streams, is just 100 feet from the door of this late-nineteenth-century inn that has been brilliantly restored by Larry Rockefeller and that is listed on both the New York State and national registers of historic places. There are 20 guest rooms, a wonderful Victorian bar, tennis courts, indoor swimming pool, fitness room, 30 miles of hiking and cross-country skiing trails, excellent food … in short, it's a wonderful inn with every amenity. I think that for what you get it's reasonable. I also think it's very special.

Captain Schoonmaker's Bed & Breakfast ■ 913 Route 213, High Falls 12440. Phone: 687-7946. Web site: www.captainschoonmakers.com

On a pretty stream—where you also can fish—and located between New Paltz and Kingston, this rather cozy B&B offers a comfortable stay at a reasonable price.

The Inn at Stone Ridge ■ Route 209, Stone Ridge 12484.
Phone: 687-0736. Web site: www.innatstoneridge.com

On the exterior, this lovely old Dutch stone house built in the eighteenth century is a gem. Set on 150 acres, the inn itself is on a rise and surrounded by well-tended lawns with lovely old trees and flowerbeds. There even is an apple orchard. As for the interior, I find the bedrooms uninteresting at best. A pity. You can also rent the entire house by the day, week or month.

Saugerties Lighthouse ■ Talk about staying on the river. You can't get much closer than this lighthouse with its two comfortable bedrooms. Phone: 247-0656. For complete information, go to the web site: www.saugertieslighthouse.com

WHERE TO EAT

Aroma Thyme Bistro ■ 165 Canal Street, Ellenville. Phone: 647-3000. Web site: www.aromathyme.biz

I like this restaurant. The chef-owner, Marcus Guiliano, is something of a health nut, but don't panic. What he does with food is healthy, sure, but it's also delicious and original without being cute. Very good fish and meat dishes, but the vegetables are really special. Don't like vegetables? You'll like these. He also has an excellent and reasonably priced wine list. Come to think of it, the food is reasonably priced, too. Try it.

The Bear Cafe, Bearsville ■ Phone: 679-5555.
Web site: www.bearcafe.com. On Route 212 near Woodstock.

The Bear Cafe has an American menu. It's good, probably the best in Woodstock, but for me the attraction here is lunch on the terrace by a stream. You should also know that about ¾ of Manhattan's Upper West Side residents will be sitting around you. Very pleasant on a summer day. Reasonably priced. Dinner 5–11 every day but Tuesday. Reservations suggested.

Le Canard Enchaîné ■ 276 Fair Street, Kingston. Phone: 339-2003.
Web site: lecanard-enchaine.net

Not bad. Not bad at all. This attractive French bistro is named after the most famous satirical newspaper in France. The food is typical bistro fare including a very good cassoulet, there's a very popular bar, the wine list is well chosen, the service is good and the prices are reasonable. Certainly it's the best dining in Kingston. And it's open for lunch, too. One note: weekends there's music beginning around 8.

DePuy Canal House ▨ High Falls. Phone: 687-7700.
Web site: depuycanalhouse.net. On Route 213. (See page 114.)

One of my favorite restaurants in the Valley. Prix-fixe dinners and à la carte selections available. Unless you have a very large appetite, stick with the à la carte selections.

La Duchesse Anne ▨ Mt. Tremper. Phone: 688-5260.
Web site: www.laduchesseanne.com. Intersection of Route 212 and old Route 28. About 20 minutes from Woodstock.

A crowded, noisy, dark but friendly and moderately priced restaurant that supposedly specializes in Breton food but really makes basic French. The food is reasonably good but certainly not memorable.

The French Corner ▨ 3407 Cooper Street (off Route 209 on Route 213 S.) Stone Ridge. Phone: 687-0810. Web site: www.frcorner.com

This is a good, solid French restaurant whose chef, Jacques Qualin, worked in several famous Manhattan restaurants. He is from the Franche-Comté, and his food is influenced by that region and by the rich produce of the Valley. And it's very good. A little pricy but worth every cent, and in a most attractive setting. (There's also a very reasonable prix fixe menu.)

Locust Tree Inn ▨ New Paltz. Phone: 255-7888. (See page 119.)

Loretta Charles ▨ Route 28 in Shandaken. Phone: 688-2550.

A pleasant country restaurant with a working fireplace and a pretty setting on the Esopus Creek. There also is a wood-burning grill and a menu that includes mussels and frogs' legs and chicken roasted on the wood fire. Comfortable and informal.

The Main Course ▨ 232 Main Street, New Paltz 12561. Phone: 255-2600.

This is an unpretentious, even homely restaurant, but very good— soups, salads, interesting specials—and very inexpensive considering what you get. Located in a small shopping plaza.

Miss Lucy's Kitchen ■ 90 Partition Street, Saugerties. Phone: 246-9240.

Country décor, country warmth—kitchen gadgets on the walls, wooden chairs, café curtains, friendly hosts. Down home, even if the owners are from New York City (they owned Grove Restaurant in the West Village.) It's also kid friendly—there's a $5 child's menu—and the entrée prices are reasonable, too.

The Red Onion ■ 1654 Route 212, Saugerties/Woodstock. Phone: 679-1223. Web site: www.redonionrestaurant.com

If you're looking for good food, well prepared and at a decent price, you've found the restaurant. From hamburgers to steaks and seafood, it's all here. Nothing fancy, just comfort food at its best. Good wine list, too.

Dutchess County
Area Code: 845

WHERE TO STAY

Alumnae House ■ Vassar, 161 College Avenue, Poughkeepsie 12603. Phone: 437-7100. Web site: www.aavc.vassar.edu/vq/articles/ Alumnae-House-Celebration.

No, this is not a dormitory-style residence. It's a Tudor-style mansion that was built in 1924 and now has been completely renovated. It's comfortable and very reasonable, and it's only a block from the main campus at Vassar. There also is a dining room serving quite a good breakfast.

Beekman Arms and Delamater Inn ■ 6387 Mill Street, Rhinebeck 12572. Phone: 876-7077. Web site: www.beekmandelamaterinn.com

The Beekman Arms, at the center of Rhinebeck on Route 9, claims to be the oldest in continuous operation in America. The Delamater Inn (see page 155) is operated by the same management. There also are other buildings, some with fireplaces. If you reserve be sure to ask what is available and where. I prefer not to stay in the inn—the rooms are cramped.

Belvedere Mansion ■ 10 Olde Route 9, Staatsburg 12580.
Phone: 889-8000. Web site: www.belvederemansion.com

Want to live like the nineteenth-century Hudson River gentry? This is about as close as you can get. The house, very near Rhinebeck, is on the Hudson and provides stunning views of the river and the Catskills. The rooms are attractively decorated and comfortable. And there also is a restaurant. (See page 176.)

Bullis Hall ■ P.O. Box 630, 88 Hunns Lake Road, Bangall 12506.
Phone: 868-1665. Web site: www.bullishall.com

This rather splendid inn is a member of the exclusive Relais & Chateau group and is correspondingly expensive and luxurious and runs like clockwork. It is housed in a very handsome Greek Revival building that dates from 1832, with its own restaurant, between Rhinebeck and Millerton. Being in the center of the hunt country, it is unsurprising that the inn has connections with the local shooting and hunt clubs. Beautifully decorated, filled with antiques, Italian linens and Frette bathrobes and slippers, a Bose music system, a wooden cruiser berthed on the Hudson for excursions … there even is a concierge and a social secretary(!) If you're feeling flush, stay here. This certainly ranks as among the best in the Valley.

The Gables at Rhinebeck ■ see page 156.

The Lakehouse Inn ■ P.O. Box 398, 401 Shelley Hill Road,
Stanfordville 12581. Phone: 266-8093.
Web site: www.lakehouse-rhinebeck.com

Fireplaces. Jacuzzis. Lakefront views. Private decks. Very attractively furnished "guest quarters," as they put it. You think this comes cheap? Most of the rooms have all of the above, and it is very expensive. But it also is very attractive.

Old Drover's Inn ■ Old Route 22, P.O. Box 100, Dover Plains 12522.
Phone: 832-9311. Web site: www.olddroversinn.com

For many years the proprietor of this inn was Alice Pitcher, and she brought great glory to Old Drover's including Wine Spectator's Award of Excellence and membership in the prestigious federation of the world's luxury hotels, Relais & Chateaux. Then she left and, quite frankly, the new ownership let things slide. Well, she's back, and the inn is back on track as one of the best places to stay in the Valley.

The inn is old; part of the building dates from 1750, the rest from 1810, and it is very beautiful. Personally, I count this as one of my favorites. I suppose it's because I enjoy things on a small scale, but it also could be the fireplace in three of the four bedrooms (my favorite is the Sleigh Room) or the murals in the Federal Room (particularly the one with an enormous urn filled with red tulips) or the taproom with paneling so dark it has an ebony glow. It's all of these things and more. For part of that "more" see page 180.

The Poughkeepsie Grand Hotel ■ 40 Civic Center Plaza, Poughkeepsie 12601. Phone: 485-5300. Web site: www.pokgrand.com

The good news is that at last there is a decent hotel in Poughkeepsie, and it's comfortable and clean. There also is a health club. However, I much prefer the Inn at the Falls (see page 174).

Troutbeck ■ 515 Leedsville Rd., Amenia 12501. Phone: 800-978-7688. Web site: www.troutbeck.com. Reservations required.

The price is stiff, but this is one of the more beautiful settings in the Valley. The original owner was a man named Joel Elias Spingarn, a most interesting individual. He was a founding member of the publishing firm of Harcourt, Brace as well as of the National Association for the Advancement of Colored People (NAACP), ran for Congress, wrote several books (including one on literary criticism in the Renaissance) and, last but not least, grew the largest collection of clematis in the world at Troutbeck. "It is the obsession of my leisure hours," he said.

Today the inn is set on 442 acres, with magnificent old sycamores in front, and elsewhere there are a lake and streams, a solar-heated pool, pool house, two tennis courts and walled gardens. All the accoutrements, in short, of an estate, which is exactly what it is. To be more specific, an English country estate. The handsome stone Tudor house with leaded windows was built in 1919 and this is how architectural historian Lewis Mumford once described it: "Nestled under a hill, secure against even visual intrusion, [the] house cultivates its innerness; though numerous doors open onto lawn and terrace, Troutbeck itself gives a sense of being snug, protected, inviolate." At these prices, it should be. Sinclair Lewis liked it too, mentioning primarily the "cathedral of trees" around the building. In any case, the house has been impeccably restored and beautifully decorated. There's also a garden house and an old farmhouse for guests, covered and heated indoor and outdoor pools and an exercise room.

BED & BREAKFAST INNS

Inn at the Falls ■ 50 Red Oaks Mill Road, Poughkeepsie 12603. Phone: 462-5770. Web site: www.innatthefalls.com

This 36-room facility really is a hotel, although they style themselves as a Bed & Breakfast hotel. Many rooms have a view of Wappingers Creek and the falls, and an extensive continental breakfast is included in the price.

The Mill at Bloomvale Falls ■ Route 82 at Route 13, Salt Point 12578. Near Millbrook. Phone: 266-4234.

This, a real charmer, on the National Historic Register, is an eighteenth-century stone mill with a splendid waterfall. The mill has been brilliantly restored and rejuvenated. Of the four bedrooms, three overlook the waterfall, while the fourth has a view of the courtyard and its fountain. The property includes 24 acres of land on which you can canoe, fish, swim, hike and, in winter, cross-country ski. A complete breakfast is included, and children over 12 are welcome.

Olde Rhinebeck Inn ■ 340 Wurtemburg Road, Rhinebeck 12572. Phone: 871-1745. Web site: www.rhinebeckinn.com

A very pleasant find with good-looking rooms and an attractive setting that led it to be voted as one of the 10 best inns in North America. I think that's pushing it, but it is nice, and the service is exemplary. There also is a cottage available.

The Red Hook Inn ■ 7460 South Broadway, Red Hook 12571. Phone: 758-8445. Web site: www.theredhookinn.com

This is right on the main drag—Route 9—but the six rooms are very comfortable and nicely decorated, the price is right, and there's a relaxed ambiance that I find appealing. There's also an adequate to good restaurant. (See page 181.)

Simmons' Way Village Inn & Restaurant ■ Main Street, Route 44, Millerton 12546. Phone: 518-789-6235.
Web site: www.simmonsway.com. (For the restaurant, see page 181.)

Millerton is a pleasant village very near the Connecticut border and is surrounded by six prep schools, so it is important to reserve well in advance if you are thinking of staying here during the school year. The house, right in the center of the village, is big and rambling with a particularly inviting front porch. It was built in 1854 and extensively remodeled in 1892 as the Queen Anne structure you see today. The common rooms downstairs both have fireplaces. There are nine rooms, all with a private bath or shower, and the beds range from canopy to brass to pine spool beds.

Whistlewood Farm ■ 11 Pells Road, Rhinebeck 12572.
Phone: 876-6838. Web site: www.whistlewood.com

Just outside the village of Rhinebeck, the décor is eclectic—in one room an antique canoe is suspended from the ceiling—but it all works, and works well. It's a very pleasant B&B that is, when all is said and done, country elegant. And the prices are very fair. Well worth your consideration.

WHERE TO EAT

Allyn's Restaurant & Cafe ■ Route 44 (4 miles east of Millbrook), Millbrook. Phone: 677-5888. Web site: www.allyns.com

The chef-owner is Allan Katz, who decided that the name of the restaurant should have a twist—hence the "y." It is the favorite restaurant of those who live in Millbrook, and I would agree that it serves the best food here. One reader writes that "200 years ago the structure was a farmhouse. Now that space is comfortably decorated in a semiformal manner. Less formal is the Cafe, decorated with a long mural representing Millbrook." There is a fireplace, and in winter competition can be fierce to capture one of the three tables there. Patio dining in the summer.

Beekman Arms: Traphagen Restaurant ■ Route 9, Rhinebeck.
Phone: 876-1766.
Web site: www.beekmandelamaterinn.com

The taproom and greenhouse are two attractive spaces, but the food is mediocre, and Rhinebeck now has much better restaurants.

Belvedere Mansion ■ 10 Olde Route 9, Staatsburg. Phone: 889-8000.
Web site: www.belvederemansion.com

A beautiful setting. Antiques, candlelight, painted ceiling … restrained elegance, I would call it. Wonderful for a romantic evening. As for the food—it's good—one of the better places to dine around here. Combined with a night at the inn, I can't think of a nicer way to spend a weekend.

Calico Restaurant and Patisserie ■ Route 9, Rhinebeck.
Phone: 876-2749. Web site: www.calicorhinebeck.com

This tiny little restaurant (seven tables) is directly across from the Beekman Arms and offers surprisingly sophisticated and good food at both lunch and dinner as well as a good and substantial wine list. It's also open for breakfast—pastry and coffee. The menu is posted outside, but get there early as it fills up fast, and make a reservation for dinner. And the pastries are delicious. An old favorite of mine.

Cascade Mountain Winery & Restaurant ■ Amenia (3 miles north of Amenia light, a left off Route 22). Phone: 373-9021.
Web site: www.cascademt.com

Henry James once said that the words *summer day* are the most beautiful in the English language. You should spend one here. In summer, a lunch outside on the porch is one of the more delightful ways to spend the early afternoon. Not only is the drive here lovely, the setting is charming, the service friendly and efficient and the food first-rate. It's very popular, so be sure to call and reserve, but I can heartily recommend it as an all-around joy. And the Cascade seyval blanc is a perfect accompaniment. Open: Lunch, Thursday–Sunday.

China Rose ■ Shatzell Avenue, Rhinecliff. Phone 876-7442.

If you leave your car at the Rhinecliff Amtrak station, you have to pass this quirky little restaurant perched on the hill with a terrace overlooking the Hudson. Inside, the decor is Victorian, the food Chinese-inspired, reasonably priced, and quite good. A nice find and a great way to be on time for the train. No reservations, so waits can be long on the weekend. Watch out for the delicious sake margaritas—or make someone else the designated driver.

Copperfield's ■ Route 44 (2 miles west of Millbrook), Salt Point. Phone: 677-8188.

More informal than Allyn's, it also is cheaper. It's not as good, either. Frankly, I don't know why it's so popular.

Cozy Corner ■ Route 44, Amenia. Phone: 373-9379.

This is an old-fashioned diner with all that implies—huge pancakes with sausage, great sandwiches and hamburgers—also outsized—and homemade pies and cakes. My favorite—the outrageously thick milk shakes. It's only open in the morning and early afternoon (until 2). Go. Indulge.

The Culinary Institute of America ■ Hyde Park. Phone: 452-9600. Restaurant reservations: 471-6608. You also can reserve on line: www.ciachef.edu/restaurants/default.asp. On Route 9 between Hyde Park and Poughkeepsie.

The CIA, as everyone calls it, primarily resides in an enormous red-brick Georgian colonial building that formerly was a seminary. (You'll see the old chapel as you come up the drive.) Its purpose is to educate around 2,000 students at a time in the culinary arts and baking and pastry arts, which it does well and thoroughly; chefs in good restaurants across the country have graduated from here, and graduates are among the most sought after in the food service and hospitality industry.

Five award-winning, student-staffed restaurants are open to bedazzle the public: **American Bounty Restaurant, Apple Pie Bakery Café, Ristorante Caterina de'Medici, St. Andrew's Café,** and **Escoffier Restaurant.** The service at all of them is perfect, as you would expect, but it's also rather endearing because they're trying so hard.

All of the dining rooms are extremely popular, not only because they can be quite good but also because they have received an enormous amount of publicity. The result: You must reserve well in advance for a Friday or Saturday night. As the CIA itself is careful to point out, these restaurants are "staffed by students in the final course of the Institute's 21-month curriculum and are intended to enhance their education," and although the restaurants generally are tops, there can be the occasional slip.

Of them all I have two favorites. The first is The American Bounty: It's warm, inviting and comfortable; a very handsome room. The seasonal menu takes advantage of regional ingredients, and everything is prepared and presented with great style and loving care. American wines, of course. The second is Ristorante Caterina de'Medici, set in a Tuscan Villa known as the Colavita Center for Italian Food and Wine and with five distinct dining areas. Colavita has invested its money well. The menu is wonderful, with regional ingredients and wonderful Italian recipes. They also have an excellent Italian wine list, as well as Italian beers and aperitifs.

The Escoffier Restaurant uses French recipes "prepared true to the principles of legendary chef Auguste Escoffier, but with a lighter, contemporary touch." My impression is that this is most people's favorite. There are two rooms here; I prefer the one with the bar—a particularly handsome one with stunning sconces—because it's more intimate than the main dining room and also because you can watch the students cooking. The international wine list deserves, as you would expect, high marks.

St. Andrew's Café has contemporary food in a family-friendly setting and features salads, sandwiches, wood-fired pizzas and main course entrées. It's fun. And so is the Apple Pie Bakery Café, again informal and very big on baking and pastry. Café cuisine, and you also can take food out from here.

40 West ■ 40 West Market Street, Rhinebeck. Phone: 876-2214.

An old blacksmith's shop that now is an attractive restaurant. New American cuisine, good, unpretentious, friendly staff. I particularly like the duck.

Gigi Trattoria ▓ 6422 Montgomery Street, Rhinebeck.
Phone: 876-1007. Web site: www.gigitrattoria.com

Italian, obviously, but with an original flair where the chef takes old standards and gives them a new twist. It is, arguably, the best Rhinebeck has to offer, and the food is reasonably priced. A word of warning: they only take reservations for large parties, and therefore it can be tough to get in—it's very popular.

Harralds ▓ Route 52, Stormville. Phone: 878-6595.
Web site: harraldsrestaurant.com

Harralds, a particularly attractive country inn set on well-tended grounds, is very much in the grand manner, featuring impeccable ervice, elegant food and fine wines (with prices to match). Sometimes the food can be a little too rich and a little too carefully thought out; one would like more straightforwardness and less sauce. Still, the quality of everything offered is first rate and the dishes are prepared and presented with consummate care. The trout, for example, comes from a pond you pass on the way in, and the duck is perfectly roasted. Portions are generous, too. I should also add that the restaurant has received several awards.

Irving Farm Coffee House ▓ 44 Main Street, Millerton.
Phone: 518-789-6540. Web site: www.irvingfarm.com

When the sign on the door says that you must wear a shirt and shoes, it makes me wonder about the quality of what's inside. But, in this instance, never fear. From morning until evening, this very pleasant sandwich-pastry-coffee spot offers very good "eats" and pleasant service. They also sell beer and wine, and their own coffee, which comes in an endless array of estate grown beans and blends and from a variety of locations. Next door is the Millerton Movie House, and before the show it gets crowded. What I most like—you can take your paper, read as long as you like, and no one gives you dirty looks. By the way, they have a sister restaurant in New York City—71 Irving Place Coffee & Tea Bar.

Le Pavillon ■ 230 Salt Point Turnpike, Poughkeepsie. Phone: 473-2525.

This is a real country French restaurant in a cozy old house. I like it for its good food and relaxed ambience. The chef-owner, Claude Guermont, a former chief instructor at the CIA's Escoffier Room, was trained in France, but his food here is a combination of both French and American elements with a nouvelle cuisine bias. It is not, however, a bastion for nouvelle; Guermont uses the best of this, plus classical and regional cooking to create solidly based dishes with an original touch. Game—pheasant, quail, partridge, venison—is always represented, as is a fresh fish of the day. Service is friendly, prices moderately expensive, and though the environs of Poughkeepsie may not be your idea of dinner in the country, you will be very happy here.

Le Petit Bistro ■ 8 East Market Street, Rhinebeck. Phone: 876-7400. Web site: lepetitbistro.com.

The general feeling—mine included—is that this is a good little French bistro made even more appealing by the fact that you can dine without going bankrupt.

Locust Tree Restaurant ■ 215 Huguenot Street, New Paltz. Phone: 255-7888. Web site: www.locusttree.com. See page 119.

Mabbettsville Market ■ Route 44A, Mabbettsville (near Millbrook). Phone: 677-5284. Web site: www.mabbettsvillemarket.com.

This is a nice find. If you're on the road and just want to get some prepared food, stop here. You'll find everything from sandwiches and soups to hors d'oeuvres and salad platters. There also are a wide variety of cheeses and a wood-burning grill for meats and chicken. Excellent desserts. Perfect choice for picnic fare.

Old Drover's Inn ■ Old Route 22, Dover Plains. Phone: 832-9311. Web site: www.olddroversinn.com

Outsize drinks, delicious food—cheddar soup is one of my favorites (and of everyone else's, too)—impeccable service. This has got to rank as a wonderful experience.

Roasted Garlic at The Red Hook Inn ■ 7460 South Broadway.
Phone: 758-8445. Web site: www.theredhookinn.com.

Food is good here and the prices are reasonable. Nothing terribly fancy—there's a Near Eastern bias, but there also are hamburgers, shrimp, and so forth—but well prepared, and the atmosphere is relaxed and welcoming. Not a bad choice, particularly if you're attending something at the Bard Music Festival and want a bite before the event.

Santa Fe ■ Broadway, Tivoli. Phone: 757-4100.
Web site: www.santafetivoli.com

Some readers call the food at the Santa Fe Southwestern. Others call it Mexican. Obviously the chef has an imagination. I like it here and it's the best Southwestern/Mexican food around.

Martha's at Simmons' Way Village Inn and Restaurant ■ Main Street, Millerton. Phone: 518-789-6235.

This inn (see page 175) also has an attractive and full-blown restaurant whose menu changes with the season. In addition, it has an excellent wine list. The food is good and is both presented and served with style. A pleasant find, this.

Star Grill ■ Franklin Avenue, Millbrook. Phone: 677-5600.
Web site: the stargrill.com

A fun "in" spot in Millbrook, this attractive American restaurant uses local ingredients in innovative ways that invite repeat dining.

Terrapin ■ 6426 Montgomery Street, Rhinebeck. Phone 876-3330.
Web site: www.terrapinrestaurant.com

This actually is two restaurants, what they call a bistro/bar with light fare—sandwiches, soups, tapas, etc—and the regular restaurant, which is rather attractive. All in a converted church. I really don't like the bistro/bar. Service is, to put it kindly, lackluster, but at least it matches the food. As for the restaurant, the food is considerably better (even the same tapas seem better here) but still, it doesn't do it for me.

Troutbeck ■ Amenia. Phone: 373-9681. (See page 173).

Dinner here is good but not great; but the country setting and dining rooms are very pretty, the service friendly. A pleasant experience if not a gourmet's delight. Expensive. Open: Wednesday–Saturday nights 6:30–9, Wednesday–Saturday lunch 12–2; Sunday brunch 11:30–2:30. Reservations required.

Finally, Dutchess County is the home of two handsome diners. In Red Hook, a short distance north of Rhinebeck, **The Historic Village Diner** at 7550 North Broadway (phone: 758-6232; web site: www.historic-village-diner.com) is a beautifully preserved stainless-steel diner that is listed on both the state and national Historic Registers. The food is good, too. **The Millbrook Diner** on Franklin Avenue in Millbrook (phone: 677-5319) also is a stainless-steel survivor and has reasonably good food.

THE LOWER HUDSON

From Putnam County to New York City

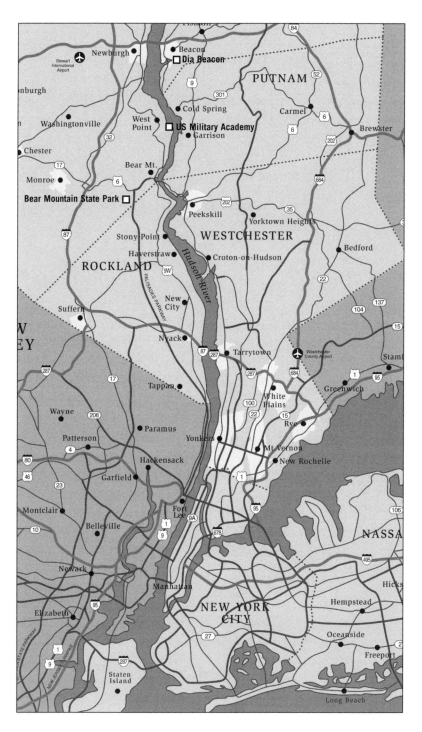

THIS IS AN AREA of near-violent contrasts: the most dramatic scenery on the river in the Highlands, the total ugliness of industrial concentration near New York City, the widest and narrowest points of the Hudson, the astounding beauty of the Palisades facing the grimy, falling-down piers, extreme wealth on baronial estates in Westchester County, dire poverty in old urban centers such as Newburgh. Here you will enjoy museums and buildings and scenery of extraordinary interest and then, within only a few miles, come upon scenes of horrendous urban development.

The pace is different here, too; nervous energy radiates out from New York City, shattering the unity of the area into a vast urban-oriented, dependent complex that reflects in a crazy-quilt way, the economy and vitality of the metropolis to the south. Sometimes the river seems to shrink to insignificance in the midst of it all, but don't be fooled. It is still the unifying link, an oasis of natural beauty that—no matter what man has tried to do—maintains its beauty and dignity. It just is, a great fact that moves on through it all, to its final destination far out in the Atlantic.

A Perfect Weekend in the Hudson Highlands

It sometimes happens when you arrive in a particular setting or place that you know this is it—here is the essence, good or bad, of the area you're exploring. In the Valley, that place is Cold Spring. Here and nearby can be found the most dramatic scenery not only on the Hudson, but it must also rank among the most beautiful areas in the entire nation as well. You'll find the best-situated inn for river views, some of the best restaurants, the most beautifully restored of all houses, West Point and Storm King, fine antique shops and excellent museums—plus a whole lot more. It is an ideal place to spend a weekend, or longer, just absorbing this magnificently complex region, in terms of both nature and of history, that constitutes the Hudson River Valley. What I describe below would take more than a weekend, but you have the luxury, then, of picking and choosing, and you can always come back for more. You'll certainly want to.

THE SETTING

Cold Spring is in the Hudson Highlands, a 15-mile length of the river that hasn't changed much since Henry Hudson first sailed past in 1609. The highest mountains on the river are here, rising straight up from the banks, and the Hudson reaches its greatest depths here, as well. According to the most prevalent geological theory, at this point the Hudson met another river forcing its way north—all of this occurred many thousands of years ago—and created the river we know today, where ocean tides sweep as far north as Troy. Bordered on the north by Storm King and on the south by Dunderberg Mountain, all the mountains within this area are so steeply sloped that building development is well-nigh impossible. What's more, today the region is protected further by the 52,000-acre Palisades Interstate Park and the 16,000-acre United States Military Academy reservation at West Point.

It is a stunning sight at any time of the year, but I particularly love it in the fall, the mountains ablaze with colors so vibrant and alive they seem to flow down the sides to spread out and shimmer on the blue palette of the river. One October, when I was staying in Cold Spring for a few days to enjoy it all, I would get up early each morning and look out my window to see a thin luminous cloud hovering over the river, a quicksilver stripe dividing the reds and greens and golds and browns of the mountains from the intense blue of the water. Slowly it would rise and dissipate, a gauzy mystical curtain, and the Highlands would appear, fully exposed in all their glory. It is the kind of scenery that draws you into its very essence, making you forget everything but the verity of those old clichés concerning water and seasons, life and death, and—I have got to say it—truth and beauty.

Putnam County

Cold Spring

Cold Spring is a small, pretty nineteenth-century village in Putnam County that does not, thank God, compete in any way with the surrounding scenery. On weekends it can be crowded, for Main Street is now packed with about two dozen antique shops of varying quality that draw people like flies to honey. You should plan on a day visiting them—some have very good material. Still, you can spend a pleasant hour or two wandering through the different establishments; they carry everything and more—from furniture, paintings and prints to old pewter, china and glass to contemporary crafts, jewelry and "fabulous fifties" dreck.

George Washington supposedly gave the town its name during the Revolution, but nothing much happened after that until the War of 1812, when President James Madison ordered a munitions foundry to be built here. It eventually constructed the nation's first iron ship and also the Parrott gun, a fieldpiece later used extensively in the Civil War. A man named Gouverneur Kemble (1786–1875) was appointed the foundry's first director, and it was he we also have to thank for the loveliest building in Cold Spring as well as one of the most charming in the entire Valley, the **Chapel of Our Lady**.

You reach the Chapel by going down Main Street toward the river. Turn left just before the railroad track (there's a sign there directing you to the Hudson House—more on that later) and then, once over the bridge covering the tracks, turn left again and, within a few feet, you will be at the back of the Chapel. Walk up the little steps, and you are on a small bluff looking out across the river. Kemble donated both this site and the funds to build the Chapel, which was completed in 1833.

The building, small and simple, with a handsome front portico supported by four columns in the Tuscan order, contains only one room. Thanks to the efforts of concerned citizens in the Valley, it has been perfectly restored. Originally a Catholic chapel, it is now an ecumenical church serving the entire community. (And more. Once, after I had mentioned the Chapel in an article for *Travel & Leisure* magazine, a young woman wrote me to say that she had traveled some distance to see the

Chapel. She liked it so much, she told me, that she planned to be married there. That was nice to hear.)

The Chapel and view have always been a favorite of artists, but the most famous rendering of it—and certainly my favorite—is by William Henry Bartlett (1809–54), an Englishman whose rendition of the Chapel first appeared in London in 1840 in a book called *American Scenery* that became a classic of its time. In the latter half of the nineteenth century, Bartlett's prints served as inspiration to such American painters as Thomas Chambers and Samuel Gerry as well as to countless folk artists. Bartlett's views of the Hudson, including this one, can still be found in antique and print shops at reasonable prices and make a wonderful memento of your time spent in the Valley. (In fact, if you go up Main Street, past the light and into Nelsonville, there, at 255 Main Street, you'll see **Hudson Rogue Company.** They offer a good, fairly priced selection of autographs, books and prints, including those of Bartlett, and are well worth visiting. Phone: 845-265-2211.)

The Chapel is a favorite landmark of all those who sail the river, for it has a dignity and simplicity that is deeply moving. I remember that I first saw it one summer night, when it is softly floodlit, and it seemed so alone, somehow, not in a sad sense but so uniquely itself that nothing could touch it. Another time, on a dreary February day, I watched a wedding party being photographed there, under the handsome wrought-iron chandelier ablaze with red candles, and I thought how wonderful it would be to have the mileposts of one's life—births, marriages, deaths—recorded here in this Elysian setting that combines so brilliantly the best both man and nature have to offer.

When you leave, instead of turning back over the bridge, go straight to the end of the street, turn left and, at the end of the block on your right is **Hudson House**, the inn with the best river setting in the Valley.

The first thing you'll notice is that you're right on the banks of the river, facing a small pier where steamboats used to dock and home to a little bandstand covered with a bright red roof. It's impossible, of course, not to walk out to the end of the pier before going into the inn, and once there you have still another spectacular view. To the south lies West Point, its chapel tower clearly visible against the sky. To the north, Storm King, somber and handsome, which Vincent J. Scully, Jr., the famous architectural historian and author, termed "a dome of living granite, swelling with

Hudson House offers splendid views of the Highlands from the unspoiled setting of Cold Spring.

animal power. It is not picturesque in the softer sense of the word but awesome, a primitive embodiment of the energies of the earth. It makes the character of wild nature physically visible in monumental form." (The mountain was originally called Butter Hill, anathema to one Nathaniel Parker Willis [1806–67], a now-forgotten writer-editor whose estate, "Idlewild," was in Cornwall on the west bank and who wrote the already-mentioned *American Scenery* that William Bartlett illustrated. It was Willis who thought up the romantically descriptive Storm King and won the campaign to have this become the mountain's official name.) By the way, usually there are some swans here and a few ducks, so if you have any cookies or crackers in your car, bring them along with you and make some new, extremely greedy friends.

Now it's time to look more closely at the inn, a three-story clapboard structure with dormer windows and a porch running around the second floor. Built in 1832 to house steamboat passengers, it was on its last legs in 1980 when it was bought and, a million or so dollars later, restored—or, more accurately, transformed into a delightful country inn, many of whose rooms look directly out on the river. Each guest room was furnished with country antiques and decorated with individual flair. Very pleasant, and a welcome comfort to the traveler.

Downstairs, three of the small dining rooms with comfortable, painted Windsor chairs face the river, and don't be afraid to kill to get a window table. On the street side is the small bar and long, nicely furnished lounge, with a roaring fireplace in winter and where guests also eat when the dining rooms are full. As for the food, it's passable, but only that.

For one of your weekend nights, though, I strongly suggest that you eat at **Plumbush**. The food is excellent and prepared with great care, the dining room inviting and the service superb—all at a reasonably expensive price. Go back up Main Street to Route 9D, turn right, and you'll see a sign for the restaurant on your left after you've driven a mile or so. Plumbush is in an old, rambling barn of a house once owned by a woman with the grand-sounding name of Marchesa Rizzo dei Ritii; her maiden name was plain old Agnes Shewan.

The menu is primarily continental/American. The wine list is more than adequate and, like the food, fairly priced. This is one of the more pleasant places to dine along the Hudson.

WHAT TO SEE AND DO

Boscobel ■ Literally a stone's throw beyond Plumbush is the entrance to Boscobel, an architecturally magnificent building that, of all the Hudson River houses, has the most spectacular interior. Overall, it is the finest example I know of the New York Federal period (roughly 1780–1820) in terms of architecture, furniture and decoration. And, certainly, Federal was one of the most elegant styles in our history.

Placed high over the river, with views extending for miles, the exterior of Boscobel glows in its original colors—a creamy white for the trim, yellow ochre for the walls. It resembles an airy, elegant stage set, with the blue-gray Hudson an ever-present motif. This feeling is reinforced by the carved wooden swags between the columns that set off the balcony on the second floor. Surrounding the mansion is a landscape of lawns, woods, gardens and orchards.

The house was the dream of States Morris Dyckman, a descendant of early Dutch settlers, who was born in New York City in 1755. A Loyalist during the Revolution, Dyckman went to London for the duration, returning to this country in 1789. In 1804, he and his wife, Elizabeth, began planning the country estate they decided to call Boscobel, both because *bosco bello* means "beautiful woods" in Italian and also in memory of the Shropshire forest where Charles II hid himself inside an oak tree after being defeated by Cromwell at the Battle of Worcester in 1651.

But Dyckman died in 1806, before the house was completed (the architect, by the way, is unknown), and it was left to Elizabeth to finish. Boscobel remained in the family until 1888, then fell on hard times. By 1954, demolition seemed inevitable; in 1955, a check for $35 bought the house from the federal government, and plans were made to tear it down. Like all good stories, though, this one has a happy ending. The house was saved, moved to its present site, a few miles farther north, and rebuilt, primarily through the generosity of Lila Acheson Wallace, co-founder with her husband, De Witt, of *Reader's Digest*. Boscobel Restoration, a nonprofit group, was set up to handle the refurbishing of the mansion, and in 1961 it was opened to the public. Then, in 1975, a copy of a list of States Dyckman's possessions was found that indicated the furnishings were quite different from what the house now contained. Mrs. Wallace again came to the rescue; the offending collection was sold and, within two years, the New York Federal furniture you presently see was put in its place.

Once through the front door, you enter the great hall, which faces a magnificent central staircase that rises to a landing with a huge Palladian window. The staircase divides to the left and right and continues to the second floor. Doric columns support three arches that separate the hall into two sections.

Because the hall's architecture is so beautiful, the restorers decided that the decoration should emphasize its detail. A wallpaper was found in the 1804 Medford Inn in Massachusetts and reproduced for Boscobel. The pattern resembles carved stonework in tan and buff, and the doors, columns and trim are painted in a period ivory color. The floor of the great hall is covered with a floor cloth—very similar to our linoleum—that has

The orangery at Boscobel. The house and setting are among the most beautiful in the country, the restoration a triumph of research and taste.

been hand-painted to look like marble and is based on a pattern found in a book published in the late eighteenth century. The doors on the principal rooms on the first and second floors have been stained to look like mahogany, based upon paint evidence found on an original door.

To the right of the hall are the parlors. In the front one, most of the furniture is by, or attributed to, Duncan Phyfe, the great New York cabinetmaker, and the chairs and sofa are covered in a brilliant lemon-yellow moreen. There are other Phyfe pieces throughout the house, making it almost a museum of his work.

A portrait of Elizabeth Dyckman—feminine and pretty, although rumor has it that she was tight with a dollar—hangs over the sofa, and the draperies are reproduced from period ones found in the attic of another Hudson Valley home. And here, as almost everywhere in the house, fresh flowers in Chinese export bowls give the impression that the owners have stepped out only for a moment, leaving instructions that their visitors be made to feel at home. Behind this room is a second parlor that includes part of States Dyckman's library and his portrait by an unidentified artist (ca. 1785).

Recross the hall and you enter the most beautiful part of the house, the dining room. The proportions are ideal, the carving of the architectural detail that of a master craftsman, the colors warm, soft and inviting. The design of the mantelpiece, as for those in the parlors, is similar to plans in William Payne's *The Gentleman and Country Builder's Companion* (1794). The dining-room table is spectacular—in three parts, with the center section in front of the window facing the Hudson. It can seat 24 when put together, but in its present, reduced state it is set for 6, with some original pieces including Elizabeth's monogrammed silver.

Two Federal sideboards, early and late period, stand against the walls, and the chairs, their backs and legs carved to imitate bamboo and painted a soft cream with green trim, are similar to the ones Elizabeth Dyckman had bought in New York. The whole feeling of the room—straight lines offset by graceful curves, symmetrical outlines, even fragile construction—is one of repose. In a small pantry behind the dining room are cupboards filled with blue-and-white porcelain.

On either side of the staircase landing, there are pictures of Elizabeth's great-grandparents, done in 1726 by portraitist John Watson. At the head of the stairs is a painting of Narcissus by Benjamin West. To the left are a guest bedroom, a dressing room and Elizabeth Dyckman's own room. Hers, of course, is the most beautiful, with its Phyfe canopy bed, needlepoint rug and portraits of her husband and son.

The central part of the upstairs is taken up by an enormous library-sitting room whose floor-length windows open onto the balcony. Two of Boscobel's most beautiful pieces of furniture are here: a bookcase with desk, again attributed to Phyfe, with the arms of Thomas Witter Chrystie, a New York attorney, the first-known example of any New York furniture bearing a coat of arms; and an octagonal card table covered in green baize and leather, which was found lying in pieces against a furnace in the nearby village of Cold Spring. The other two rooms on this floor are a maid's storage room and the housekeeper's room, which also served as the nursery and is complete down to a crib of the period.

The basement once consisted of a root cellar and two kitchens. Now it is devoted primarily to exhibition space. In a way, this is the heart of the house, for here you find the original material that set the tone for the restoration. There are family documents and the china, glass and silver purchased by States Dyckman in England; a medallion carved from a piece of the Royal Oak in the forest of Boscobel in England; even examples of china with companion bills alongside describing the English country scenes painted on them. Look, also, for two pairs of portraits of Hudson Valley gentry, one pair by Ammi Phillips, the other by Ralph Earl; they are masterpieces of their kind. You exit out into the grounds through the restored kitchen, warm and comfortable with Hudson Valley chairs and tools of the time.

Boscobel is set on 45 acres of land, about 15 of which are landscaped. In the spring, 2,800 tulips and flowering fruit trees greet the visitor. In spring, too, there is an annual Snapping Turtle Walk that takes place in June, when they stroll across the grounds on their way to lay their eggs. Call in early June for more information. In summer a formal rose garden scents the air. All the grounds are open to the public. In 1997 a Woodland Trail was opened on 25 acres to the south of the formal grounds and features spectacular views of the Hudson. Rustic shelters are conveniently placed along the 1-mile trail, and a self-guided trail brochure is available at the reception center.

There is also a well-stocked gift shop with everything from candles and soap and 20-cent candy sticks to reproduction china. In the fall, you can buy apples picked from the trees on the estate, and in winter a fire always burns in the kitchen of the mansion.

As you leave, look back. Your view is framed by the alley of hemlock hedges … and there, at the other end, is one last view of the Hudson, now silver in the reflected light.

**Boscobel is open daily except Tuesday, April–October 9:30–5.
The last tour is at 4:15. In November and December 9:30–4,
with the last tour at 3:15. Closed January, February and March,
Thanksgiving and Christmas Day.
Phone: 845-265-3638. Web site: www.boscobel.org**

Constitution Marsh Audubon Center and Sanctuary ▪ Lovely … serene … unique … all true, and the marsh is almost immediately adjacent to Boscobel going south. You take a right onto Indian Brook Road, and that brings you to the parking lot. If you're at all interested in nature, birds, plants, fish, and wildlife, this is the place for you—200 bird and 35 fish species have been identified here. In essence, it is a 270-acre marsh, one of the few remaining Hudson River tidal wetlands and now a public wildlife sanctuary. It also is unique because it can range from primarily freshwater to brackish to saline depending on the season and the runoff. You should plan on one to two hours here.

The visit begins at a parking lot with only eight spaces (I would get there early) at the top of a steep drive that will bring you down to the Education Center. Wear sturdy shoes or boots. You particularly will need them on the trail to the marsh. The Center is small but has tanks filled with various forms of marsh life. (In spring there is what they call the "phoebe cam," a live video camera focuses on nesting Eastern phoebes. I haven't seen that yet, but it sounds wonderful.) From there you take the fairly rugged woodlands trail to Jim's Walk, the boardwalk named after a former manager and warden of the sanctuary. Once on Jim's Walk you are, quite literally, walking on the waters. Needless to say, the Hudson River views are glorious, especially the one up to Storm King Mountain, and the marsh life surrounding you is almost overwhelming in its richness. There are wooden benches where you can relax and try and take it all in and there is informative signage. Basically the walk is shaped like the letter P, with short diversions off the main boardwalk. It's one of the most relaxing experiences I know of.

There also is a **public canoe program** that lasts about two hours and is led by a marsh naturalist. Reservations are required for all canoe trips and there is a fee. Trips are tide and weather dependent.

Constitution Marsh Audubon Center and Sanctuary is open from 9–6 during Daylight Savings Time, 9–5 the rest of the year. Admission is free. Phone: 845-265-2601. Web site: www.ny.audubon.org/cmac.htm

Manitoga: The Russel Wright Design Center ▓ First the man. Russel Wright (1904–1976) was one of the most famous designers of his time (the 1930s, '40s and '50s) and designed everything from furniture, accessories, dishes and glassware to table linens, rugs and art pottery. He was the first in a line currently headed by Martha Stewart. Once, when one store announced they would be displaying his latest creations on such-and-such a day, the lines were so long that the police had to be called to control the crowd, and his American Modern dinnerware sold 80 million pieces over 20 years. He also was the first designer to use his name on his wares. Today some of his more popular designs have been reissued, and some are available in the gift shop at Manitoga. (But not my favorite—the Big Bertha cocktail shaker whose top is shellacked cork. It is the epitome of the '30s, right out of a Fred Astaire film.)

Wright, with his wife Mary, bought the Manitoga property—the word means "Place of the Great Spirit" in Algonquin—in 1942. It was, in the words of his daughter, "a ravaged landscape" thanks to over a century of quarrying and lumbering. (Some of the granite quarried here was used in the New York Public Library building.) Over more than 30 years, until his death in 1976, Wright would redesign and refurbish the landscape, moving a stream, for example, to culminate in a waterfall into the old stone quarry, which became a natural pool in front of the house; planting native flowering species; moving boulders; planting trees and bushes (particularly a dazzling display of laurel); and so on. He also designed more than four miles of paths that wander over the 75-acre property that he called a "garden of woodland paths" and that link to the Appalachian Trail.

The tour of the house and a bit of the landscape begins at Mary's Meadow and continues on around the former quarry, ending at the house, which is on 11 levels and, at the top, is divided into the main house and a studio. The house is eccentric but thoroughly interesting. Each doorknob is different, for example, and a cedar pole rises up from the living room as a support "column." It is a house of contrasts. For example, there are boulders in the house as well as an elegant Korean ancestor portrait. In fact, the influence of Asia and Asian artifacts can be seen throughout both buildings. Huge windows look out on the waterfall, and very beautiful laminated grasses, leaves and flowers are used on sliding doors. But is the house as a whole beautiful? I don't think so, but I'm not sure it was meant to be. It is, instead, a melding of nature and architecture and design that jumbles outside and in into a true union. It definitely is worth seeing.

House and landscape tours at Manitoga are available from April through October. Daily tours: Monday–Friday, 11; Saturday and Sunday, 11 and 1:30. Advance reservations are strongly recommended. Self-guided hikes: Daily during daylight hours. Phone: 845-424-3812. Web site: www.russelwrightcenter.org

Stonecrop Gardens ▪ This is a real find, and no one interested in plants and gardens should miss it. The 63-acres of gardens, fields and woodlands are located outside Cold Spring on Route 301 and originally were part of the home of Anne and Frank Cabot, who created the truly beautiful gardens. In 1992, it became a public garden and its director has taken the property to new heights. According to their literature the gardens serve four basic purposes, as: "a series of display gardens illustrating the range of plants that can be grown on a windy hilltop in a Zone 5 climate; a source of seeds and plants of the species and cultivars grown therein; an educational resource for the amateur and professional gardener that demonstrates how plants can be grown and how they may be combined for aesthetic effect in appropriate settings; and an illustration of the elements involved in garden design."

The display gardens cover about 12 acres, and there are 29 (!) separate areas that display different gardening aspects. There is a Fern Vista and an Enclosed Flower Garden, a Pond Garden and a Woodland Garden, a Himalayan Slope Garden (I'll let you think about that one) that has a swimming hole fed by a very pretty stream, and a Lake and Hillside Garden. To give you an idea of how serious the whole project is I'll quote what they have to say about the Alpine House. "The northernmost greenhouse attached to the Potting Shed is a display Alpine House. Here the choicest alpines are grown and propagated. This house also includes a small room for tropical plants and a mist propagation bench. Considered to be those species that grow at high elevation, usually above the tree line, alpines are dwarf in stature, often growing in a mat or cushion form. ... The Alpine House is equipped with air conditioning and a refrigerated bench to help combat the heat and humidity of our northeastern summers."

Every time I'm there I develop a new favorite spot, but overall what I like is that the garden is cottagey-messy. By that I mean there is no formality—it is far more English than French or Italian,

They also have a sales bench where plants propagated there are sold—mostly alpines and woodland perennials, but I've also bought more ordinary plants such as rudbeckia and some grasses. I've been back several times, and I can't wait to go again. Another plus—when I've been there I've had the gardens mostly to myself.

Stonecrop Gardens is located 5 miles east of Cold Spring on Route 301 and 3.5 miles west of the Taconic State Parkway (the Cold Spring exit).

The gardens are open: April–October, Monday–Friday and the first and third Saturday of each month, 10–5. Guided tours available by appointment. Phone: 845-265-2000. Web site: www.stonecrop.org

The Hudson Valley Center for Contemporary Art ■ 1701 Main Street, Peekskill. Phone: 914-788-7166. Web site: www.hvcca.com.

Like several other formerly-run-down-and-uninteresting towns on the river, Peekskill is perking up. Certainly one of the most important reasons is the advent of HVCCA, which is housed in a 12,500-square-foot space right on Main Street.

Their mission statement says it all: "The Center is dedicated to the development and presentation of new art, exhibits and interdisciplinary programs that enrich our understanding of contemporary art, its contexts, and its relationship to social issues. HVCCA is also committed to the enrichment of Peekskill, a multicultural community that has recreated itself as a major arts destination. HVCCA operates a 12,000 square foot exhibition space and is the primary sponsor of the Peekskill Project, an annual city-wide exhibition of site-specific artwork work."

Currently HVCCA offers changing exhibitions, an artist-in-residence program, lectures, panel discussions and other outreach programs for adults and students, and special projects. In the short time they have been in existence they have accomplished a great deal, and a visit here is worth a special trip or certainly could be tied in with a visit to DIA:Beacon (see page 164). As for the annual Peekskill Project, which takes place over several weekends in the fall, it really does involve the entire town and can range from tours and video screenings to artist talks and panel discussions as well as indoor and outdoor site-specific works.

Rockland and Orange Counties

Nyack

As a small river town only about 40 minutes from midtown Manhattan, Nyack is as unspoiled as any on the west bank and can make a very nice focus for a day. Actually, there are three Nyacks—Upper Nyack, Nyack and South Nyack, one on top of the other and all really quite small—and all are repositories of spectacular examples of Victorian architecture in all its phases. It is amazing so many examples have survived. No wonder the villages have been so popular with artists and weekenders.

Begin in Nyack, just across the Tappan Zee. The two primary streets are Main and South Broadway. Both are crammed with antique shops, restaurants, art galleries and crafts dealers, and assuming you arrive in the morning with an hour or two to enjoy before lunch, you will find there is plenty to keep you occupied. Two places I like to visit: **The Pickwick Bookshop** (phone: 845-358-9126) at 8 South Broadway, pleasantly overflowing and with a wonderful selection of Hudson River-related books, and the **Hand of the Craftsman** (phone: 845-358-6622) at 152 Main Street, which has an extraordinary collection of kaleidoscopes ranging from just a few dollars up to the thousands.

Lunch can be had at any number of places, but I would suggest you go to **The River Club** (phone: 845-358-0220), at the foot of Burd Street, one block south of Main Street. It is the only waterfront restaurant and offers splendid views of the river and the Tappan Zee Bridge. The food at lunch runs from salads and burgers to a sandwich board and various specials.

After lunch, I would head back to the car and go up North Broadway where, at 82, you will come upon **The Hopper House** (1858), the childhood home of Edward Hopper (1882–1967), and where his sister lived until her death in 1965. Hopper probably is the most important realist painter this country produced in the twentieth century. His paintings are familiar to all of us, and his disturbing ability to portray loneliness, silence and solitude and a strange kind of eroticism makes him unique among American artists. Today it has been restored and transformed into a community cultural center and exhibition space and is well worth a visit. (Open: Thursday–Sunday 1–5. Phone: 845-358-0774.)

Now, for about 2 miles, until the road ends at the foot of Hook Mountain, you pass some wonderful examples of grand Victorian architecture—including the house of the late actress Helen Hayes, on your right, white with black shutters and an elaborate widow's walk, bordered by a brick wall. But this is really only one of a series of very handsome houses that are worth going out of your way to see.

Watch on your right for the sign for Van Houten Street and, beneath it, a sign for the Julius Petersen Boatyard. Turn here and go down to see a completely unspoiled, working marina. Be sure to visit the shed at the end of the marina and take a peek inside; to your right is a house that has very casually been incorporated into the shed's structure and, yes, someone does live there.

Go back up to North Broadway and continue on to its end to Nyack Beach State Park. This is one of the loveliest river locations on the west bank, with some idyllic spots for picnicking. There also is a trail, just under two miles, along the shoreline, easy and beautiful walking that you really should take in.

Now you can go back down North Broadway to South Broadway and turn left at any street. This will bring you to Piermont Avenue, running parallel to South Broadway, which you now can follow to charming little Grand View or farther south to Piermont, newly revitalized with shops and stores and restaurants and tourists, or on to Sneden's Landing or a few other of the old river towns, not much changed visually from their period of prosperity in the nineteenth century, and, again, offering interesting houses and architecture and great river views. (Piermont, by the way, is the home of **Xaviar's in Piermont**, which many feel is one of the best restaurants in the Valley. See page 250.)

West Point

The mission of the United States Military Academy is "to educate, train and inspire the Corps of Cadets so that each graduate is a commissioned leader of character committed to the values of Duty, Honor, Country; professional growth throughout a career as an officer in the United States Army; and a lifetime of selfless service to the nation."

West Point is within easy driving distance of Cold Spring. Go south on Route 9D to the Bear Mountain Bridge, cross the Hudson into Orange

County, and then go north on 9W, following the West Point signs and eventually getting on Route 218N, which will take you right to the grounds of the Academy. Stop first at the **Visitors Center**, open daily 9–4:45, except Thanksgiving, Christmas and New Year's Day. (On Thanksgiving, Christmas and New Year's Eve, this facility closes at noon.) Here you can look at displays and films concerning the Academy, pick up informational literature and explore the gift shop. Be sure to include a map of the grounds, vital to your getting around easily.

(Mention of the Bear Mountain Bridge gives me an opportunity to tell a wonderful story. It seems that Mrs. E. H. Harriman, wife of the railroad tycoon and mother of the late Averell Harriman, onetime United States ambassador and New York State governor, found it highly inconvenient to go from her estate on the west bank to visit her friends on the east bank, so she decided to build a bridge to solve her problem. Friends and advisers all told her she was a fool—politely, of course—but Mrs. Harriman smilingly ignored them and forged ahead, not at all daunted, spending a rumored $5 million to create her "little time-saver," which also turned out to be, for the time, the longest suspension bridge in the world. When it was finished, she promptly put a tollbooth at the western entrance; in 1940, when the bridge was sold to New York State, the proceeds plus the tolls netted the Harrimans a nice little bundle. I don't know if the details are true—I hope so—but it certainly is true that the Harrimans built this, the loveliest bridge across the Hudson outside New York City and soaring 185 feet above the river.)

HISTORY

With the onset of the Revolution, it became immediately apparent that the Hudson would have to be secured against the British. For one thing, it was the natural invasion route from Canada and, for another, if it ever fell under British control, that meant New England would be cut off from the rest of the colonies. Congress appointed a committee under George Washington to study the matter and they quickly concluded that the best stronghold was in the Highlands. Here it was easiest to protect the water corridor and, in addition, this was also where the major northeast-to-southwest land routes lay that could be used by the American Army to move supplies and men between New England and the Middle Atlantic colonies.

This all happened in 1775. By 1777, because of bickering, stalling and general inertia—plus the appointment of a Dutch botanist with almost nothing to recommend him to the post of military engineer—very little had been done. The Hudson still lay open to the British. That same year General Burgoyne did, in fact, come down from Canada (see page 23). In late summer General Sir Henry Clinton sent a message to Burgoyne that he would be moving north to assist him. It was already too late. The message reached Burgoyne on September 21, 1777, just after the first part of the Saratoga campaign had ended so badly for him and his men.

On October 3, Clinton began his move, and by October 6, he had defeated the American forces in the Highlands. The river was now open all the way to Albany, and the elated British proceeded farther north to burn Kingston (see page 109) and Clermont (see page 66). That's when they got the news that Burgoyne had been forced to surrender. Clinton's troops fell back to New York City, leaving the Hudson safe once more in American hands.

Even after that, the Americans didn't learn their lesson. They dithered about until 1778 when they finally got together and decided that West Point should be fortified and occupied as a post. It has never been unoccupied since. Things looked even better after the appointment of Colonel Thaddeus Kosciuszko, a French-trained Polish army officer, as chief engineer, and he began fortifying the entire surrounding area as well—work that continued far into the next year. By the time Kosciuszko was finished, the Americans had a fortified area greatly ahead of its time: several mutually strong points along the river instead of one fortified position as had been the rule throughout the eighteenth century.

It was in 1778, too, that the Great Chain between West Point and Constitution Island was put in place to prevent British ships from sailing up the Hudson. The chain was a major undertaking for its time. The iron came from New Jersey and the lower Catskills. The forged links were taken north of West Point, joined together to form the chain, and then fastened to logs that served as floats. These carried the chain downstream to the points on both shores where it was to be anchored by huge blocks of wood and stone. (An earlier chain between Fort Montgomery and Anthony's Nose had been put in place in 1776, but it soon broke. As for this one, no enemy ship ever came this far upriver after 1778 to test its effectiveness.)

The next—and last—real threat to the security of West Point was the treason of Benedict Arnold. After his inspired actions at Saratoga (see page 35), the height of his glory, Arnold's career slid slowly downhill. Posted to Philadelphia, he did so poorly that he was reprimanded by Washington and even faced a court-martial. The one bright light for him was Peggy Shippen, the ravishingly beautiful 18-year-old daughter of a Tory sympathizer, whom he married in 1779. No one seems to know exactly what role Peggy, who came from a prominent Philadelphia family, played in Arnold's eventual betrayal, but it was around this time that he made contact with Captain John André, aide to General Clinton, and offered his services to the Crown.

Clinton soon let Arnold know what he wanted—West Point. And, for $20,000, Arnold said he would deliver it up. It was at this stage that Washington decided to use Arnold as an auxiliary commander of his left flank in an attack on New York City. Arnold begged off, asking for command of West Point instead. For some reason, Washington relented and gave it to him.

On September 21, 1780, André sailed up the Hudson on *HMS Vulture*—the same ship, incidentally, that had been used by the squadron sent to burn Kingston and the Livingston estate at Clermont—and met Arnold on shore south of Verplanck's Point. Unfortunately for André, the Americans (under Colonel James Livingston, appropriately enough) began shelling the Vulture, forcing the ship to retreat southward. André was left stranded (literally high and dry, you might say). On his way back to rejoin the British lines he was captured, tried and hanged as a spy. Arnold himself narrowly escaped being caught, but went on to serve in the English army as a brigadier general, leading troops in both Virginia and Connecticut. In 1781, Arnold left the colonies for England where he and Peggy lived in disgrace and poverty until his death in 1801.

After these events the war shifted elsewhere and although Washington and others had strongly urged the founding of a national military academy to provide professional officers—it "has ever been considered by me as an object of primary importance to this country," Washington pleaded—it wasn't until 1802, under President Thomas Jefferson, that legislation established the United States Military Academy at West Point. The Academy first opened its doors that same year, on Independence Day, with 10 cadets. Today there are about 4,000 men and women at the Academy, representing all 50 states as well as our territories and possessions. Its graduates have dominated the leadership of all our wars from the Civil (both Grant and Lee) to the present. (It is sobering to realize that in the War Between the States, of the 60 major battles, 55 were commanded on both sides by West Point graduates.)

The Academy Grounds ■ Your first stop after the Visitors Center should be at the **West Point Museum**, located in Olmsted Hall, to the right of and slightly behind the Visitors Center. I am not a military buff, but I would strongly urge you to begin your visit here for two reasons: It makes a perfect introduction to the Academy; and visiting it provides a unique and fascinating experience. This institution, with about 2,000 military relics on display from its collection of more than 45,000 (more than any other such edifice in the western hemisphere), has everything brilliantly presented—from its clear, concise signage explanations to its perfectly arranged display cases and exquisite dioramas to the taste and sensitivity in the treatment of the material.

The collection is shown on four levels. On the lowest two levels, where I would suggest that you begin your visit, are the Large Weapons and Small Weapons galleries, the latter set on a balcony overlooking a small space that contains—take a deep breath—guns, howitzers and mortars; antitank weapons; a World War II jeep (please note the wonderful Bill Mauldin cartoons above it); a 1917 tank; a 1916 staff car; a machine-gun display; a hand-grenade display; detailed paintings of the D-day invasion, the invasion of Normandy and a "chart of the relative importance of the weapons of land warfare on the battlefields of the world"; two large carved eagles, one Nazi, one American; the "Fat Man" atomic bomb case, representing the second bomb used in World War II, this one over Nagasaki ... and more!

I tell you this not to be daunting but to give you some idea of how varied the collections are. And even though this space truly is small, relatively speaking, so cleverly are the displays arranged that there is no sense of crowding or confusion.

There are two galleries on the entrance floor, the History of Warfare and the West Point Gallery. The former extends from ancient warfare to the nuclear age, using drawings, reproductions, models and weapons—as is true in all the galleries—as well as superb dioramas and models, photos and posters. Without ever condescending to the visitor, this immensely complex subject is presented in a forthright, lucid manner that makes each phase of the installation simple and clear.

There also are some fascinating objects—Goering's baton, ivory and mounted with 20 golden eagles and 20 platinum crosses, while the end knobs of gold are encrusted with 640 diamonds, and a nasty little presentation pistol of Adolf Hitler, for instance. But what lingers is the overall dignity of the presentation, ending with the simple panel called Reflections that contains quotations on war ranging from Thucydides to Eisenhower, and including my favorite, a quotation from Robert E. Lee: "It is well that war is so terrible—we would grow too fond of it."

The West Point Gallery is, to me, the most interesting of all because of the excellent presentation of what is, after all, a fascinating history. What particularly interests me is the detail devoted to the breadth and quality of the education cadets have always received. And, again, there are those wonderful touches that do so much to bring history alive: For instance, off in a corner is a drawing done by William Tecumseh Sherman while he was at the Academy in 1838, and right next to it is a watercolor by Cadet Ulysses Grant from 1841. The Sherman, academically correct and lifeless as ice water, is of the Italian sculptor Antonio Canova's work "Theseus and the Centaur." But the Grant, a study of Indians, is wonderfully fluid and alive. It provides a fascinating and curious look into Grant's persona—particularly when one knows that Grant never really showed any interest in the fine arts.

Upstairs are two more galleries, one devoted to the history of the United States Army, the second to American wars. I would see them in that order, once again appreciating and admiring the intelligence and imagination behind the presentations and the quality of the materials, and ending at the most moving display of all—a wall listing the names of all those from West Point who have been awarded their country's highest honor, the Medal of Honor.

The West Point Museum is open daily 10:30–4:15, except for January 1, Thanksgiving and Christmas Day.

From the Museum, stop at the main entrance, Thayer Gate, and ask the Military Police for directions and parking information for the most famous view on the Hudson, **Trophy Point**. You've seen it a million times in movies and photographs, but it remains a thrill, nonetheless, viewed "live": the great river coming down right through the Highlands and the Catskills a hazy blue in the far distance. In combination with the surrounding monuments, particularly the nearby Battle Monument inscribed with the names of 2,230 men killed in the Civil War, it is guaranteed to bring out the most latent feelings of patriotism.

Your next stop should be the **Cadet Chapel** (1910), for me a curiously unsuccessful building. The architect was Bertram Grosvenor Goodhue (1869–1924) of the firm Cram, Goodhue & Ferguson, who designed a number of other buildings at West Point. My favorite work of theirs, though, is in New York City—St. Thomas' Episcopal Church (1914), which, like the Chapel here, is also a Gothic building. During the first three decades of this century, Cram, Goodhue & Ferguson were considered the country's foremost church architects and primary exponents of the Gothic style. Goodhue himself also designed St. Bartholomew's Episcopal Church (1919) in New York, the Los Angeles Public Library (1924) and the Nebraska State Capitol (1928) in Lincoln, considered to be his masterpiece.

There's no denying that this chapel has a handsome exterior, and its spectacular location high above the campus adds to its sense of dominance. In fact, it's most beautiful when seen from afar ("distance lends

Fat and sassy, the pleasure boat Commander *chugs by the looming gray walls of West Point, which seem faintly disapproving of the intrusion.*

enchantment …"). Yet it is cold, even to the point of sterility. Is it the forbidding battlements and crenellated towers? Or could it be the strangely lifeless gray of the West Point granite from which it is built? Gothic should be soaring and elevating, but this building doesn't soar, it looms. You feel almost unwelcome approaching it.

The interior, thankfully, is less forbidding, and here the verticality of the architecture does indeed soar. Then there is the stained glass, all of which was designed by William and Anne Lee Willet of the Stained Glass and Decorating Company in Philadelphia. Not terribly good, I think. But what makes the interior seem so austere are the stone floors and arches and the brown brick walls and surface between the ribs of the vaults—not to mention some particularly ugly lights on the side walls and below the triforium made of opaque glass and using fluorescent bulbs. Taken all in all, there is, admittedly, a very real sense of dignity to the place, and I suppose many would consider this interior to be on a scale that might be termed awesome. (Open: Daily 8–4:15.)

Far more interesting, I'd say, is the lovely **Old Cadet Chapel** (1836), which stands at the entrance to West Point's cemetery. Greek Revival in style, with four white Doric columns, the exterior has a quiet, simple elegance that is most effective. Inside, white Ionic columns support the curved ceiling, nicely setting off the plain wooden floor and carpeting and the pews with their handsome wooden armrests, while the clear glass windows, wide and rounded at the top, let the light flood in. There's an unpretentious, even virile dignity here that I miss in the new chapel. At the front, behind and above a red velvet screen topped by a gilded eagle with spread wings, is a mural representing War (a Roman soldier) and Peace (a young woman—dressed in white, naturally).

Far more moving, though, are the simple black marble plaques with gold lettering dedicated to early American officers, which cover the walls between the windows, and also the handsome old cannons, embedded in those same walls, snub snouts pointed at the ceiling. For me this chapel sums up and symbolizes the values and traditions of West Point better than anything else on the grounds, and gives a special, even unique, insight into the history and meaning of the Academy.

Open: Daily 8–4:15. For tour information phone 845-446-4724. Web site: www.usma.edu/visiting.asp

A River Cruise on the *Commander*

If, when you enter the gates at West Point, you turn right at the first divide in the road, you will come down to the river and to a pleasant little park with picnic tables scattered about along the bank. It is from here that you can board the *Commander* for a delightful and scenic cruise, usually north to Bannerman's Island (see below). The boat looks more like a jolly toy than a real operating vessel, with its green-and-white-striped awning over the top deck and its chubby outline, and it puts you into an appropriately festive mood. The last time I enjoyed her hospitality we left about 12:30. Because it was toward the end of the season, a crystal-clear and brilliant September day, not many people were aboard, and even fewer were on the exposed top deck to enjoy the autumn colors and the passing river landscape.

The next time I'd like to go in the evening; I've watched her pass by at dusk on private charter, lights ablaze, from Cold Spring. That would be a fine way to see Bannerman's Island, one of the more romantic spots in the Hudson. (Francis Bannerman was a dealer in U.S. Army and Navy surplus

One of the manifold pleasures of back roads is coming upon dignified, well-designed old homes like this one nestled deep in the country.

equipment who bought up most of the weapons captured in the Spanish-American War—at the age of 14. Eventually he became the country's biggest surplus arms dealer. He built a huge warehouse and store on lower Broadway in New York City, but the city fathers decided that this was not the world's best location for munitions and told him he would have to move. He did. To the 7-acre Bannerman's Island, where he dredged out a small harbor and built his arsenal. Then he decided to build as his summer home a Scottish castle, with a bridge over a moat and crenellated towers. He even brought in special soil for the formal gardens. He died in 1918, before the house was completed. In 1920 there was a huge explosion that sent a section of the tower hurtling into the Hudson, but the family continued to summer here through the 1930s. In 1967 the family sold the island to New York State, and in 1969 a major fire gutted the buildings. Today the island is a part of the Hudson Highlands State Park. It's dangerous to go ashore because the buildings are in such an advanced state of decay, but that doesn't seem to deter most people. Seen from the deck of the boat as it cruises past, it is a wonderful sight, this rugged, romantic ruin just north of Storm King. There is now a Bannerman Island Cruise Tour sponsored by the Bannerman Castle Trust, Inc., and the Bannerman Island Educational and Cultural Project.

For information, phone 845-831-6346.
Web site: bannermancastle.org

The *Commander* is operated by Hudson Highlands Cruises, Inc., in Cornwall-on-Hudson. They also offer cruises from Peekskill on the last Saturday of the month. (Phone: 845-534-7245, or e-mail: hudsonhighlandscruises.com.) It operates from May through October, with cruises each day leaving from West Haverstraw and West Point. Call in advance for reservations and detailed information on cruise choices.

Storm King Mountain

When you are ready to leave West Point, follow the main road north and, as you exit the grounds, turn right on 218, here a narrow, winding, two-lane country road that passes through woods, then rises and takes you along Storm King and to a breathtaking view of the Highlands. There are several places along the way where you can pull your car off the road to enjoy the view, but by far the best is a tiny spot, big enough for only a car or two and at the highest spot on the drive. From here the river can be seen at its most majestic as it passes between the mountains. Trains on the opposite bank are toys, cars seem as small as ladybugs, a seaplane passes below you, pleasure boats become whitecaps on the swelling flow. But what you are most aware of is the wind, the river and the utter tranquility of the scene at your feet.

It was here that, back in the 1960s, Consolidated Edison of New York decided to build a power plant, the largest of its kind in the world—it could have drawn six *billion* gallons of river water each day into its storage reservoir—at the base of the mountain. Fortunately, it was one of those proposals that galvanized people into action, and up and down the Hudson residents rose in wrath. Con Ed eventually backed down, thus ensuring—forever, one hopes—that the mountain remains an undisturbed natural treasure for all to enjoy.

A VERY SPECIAL MUSEUM IN ORANGE COUNTY

The Museum of the Hudson Highlands ■ Continue north, descending the mountain, and you will discover, as you approach Cornwall, the Museum of the Hudson Highlands, a regional history museum. I decided to drop in. What I discovered was an ideal spot for children and an endearing tiny museum for adults. I urge you to go there.

The museum's purpose is to focus on the diversity and splendor of the Hudson Valley's natural history, which it accomplishes at its two locations. The original site, Museum on the Boulevard, located on the Boulevard off Hasbrouck Avenue, is a handsome, rustic stone-and-wood building surrounded by a forest. There's even a stream flowing beneath the galleries; a more charming setting would be hard to find. Set up in 1959 specifically to provide children with educational and recreational programs unavailable locally, the museum now engages in other activities, such as the Ogden Art Gallery and the Nature Shop. Currently museum staff and volunteers are working on a lecture series featuring speakers who are expert in various nature disciplines, antiques and art.

But that's enough background; on to the exhibits. The Natural History Wing is my favorite, for here are the live mammals, birds, reptiles and fish that make it so much fun. What's more, all are native to the Hudson. I really like the owls—they always look so silly to me rather than wise—but my favorite is a crow who screeches "Hello!" periodically but doesn't look like he really means it. There's even an Indian wigwam. Needless to say, kids go wild here and have to be dragged away.

I wasn't in any rush myself to leave, but when I did I discovered that there are self-guiding nature trails through 70 acres of mature forest. I wasn't quite ready to explore them all, but I walked enough to know that I would like to come back, perhaps with a picnic on some perfect summer day. (If you're not in a picnic mode and are there at lunchtime, try **Painter's** in Cornwall. See page 252.) And, anyway, I want to hear the crow do his routine again.

A second location, the Kenridge Farm 177-acre historic property in Cornwall, is right off 9W and offers many programs and activities at the farm for people of all ages. There are two ponds, a self-guided nature trail, a historic sheep trail, meadows, wooded areas, a large nineteenth-century hay barn, a sugar bush area for maple sugaring, a farmhouse with conference and meeting rooms ... and on and on, including many special events and festivals.

Museum on the Boulevard is open: Thursday–Saturday, 10–4, Sunday, Noon–4. Kenridge Farm Location: Gallery open: Saturday and Sunday, 12–4. Trails daily dawn to dusk. Admission: Donation. Phone: 845-534-7781. Web site: www.museumhudsonhighlands.org

Newburgh

If you continue on Route 218 you will soon come to Route 9W. Take it north to Newburgh. This is one of the saddest sites on the Hudson, for the once lovely river town was largely destroyed by an urban renewal program that tore down but did nothing else. It could have happened in Kingston, too, except that men like Fred Johnston (see page 109) stopped it and, instead, restored what they had. Newburgh had no such luck. (There is some good news, though; people are beginning to move there and buy up some of the older houses at bargain-basement prices. In addition, the 3.5-acre landscape designed by Frederick Law Olmsted and Calvert Vaux in 1895 in honor of Andrew Jackson Downing has been restored. Tours can be made by appointment. Phone: 845-565-5559. There also is a website that not only gives you an idea of the park but also some of the more attractive architecture remaining in Newburgh as well as other interesting material: www.newburghrevealed.org/photojournalajdowning.htm.)

Washington's Headquarters ▇   84 Liberty St. Open: mid-April to October, Wednesday–Saturday 10–5, Sunday 1–5.

Phone: 845-562-1195. Web site: www.nysparks.state.ny.us/sites/info.asp?siteID=30

After the Battle of Yorktown in 1781, it was still necessary to keep the Continental Army together until the negotiations leading up to the Treaty of Paris—which formally acknowledged the independence of the United States—could be completed. Therefore, the army encamped at nearby New Windsor in late October of 1782 while, from April 1782 to August 1783, Washington took up residence in this house, which then belonged to members of Jonathan Hasbrouck's family. (Hasbrouck, a successful farmer and merchant, served in the military as a colonel but was forced to retire in 1778 because of ill health. He died in 1780.) The house descended through the family until 1850, when New York State bought it to preserve as a historic site, the first publicly operated historic site in the United States. It was during his stay here that Washington authorized and awarded the Badge of Military Merit, forerunner of the Purple Heart.

You first enter an adjacent museum that is, in many ways, more interesting than the house itself. There's an excellent slide presentation here and, even better, the permanent exhibits contain much interesting memorabilia relating to the Revolution. Then, when you are through, a guide will take you to the house with its view across the Hudson to the east bank. The building is tiny, and it's hard to imagine it as the headquarters for the general of a victorious army. When the Marquis de Chastellux, who had fought with Washington during the Revolution, came here to bid his final farewell before returning to France, he noted that only one room was "tolerably spacious" and that even that one was broken up by seven doors and one window. He was wrong; there are eight doors in this room, the first that you will visit.

There are eight rooms in all, and the tour is well conducted and generally informative. Outside again, take a look at the rather startling "Tower of Victory," a monument put up on the centennial of the signing of the Treaty of Paris, which Washington learned about in this house.

Knox's Headquarters ▪ Forger Hill Road, Vails Gate. Open: Memorial Day through Labor Day, Wednesday–Saturday 10–5, Sunday 1–5.

Web site: www.nysparks.state.ny.us/sites/info.asp?siteID=16

A moderately interesting 1754 Georgian-style stone house that was owned by a wealthy merchant and miller named John Ellison. General Henry Knox, Washington's chief of the artillery, used it as his military headquarters, as did generals Nathanael Greene and Horatio Gates. In addition, there is a plant sanctuary and the remains of a 1741 gristmill.

New Windsor Cantonment ▪ Temple Hill Road, Vails Gate. Open: mid-April through October, Wednesday–Saturday 10–5, Sunday 1–5.

Phone: 845-561-1765.
Web site: www.nysparks.state.ny.us/sites/info.asp?siteID=18

Here, during 1782 and '83, the Continental Army of about 7,000 officers and enlisted men encamped in the most successful winter encampment of the Revolution while awaiting news from Paris about the final peace.

The original cantonment covered a two-and-a-half-square-mile area and contained some 600 log cabins laid out in rows along the linear patterns the army would follow in case of battle. Wood came from the nearby forests and the huts were built by the 16 soldiers assigned to each.

When the housing and other essential buildings were completed, a chaplain suggested that a large hall be constructed for religious services and public assemblies. Up it went and was named the Temple of Virtue. It was in the Temple that Washington addressed his officers and narrowly averted a mutiny arising from the affair of the Newburgh Letters, in which his officers were urged to rebel and force Congress to meet their demands for back pay and pensions.

After the war formally ended, the soldiers drifted back to their homes and the buildings were auctioned off, dismantled and taken away to disappear from history.

Today the site contains reconstructed buildings, special exhibits, a large display of original cannons, reenactments of the Revolutionary soldier's life and army-crafts displays. Uniformed staff members also demonstrate weapons and present military drills daily, and there are living history demonstrations. The National Purple Heart Hall of Honor is located here.

Storm King Art Center ■ Old Pleasant Hill Road, Mountainville. Open: Wednesday–Sunday, from first open day after April 1 to last open day before November 15, 11–5:30. Closes at 5 after daylight savings time ends. Open until 8 on Saturday evenings from Memorial Day weekend to Labor Day weekend. Daily docent tours at 2. Self-guided handicap accessible tram tours available daily, noon–4:30. Last tram tour during evening hours, 7. Picnic area with drink and snack vending machines. Special lectures, outdoor concerts, family programs and hikes.

Phone: 845-534-1115, x 136. Web site: www.stormking.org

The Storm King Art Center is a museum that celebrates the relationship between sculpture and nature. And it does so to perfection.

First, nature. The setting for this most important open-air center of contemporary sculpture, brilliantly placed about the grounds, is 500 acres of magnificent land that includes fields, lawns and woodlands. Right now the Center is re-introducing native long grasses and wildflowers into the fields. The result: islands of alfalfa, buckwheat and oats, with mowed paths through them that provide access to the sculptures. It is a wonderful idea that adds immeasurably to the ambiance.

Now the museum. You approach the museum building along a driveway bordered by trees, through which you see examples from the permanent collection of about 100 sculptures dating from the post-1945 era. All the "greats" are here—David Smith, Isamu Noguchi, Alexander Calder, Henry Moore, Barbara Hepworth, Louise Nevelson, Richard Serra and on and on ... Nam June Paik, Mark di Suvero, Ursula von Rydingsvard. It is a wonderful experience to be here, and you can easily spend the entire day—there are picnic facilities, by the way. But there is one thing you must do—rent an Acoustiguide. The descriptions of the individual sculptures are extremely well done—on some, the artists themselves talk about their pieces—and it adds immeasurably to the overall experience. One complaint: I wish that next to the work of art they would place a discreet number that is matched on the Acoustiguide. Being a total jerk about directions and such, I spend too much time looking for the matching identification on the Center's identification map.

The museum building was originally built in the French-Norman style as a residence for Vermont Hatch, a New York City lawyer, out of stones he had bought from the just-demolished Danskammer House, a famous Greek Revival residence just north of Newburgh.

Danskammer had been built in 1834 by Edward Armstrong, the son of a British officer who, although he'd fought against the patriots in the Revolution, nevertheless decided to stay in the United States after the war. The house was so beautiful that many people tried to save it from being razed, but they failed, unfortunately. In 1935, Mr. Hatch took the

All that is left of Danskammer House are these columns moved to Storm King Art Center, still regal in their lonely splendor.

remains, including the splendid Ionic columns, to form his new residence. The columns have been preserved and now stand just south of the museum on a lovely spot high above the gently rolling fields.

Each year the museum offers changing exhibits of prominent American and European artists to enhance its permanent collection. Frankly, whether you are interested in contemporary sculpture or not, the setting is so pleasant that you could go there just to enjoy the views and explore the landscape. But if you *are* at all interested, this is truly America's finest outdoor sculpture park. Don't miss it.

Westchester County

OTHER SPECIAL PLACES IN THE LOWER HUDSON VALLEY

Caramoor House Museum ■ Katonah. Open: First weekend in May to October 15, Wednesday–Sunday 1–4. Wednesday there is a recital at 11 followed by a house tour.

For tour information, phone 914-232-5035 x221.
Web site: www.caramoor.org

I first discovered Caramoor through the summer music festival held there in July and August, an event that takes place on the grounds of this grand estate either in the Venetian Theater, an exquisite, tented outdoor site whose stage is framed by an arcade of (logically enough) Venetian columns, or in the Spanish Courtyard, part of the house itself. (For information during the festival, phone 914-232-1252.)

The Mediterranean-style house was built by Walter Rosen (1875–1951), a New York lawyer, and his wife, Lucie Dodge, in the 1930s following the designs of Mr. Rosen. I find it a curious, intensely personal building; artistic treasures rest cheek by jowl with things that definitely aren't, but the overall impression is, no doubt about it, one of magnificence.

The tour takes you through the rooms on the first floor. The most striking, I'd say, is the seventeenth-century painted library that was brought over in its entirety from France and incorporated into the house, as were several of the other rooms. What one immediately notices is the glorious blue of the background, particularly on the ceiling. I've never seen its like anywhere, and it's startlingly lovely. The groin-vaulted ceiling is filled with biblical scenes in amazing colors, and the door panels are painted, too. It's an enchanting room, one you will want to linger in.

By far the most dramatic room is the immense music room, which extends the full length of the north wing of the house. High, wide and handsome, it has, for instance, a sixteenth-century carved wood coffered ceiling designed in squares and crosses with center rosettes that was shipped to Caramoor from a palazzo in southern Italy. But this room holds all kinds of surprises: sixteenth-century stained glass from France and Switzerland, a seventeenth-century Turkish rug, eighteenth-century Italian armchairs, a bride's chest from Spain, ruby velvet sixteenth-century Italian curtains, a terra-cotta relief from the workshops of Andrea della Robbia. Eclectic, yes, and some of the pieces and artworks I could do without, but definitely sumptuous and even beautiful in its own way. My favorite of all: an exquisite *Mary Magdalen* by Lucas Cranach. My second favorite: a bronze plaque of singing angels made after designs by Donatello for a church in Padua. And this is only a cursory glance at what the room has to offer.

Then there's the dining room with its hand-painted eighteenth-century Chinese wallpaper filled with birds and flowers and found near Turin, plus Grendey armchairs and side chairs, also eighteenth century, and lacquered scarlet with gilt-and-silver chinoiserie decorations. They were made in England for a Spanish duke. Not to mention Mrs. Rosen's bedroom with its colossal seventeenth-century wooden bed, carved and gilded and probably designed for Pope Urban VIII. Finally, there's the New Wing, with its early-sixteenth-century Valle d'Aosta Room and Jacobean Bedroom, both brought from the Rosens' New York home.

When you're through inside the house, clear your mind and your (by now) sated senses by taking a refreshing stroll through the grounds and gardens. They have been done to perfection and offer such pleasant surprises as Cedar Walk, with seventeenth-century stone sculptures, a Sense Circle meant for the visually handicapped but obviously enjoyable by all, and, above the festival area, eighteenth-century wrought-iron, gilded gates that are exquisitely detailed.

John Jay Homestead State Historic Site ■ Katonah.
Open: April–October, Tuesday–Saturday 10–4, Sunday 11–4.

Phone: 914-232-5651 for hours open during the rest of the year.
Web site: www.nysparks.state.ny.us/sites/info.asp?siteID=14

You pass this on your way to Caramoor, and it looks interesting. It's not, really. The home of John Jay, our first Chief Justice of the Supreme Court, it descended in his family through four generations and offers some basically mediocre period furnishings and a rather bizarre ballroom added in this century. Unless you are a John Jay fanatic or a distant relative of the family, this is something you can afford to miss.

(After the above appeared, I received a very nice letter from a woman connected with the house who pointed out that John Jay was important in our history and that "a tour of the Homestead should provide our guests with a sense of the man, his lifestyle and the culture of his day and the four generations that followed him." She also points out that "we have … a fine Gilbert Stuart painting … and a strong portrait of Jay's great-grandson by John Singer Sargent.")

Some Shops and Galleries ■ For shopping try **Yellow Monkey Village** on Route 35 in Cross River. Web site: www.yellowmonkey.com/tymv.html. This assemblage of shops in reproduction eighteenth-century buildings will keep you wandering about happily. Be sure to bring your checkbook.

The shop I like best is **The Yellow Monkey Antiques** (phone: 914-763-5848), specializing in English country pine antiques and accessories. From there you can walk over to **The Cheshire Tree** (phone: 914-763-5732), an appealing dried and fresh flower store.

Finally, in nearby Katonah, can be found **The Katonah Museum of Art**, on Route 22 at Jay Street. Open: Tuesday–Saturday 10–5, Sunday 12–5. Closed: Monday. Phone: 914-232-9555.
Web site: www.katonahmuseum.org

Founded in 1953, this nonprofit educational institution housed in a handsome building designed by Edward Larrabee Barnes presents lively, extremely interesting—six annually—exhibitions that range from the works of contemporary artists (Kenneth Noland and Ellsworth Kelly, for example) to such diverse topics as "Against the Stream: Milton Avery,

Adolph Gottlieb and Mark Rothko in the 1930s" and "Medieval Monsters: Masterpieces in African Art." Well worth a visit.

The Hammond Museum and the Japanese Stroll Gardens ■ 28 Deveau Road, North Salem. Gardens open: May–October, Wednesday–Saturday 12–4.

Phone: 914-669-5033. Web site: www.hammondmuseum.org

The Lower Hudson has several out-of-the-ordinary museums, but surely this is one of the most charming and a must for garden lovers.

The museum was founded in 1957 by Natalie Hays Hammond in memory of her parents.

What makes it so very special are the Japanese Stroll Gardens, divided into such delightful sections as The Waterfall Garden, The Azalea Garden, The Fruit Garden and The Autumn and Zen Gardens. Each is more lovely than the last and Miss Hammond has set forth its purpose and meanings far better than I could: "The translation or adaptation of the Stroll Garden, which originated in Japan and reached its perfection in the Edo Period (1615–1867), should be in terms of tranquility, providing a world apart, as well as a world within. Its calming flowing pattern offers no surprise but special points of interest symbolic of outer and inner windows from which to view the broader landscape or review one's thoughts." Miss Hammond's creation achieves all of that and more.

The museum has one other pleasing element, a restaurant called the Silk Tree Café, that offers food at moderate prices. Best of all, it's set in a shaded flagstone courtyard with a fountain surrounded by flowers. I would suggest that you lunch here before or after enjoying the gardens.

Historic Hudson Valley

An Historical Feast in Westchester County

GENERAL INFORMATION

How to Get There ▦ The five sites operated by Historic Hudson Valley in Westchester County (each discussed in full below) are all relatively close together: Sunnyside is 1 mile south of the Tappan Zee Bridge on Route 9; the Union Church of Pocantico Hills is 1 mile east of Route 9 on Route 448; Philipsburg Manor is 2 miles north of the bridge on 9—and it is from here that you visit the Rockefeller estate; and, for Van Cortlandt Manor, continue north on 9 to the Croton Point Avenue exit, then go 1 block east to South Riverside Avenue, turn right and, about a half-mile farther, you will see the entrance directly ahead. There also are summer cruises from New York City and Weehawken, New Jersey, that include Kykuit, Philipsburg Manor and Sunnyside. Reservations are required. For information on tours, call 914-631-8200. For Kykuit reservations, phone 914-631-9491. For information on boat trips, call 800-533-3779.

Hours ▦ Kykuit is open daily, except Tuesday, April–October 10–5. Sunnyside and Philipsburg Manor are open daily, except Tuesday, 10–5 April–December and weekends in March. Van Cortlandt Manor is open daily except Tuesday, 10–5. Closed for the months of January and February and on Thanksgiving and Christmas Day. The Union Church of Pocantico Hills is open April–December, weekdays except Tuesday, 11–5; Saturday 10–5; Sunday 2–5. Other times by appointment.

For all reservations and information, phone 914-631-8200. Web site: www.hudsonvalley.org

A word of advice: Don't be as ambitious as I once was and try to see several of the sites on the same day—that's exhausting.

Historic Hudson Valley, chartered in 1951 by the state of New York as an educational institution, was founded by John D. Rockefeller, Jr. The project began in 1937 when what is now Philipsburg Manor was to be torn

down and replaced by a housing development. Mr. Rockefeller stepped in
and purchased the house in 1940. Then, in 1945, a collateral descendant
of Washington Irving decided to sell Sunnyside. Again Mr. Rockefeller
came to the rescue, buying not only the house but many of the original
furnishings as well. Finally, in 1953, Van Cortlandt Manor became available and it, too, was added to the restorations project and opened to the
public in 1959 after the staff of colonial Williamsburg had restored it. In
1984, the Union Church of Pocantico Hills was opened for tours, and the
latest, and undeniably spectacular, addition is Montgomery Place in
Annandale-on-Hudson, a 400-acre estate opened to the public in 1988
(see page 144).

Today the overall collection of Historic Hudson Valley includes about
12,000 fine and decorative pieces as well as paintings, drawings, prints,
textiles and such from the seventeenth, eighteenth, nineteenth and twentieth centuries, all offering an unparalleled glimpse of life in the Hudson
Valley over a period of 300 years. It is a remarkable undertaking that has
been perfectly realized.

KYKUIT (Pocantico Hills)

I suppose the Rockefellers come as close to a nationally recognized and
admired family as this country can offer. They have achieved this eminent
position through a pattern of public generosity and philanthropy while
maintaining a respectable and dignified—for the most part—private life
that simply does not make for "sexy" media coverage. And now, as the
fourth and fifth generations are coming to the fore, one thinks more of the
family than of any individual. (I was once told that the Rockefellers' staff
sometimes request that when the family is mentioned, it be referred to as
The Family. It makes an odd kind of sense.)

Kykuit—it rhymes with high cut and means "lookout" in Dutch—
was built for John D. Rockefeller, Sr., and is the only house he ever built.
John senior's brother, William, was the first Rockefeller to settle in
Tarrytown (in the 1880s), although the Rockefellers have a long associa-
tion with the Hudson River Valley, having originally settled there; outside
Germantown, which is between Rhinebeck and Hudson, is an old
Rockefeller homestead still known as the Rockefeller Tavern. Today it has
been divided in half as two private houses.

John senior began buying this land, 30 miles north of New York City, in 1893 with the purchase of 400 acres, which included the site of the present-day house. Until 1902, when it burned, he lived in a rather undistinguished Victorian villa. He moved into another house on the estate, and it was then that his son, John junior, began to try to convince his father to build a house on Kykuit Hill.

The house the senior Rockefeller eventually built was modest by Gilded Age standards, and when you see it today, even though you know it has 40 rooms, it still seems reserved, even modest, when compared to the Vanderbilt mansion further up the river; but, then, the Vanderbilts had a building mania. And the house you see today is not the house that was originally built, which was even simpler. In fact, four architects—Dunham A. Wheeler, William Adams Delano (a distant cousin of John junior's wife), Chester Holmes Aldrich and William Welles Bosworth—were eventually involved, as was the interior designer Ogden Codman (see page 140).

The first house, which was completed in 1908, was thoroughly revised from 1911 to 1913 and reflects more the intention of John junior, as John senior would have been perfectly happy with something simpler. (John junior once expressed his intentions by noting that "I frequently said to the architects and decorator that my ideal for the house was to have it so apparently simple that any friends visiting Father, coming from however humble houses, would be impressed with the homeliness and simplicity of the house, while those who were familiar with beautiful things and appreciated fine design would say, 'how exquisitely beautiful!' This was the result obtained.")

When John senior died in 1937, John junior moved in; the superb Ming and Qing porcelains you will see are from his collection. His son, Nelson A. Rockefeller (whose own collection of Chinese ceramics is here), former governor of New York and vice-president under Gerald Ford and the most colorful of the Rockefeller brothers, moved in upon his father's death in 1960. It was he who put the most interesting stamp on the estate. And it was he who initiated the effort to give the estate to the public by willing his one-third interest in the house and property to the National Trust for Historic Preservation upon his death in 1979.

Fifteen years later, the remaining Rockefeller brothers, David and Laurence, worked out a deal with the National Trust that gave the Trust total ownership of Kykuit and its immediate surroundings of 87 acres in exchange for the Trust's one-third interest in the entire property. In addition, the Rockefellers have agreed that the Rockefeller Brothers Fund will maintain the property, while Historic Hudson Valley is in charge of the public tours.

The House, Art Collection and Gardens ▨ The van approaches the house along a gently rising road. The landscape along the first part is serene and totally unpretentious, with open spaces of lawn, handsome specimen trees, and occasional glimpses of pieces from Nelson Rockefeller's spectacular collection of twentieth-century sculpture, all of which—it should be noted—were placed by Nelson himself. (It is said that he would sometimes hover over the landscape in a helicopter while figuring out where a certain piece would look best.) And then, there you are, at the forecourt of the house.

The house is generally described as Georgian Revival. Fair enough, but I had the immediate feeling—reinforced by the interior—that somehow this was a Dutch house, not so much in style but in the overall character. Perhaps it is the slight feeling of restriction, as if the house were forced to fit into a limited space. In any case, the interior also has that feeling of Dutch stolidity. Nothing wrong with it; in fact, it is a part of the complete lack of vulgarity that this house displays, but it also is a definite part of what sets the house apart from others of its time.

The tour of the living quarters of the house only includes the first floor, and although interesting—the absolutely splendid Tang Dynasty bodhisatt-va figure set in a window that offers one of the great views to the Hudson two miles away is almost worth a trip in itself—it is the gardens and the art collection assembled by Nelson that is the real reason to come here.

The gardens were designed by William Welles Bosworth, who once worked with Frederick Law Olmsted. He began designing them in 1907, and here all sense of narrowness and restriction drops, although there is a clear and formal order of terraces, paths, pools, beds, fountains, an allée of linden trees ... each garden is its own formal room, providing views and settings unique to its own space. And throughout, usually each piece perfectly sited, is the highlight of the visit, the sculpture collection. The names roll off, a listing of twentieth-century masters that includes Picasso, Calder, Arp, Lipchitz, Noguchi, Nadelman, Tony Smith, Moore, Giacometti, Maillol, Nevelson and many more. My favorite, both because of its great beauty and its stunning placement framing a Hudson River vista of lawn, trees, sky and river, is Max Bill's "Triangular Surface in Space."

As for the art collection, Nelson converted part of the basement and underground passageways into galleries where he could display his collection of more than 100 works by virtually every major American artist active in the 1960s as well as such preeminent European artists as Braque and Picasso. It is a wonderful display of his enthusiasm for the art of his time and the catholicity of his taste. It, too, is worth a visit. And that brings up my one complaint about this tour: There's too much to see in the two hours allotted. I would hope Historic Hudson Valley could eventually set things up so that there could be this kind of overview tour and then, perhaps, one that would concentrate primarily on the house, gardens and sculpture, and another that would concentrate on the house and paintings.

In any case, it's not over yet, for before you leave there is a visit to the coach house, where there is a nice collection of historic carriages and cars.

SUNNYSIDE (Tarrytown)

The approach is much the same as Henry James described it years ago, "a deep, long lane, winding, embanked, overarched, such an old-world lane as one scarce ever meets in America." It sets the mood for your arrival at this fanciful, endearing confection of a house.

I sometimes think that if I could have my choice of any house on the Hudson, this might well be it. Irving himself described it as "a little, old-fashioned stone mansion all made up of gabled ends, and as full of angles and corners as an old cocked hat." It is all of that; if a house could be called "good-humored," it would perfectly describe Sunnyside.

Washington Irving (1783–1859), America's first great writer and still one of our best-loved, if only for his short stories based on life in the Valley such as "The Legend of Sleepy Hollow" and "Rip Van Winkle," bought this estate on the banks of the Hudson in 1835. At that time the house was a simple farmhouse built in the seventeenth century when the land was still part of Philipsburg Manor. (In the eighteenth century it was owned by a branch of the Van Tassel family that Irving would immortalize in "The Legend of Sleepy Hollow.") After Irving purchased it he immediately began remodeling to create his own romantic vision of a house with the help of George Harvey, an artist and neighbor whose own home Irving much admired. When finished, it looked almost exactly like what you see

Sunnyside still brings out the child in us, like a well-loved picture suddenly rediscovered in an old book of fairy tales.

today, with those wonderful weather vanes that Irving had taken from old houses in New York City and Albany, Dutch-stepped gables and a wisteria vine over the front door. As for the whimsical, pagoda-like tower off to the right, Irving added that in 1847.

The interior is completely without pretension, with small, rather modestly furnished rooms made for good conversation and convivial friends. The most interesting to me is the library with its well-worn, rich leather volumes, a red-curtained alcove with a divan where Irving could catch forty winks, and the wonderful, massive desk, a gift to Irving from his publisher, G. P. Putnam.

The dining room, to the left of the entrance hall, is particularly inviting, especially at Christmas when the table is set and decorated with sprays of holly, nuts, fruits and candy, while a large red bow encircles it.

In planning your visit, be sure to leave some time for strolling about the grounds. You'll enjoy the pond Irving created and called "Little Mediterranean," and you certainly should not miss some of those wooded paths that open up onto views of the river, here at its widest point and looking very awesome indeed.

When you do leave, it's worthwhile to continue south for a few minutes to Irvington to see the **Presbyterian Church** to your right on North Broadway. It was built in 1869 by James Renwick, Jr. (1818–95), whose most famous building is St. Patrick's Cathedral in New York City, but who also designed the Renwick Gallery and the first building of the Smithsonian Institute, both in Washington, as well as Grace Protestant Episcopal Church in New York. The Romanesque Presbyterian Church here in Irvington, with its exotic cupola and rough-finished stonework, has the added attraction of windows designed by Louis Comfort Tiffany, a onetime resident of Irvington. (For an appointment, phone 914-591-8124.) Just to the south is the Gothic **St. Barnabas' Episcopal Church** (1853–63), in charming contrast to its more elaborate neighbor.

UNION CHURCH OF POCANTICO HILLS

Historic Hudson Valley also offers tours of the Union Church of Pocantico Hills, located near Tarrytown, whose exquisite windows, donated by members of the Rockefeller family, were designed by Marc Chagall (1889–1985) —the eight side windows and the narthex window—and Henri Matisse (1869–1954), whose rose window here is his last completed work.

The Chagall windows have great vitality and shimmer with the passionate colors he applied directly to the glass—amethysts ranging from the deepest, moodiest purple to the purest violet, greens of a summer day, blues as deep as indigo and as pale as winter ice. But it is the Matisse that I found the most satisfying and moving. Having created an abstract design in pale blue, green, white and ochre, Matisse achieves the brilliant effect of allowing you to transcend your physical presence in the church by making the green glass translucent, so that you first sense then see the tops of trees and the sky, drawing your eye and heart out and heavenward. (According to Cary Reich, author of *Life of Nelson A. Rockefeller*, after the window was dedicated, Nelson, "never one to leave well enough alone … arranged for the Pocantico gardeners to transplant a large white pine in front of the window outside the church. The tree was positioned to mute the flow of morning sunlight through the window, adding the natural rustle of foliage to the verdant ballet of Matisse's design.")

As in any church, the windows are best appreciated during a service, and I would urge you to spend an hour here one Sunday morning, allow-

Looking across the Pocantico to the mill and Philipsburg Manor House, one of the first "industrial complexes" in the country. The Philipse family sided with the British in the Revolution and thereby lost everything.

ing the glory of these creations to wash over you, the changing light creating new bejeweled surfaces, the quiet glory of the rose window lifting your thoughts up and out to eternity.

Philipsburg Manor Upper Mills (Sleepy Hollow)

There's not a child in the world who wouldn't enjoy a visit here if only to see the gristmill. The miller will let children help him operate it and it's a lot of fun for them to watch the huge, clackety-clack waterwheel he releases to grind his corn. For adults it's an informative trip back to the early part of the eighteenth century to see how a working estate of that time operated.

Frederick Philipse (1626–1702)—his Dutch name was Vredryck Flypsen—was born in Friesland, Holland, the son of a slater, and immigrated to New York (then New Amsterdam) at the age of 21. Between 1662 and 1693, by then a very rich man, he created his estate, called the

Manor of Philipsburg and consisting of 90,000 acres. Philipse had his primary residence in Yonkers but, in the 1680s, constructed this manor house, which became the headquarters of the first industrial complex in the Thirteen Colonies. His son, Adolph, turned the mill into so successful an operation that its flour and meal were even shipped overseas, but everything collapsed when Frederick's great-grandson, Frederick III, remained loyal to the British during the Revolution and fled to London. The estate was confiscated, and the family disappeared from American history until Historic Hudson Valley revived their name through this restoration.

Before you visit the mill and the stone manor house, there is an interpretive exhibition, and there's also a café and gift shop. The tours are self-guided with costumed guides stationed in the building. The emphasis is on northern colonial slavery. The house itself is small—it was, after all, used more as a place of business than as an actual dwelling—and some of the rooms served several purposes. In Adolph Philipse's bedroom, for example, the bed could be folded against the wall when not in use. There also are two kitchens, a foreroom and a parlor, all furnished with superb examples of Dutch, New England and New York pieces.

Tarrytown's Old Dutch Reformed Church was built in the 1690s.
Its graveyard is the final resting place of Washington Irving.

The mill itself, though, is everyone's favorite, for it is in working order, and the costumed miller is only too happy to demonstrate how the whole thing operates.

When you leave, be sure to visit the **Old Dutch Reformed Church,** built by Frederick Philipse in the 1690s and lying just north of the manor. Its bell-shaped gambrel roof, old when Washington Irving wrote about it, makes it instantly identifiable as Dutch Colonial. Irving is among the famous Americans buried in the graveyard. If you wish to see the inside of the church, it's open Sunday between June and the first Sunday in October at 10 a.m., when church services are offered, or call 914-631-1123 for an appointment.

VAN CORTLANDT MANOR (Croton-on-Hudson)

Of all the buildings owned by Historic Hudson Valley, this nearly 300-year-old house is certainly among the loveliest. And perhaps because it is a little off the beaten track, I find that the tours here are generally smaller and more relaxed.

The first Van Cortlandt to come to this country was Oloff (1600–1684), who arrived in 1638. He ended up a highly successful New York businessman and a leading citizen of the city, eventually rising to deputy mayor in 1667. His name is now perpetuated in New York City's Van Cortlandt Park (see page 240), part of his original estate that eventually encompassed 86,000 acres. As for this manor, it is Oloff's great-grandson Pierre (1721–1814) who is most associated with it. Pierre lived here as a country gentleman from 1749 onward after marrying Joanna Livingston (from another famous Hudson River family—see page 67), and she, according to legend, designed the beautiful "Long Walk" that leads from the house to the tavern.

When the Revolution came, Pierre—unlike Frederick Philipse—sided with the patriots and became the first lieutenant governor of the state in 1777, serving in that position for 18 years. The house descended through the family until 1945, when it was sold. A short time later, Mr. Rockefeller bought it. Much of what you see here in the way of furnishings and other articles belonged to the Van Cortlandts.

This wonderful-looking stone and white-clapboard house has a striking double staircase leading to a pillared veranda on the second floor through which guests would enter, the service rooms being on the first

The old Ferry House and kitchen on Van Cortlandt Manor furnish much insight into what eighteenth-century inns were like. The brick "Long Walk" in the foreground leads to the manor house and is bordered by well-kept flower beds.

floor. Inside, the rooms have been restored to show the changing taste of the family from the seventeenth into the nineteenth centuries; the parlor, for instance, has Queen Anne, Chippendale and Federal furnishings as well as two handsome portraits circa 1725 and a French mantel clock dating from much later. They go well together, creating a feeling of continuity, of an actual family living here over a great span of time. But my favorite room is the dining room with its mid-eighteenth-century mantelpiece, its shelf supporting Chelsea figurines, and the rare Delft biblical tiles around the fireplace opening. There also is an excellent portrait of Ann Stevenson Van Cortlandt attributed to Ezra Ames (see page 51), painted about 1815, as well as a splendid Federal sideboard.

The downstairs is much more informal, the old parlor and kitchen filled with simpler furnishings and, naturally, more utilitarian objects. If you're lucky, one of the employees may be preparing food in the kitchen and will offer you a sample of her fare.

From the house you take the brick-paved "Long Walk" to the Ferry House. This 750-foot-long walk is bordered by perfectly maintained flower beds and there are also orchard and vegetable gardens nearby to reinforce the nice eighteenth-century bucolic feeling. Both the Ferry House, once an inn, and the nearby kitchen house were for the use of travelers who crossed the Croton River here to continue on up the old Albany Post Road, some remains of which still exist at the end of the property.

The barroom is terrific, with a stunning collection of pewter, good-looking Windsor chairs and tables. The common room is a bit more elegant and was more exclusive when it was in use, but give me the barroom any day. Upstairs are two dormitory-styled bedrooms for men and women. All in all, an interesting peek at an eighteenth-century inn—but I wonder if it ever looked this inviting and fresh and clean when it was in actual use.

ANOTHER FINE HOUSE NEARBY

Lyndhurst ■ Lyndhurst should not be missed. In fact, architecturally it is one of the most interesting houses in the Valley. It is located about one-half mile south of the Tappan Zee Bridge on Route 9 (a half-mile north of Sunnyside). Open: Mid-April to October, Tuesday–Sunday, 10–5. November–April, weekends only, 10–4. Phone: 914-631-4481. Web site: www.lyndhurst.org.

Of all the houses that line the Hudson in a stately progression and demonstrate almost every architectural style, Lyndhurst is the best in the way it complements and enhances the natural splendor of its setting. Put it down on any other spot in the world and it might jar, but here it is absolutely right and, says William H. Pierson, Jr., author of *American Buildings and Their Architects,* "when completed in 1866, [Lyndhurst] was the most profoundly intelligent and provocative house to be built in this country since Thomas Jefferson's Monticello."

The mansion was designed by Alexander Jackson Davis (1803–92), perhaps the greatest residential architect working in the Gothic Revival style that this country ever produced. Gothic Revival took its inspiration from the Gothic style of the Middle Ages and was the complete antithesis of cool, rational classicism. In its earliest phases, Gothic Revival was all emotion and picturesque eccentricity, and so when Davis was asked to build a great house atop a hill, his imagination was especially fired by the special light and unspoiled magnificence of the Hudson River Valley. His long association with Thomas Cole and other Romantic painters of the Hudson River School also stood him in good stead.

Davis erected Lyndhurst, the perfect Hudson River Gothic house, in two phases. The first began in 1838 and was planned for General William Paulding, a former two-time mayor of New York City, and his son, Philip. The second, which roughly doubled the size of the building and created what we see today, was begun by Davis in 1865 for its new owner, George Merritt, a successful merchant and inventor who wanted his house to reflect his wealth—and not in any modest way. The last family to occupy the mansion was that of Jay Gould (1836–92), robber baron par excellence, who happily bilked the Erie Railroad of millions and then proceeded to come very close to cornering the gold market, thereby causing the panic that is still referred to as Black Friday (September 24, 1869). Since Gould also controlled Western Union and the *New York World* and held vast interests in the western railroads, he could well afford Lyndhurst when he bought it in 1880. (His daughter Anna, Duchess of Talleyrand-Périgord, gave the estate to the National Trust for Historic Preservation, which opened it to the public in 1964.)

The house, set high above the Hudson with wonderful views to the north and south, has a breathtaking exterior, a fairy-tale palace of turrets

Lyndhurst is set on 67 acres of land. Not far from the house are the remains of the enormous greenhouse, of which this wing is a part. It was once world-famous for its orchid collection and currently is undergoing extensive renovation.

and towers, mysterious windows in wonderfully changing shapes and sizes, a superb veranda ... all seemingly jumbled together in a restless gray mass of Sing Sing marble with no immediately recognizable architectural plan. But look closer and walk around it: you'll soon see that it exudes an inherent logic, power and intelligence that fits it exactly into its setting. The house doesn't look "built," it looks as if it *grew*, its outlines and proportions splendidly matching the Valley it adorns. And the more you look at it from different angles and positions, the more wonderful it becomes.

My favorite place is the veranda, which manages to be a part of both the interior and the exterior of the house. You feel here as if you're moving within a wonderful limbo that contains the best of both the man-made and the natural worlds—protection from the elements in a welcoming space, yet all the joys of the outdoors. It moves, somehow—is it because of the marvelous architectural treatment of the ceiling?—and yet it appears extraordinarily peaceful and inviting. Hours could be spent here, at perfect ease, in this strangely contrasting space that somehow achieves a perfect equilibrium.

The interior, architecturally speaking, fulfills the promise of the outside. Still, for me, it's a disappointment, with second-rate statuary and paintings. It is a study in moneyed nineteenth-century gloom.

Before you leave, though, be sure to walk about the grounds. There are 67 acres in all, dotted with wonderful, ancient specimen trees, particularly copper beeches and cut-leaf Japanese maples. And be sure to visit the rose garden and the spectacular greenhouse, which seems large enough to hold half the houses in the Valley. It was fully stabilized in 1996. Built by Jay Gould in 1881 after the original structure on the site was destroyed by fire, it remains an astounding sight even in its present condition. The main building is slightly more than 376 feet long and 36 feet wide, and there are two smaller wings as well. The design echoes that of the house, although most of the neo-Gothic detail is long gone. The frame is wrought iron, one of the earliest uses of it for this kind of construction, and served as a prototype for later conservatories throughout the country.

In its day Lyndhurst was particularly famous for its collection of orchids and palms; in fact, Jay Gould's daughter, Helen, established the orchid collection at the New York Botanical Garden by giving them 230 specimen plants in 1900 from her holdings at Lyndhurst. (Originally the greenhouse here had 14 plant rooms.)

There also is a bowling alley below the house, and the carriage house has been made into a very pleasant and attractive lunchroom—the stalls are now booths—that is moderately priced and is open for lunch, 11–3, Wednesday–Sunday from May–October.

New York City and Vicinity

SOME THINGS TO SEE

Battery Park City Esplanade and South Cove ■ at Battery Park City in Lower Manhattan.

Web site: www.bpcparks.org

This marvel brings you closer to the river than any other location in New York City.

Begin by entering on the Esplanade from the World Financial Center's Winter Garden. This is at the northern end of Battery Park City and is, in itself, well worth visiting as one of the more splendid interior spaces in New York.

The Esplanade, 70 feet wide and beautifully landscaped, runs for over a mile south along the Hudson and has delightful small parks and gardens scattered along its length.

At its end, you will come out on South Cove, one of the most special parks you will ever see, nestled in its idyllic 3-acre site and with the river so close you want to lean over and let the cooling waters run through your fingers. There is something so intimate about South Cove, something so natural and inviting that it's like suddenly seeing an old friend after a long separation.

The design was the collaborative effort of three people: Stanton Eckstert, an architect who also was involved in the master plan for Battery Park City; Susan Child, a landscape architect; and Mary Miss, an artist. What they have created is, indeed, a work of art. One of their happiest notions was to strew boulders down a hillside, "allowing" an occasional one to be on the sidewalk—just as you would expect if you were walking along the river's bank. This effect ties together the landscape, river and path in a way that is so enveloping the city fades from your ken and you feel you have arrived in some half-remembered place just over the horizon of consciousness.

Other wonderful inspirations: The wooden lamp posts with their cobalt-blue glass ship lanterns, which, at night, and combined with the other lighting in the park, cast magical rainbows on the dark waters of the river. (I should point out that the evening hours are not only beautiful but safe.) I also love the observation bridge—was it purposely designed to echo the line of the Statue of Liberty's diadem?—the wonderful views of the Verrazano Bridge, the Statue of Liberty, Ellis Island and that grand architectural fantasy, the old Jersey Central Railway Terminal, the jetty that yields, swaying, to the wakes thrown up by passing boats and, perhaps best of all, at the end of the seawall, that wonderful, mysterious sound of water slapping against wood.

I like to move from bench to bench, enjoying the changing perspectives, absorbing the beauty of the flowers, trees and shrubs, watching the patterns of light reflecting from the water and then seeing the gulls swooping over all ... I've even seen flocks of ducks flying low over the water. It doesn't seem in the slightest like New York, yet I can't imagine another city it would suit so well.

One last mention—there's enough to see that I can't cover it all, but do see the Irish Hunger memorial, located two blocks from ground zero, and unconventional enough to stop traffic. The work commemorates the Irish famine of 1845–1852, and it has taken on additional resonance since 9/11 as so many of the firemen, policemen, rescue workers and office personnel were of Irish descent. The work of Brian Tolle, it is extraordinary in that it combines realism and abstraction as a realistic setting of an Irish hillside and an abandoned Irish fieldstone cottage. At the same time, it rests on a 96-by-170-foot wedge-shaped base that slopes up from street level to a height of 25 feet, culminating in a striking view of the Statue of Liberty and Ellis Island.

The Cloisters ▦ Fort Tryon Park, Manhattan (just off Riverside Drive). Open: Tuesday–Sunday 9:30–5:15; November–February, closed at 4:45. Closed: Monday. Phone: 212-923-3700.

Web site: www.metmuseum.org

I include this, one of New York's great glories and a personal favorite because, from its terraces and many of its windows, you can see views of the river that are essentially unchanged from the time Hudson first sailed up it. This building, more than any other in the city, fits brilliantly into its river landscape setting and would be totally different in feeling (and the poorer, overall) had it been placed anywhere else.

The Cloisters is a branch of the Metropolitan Museum of Art and has a collection of medieval art that ranks among the finest in the world. The building opened in 1938, and much of its contents were given by John D. Rockefeller, Jr. It incorporates within its walls a twelfth-century chapter house and Spanish apse, sections of cloisters from five medieval monasteries and a Romanesque chapel.

I don't have the space to detail all its wonders, but it would be impossible not to at least mention the Unicorn Tapestries Room with its incredible series, "The Hunt of the Unicorn," with their endlessly beautiful and complex colors and scenes. Probably woven around 1500 in Brussels, almost every inch of the surfaces are covered with flowers and plants, animals and people, all depicted in astounding detail. You could gaze at these magnificent tapestries for hours without penetrating one-tenth of their visual feast.

The Hudson River Museum of Westchester and The Andrus Planetarium ■

511 Warburton Avenue, Yonkers. Open: Wednesday–Sunday 12–5, Friday 12–8. Closed Monday and Tuesday. Planetarium hours: Saturday and Sunday shows, 12:30, 1:30, 2:30. Free Friday show, 7.

Phone: 914-963-4550. Web site: www.hrm.org

The museum displays changing exhibitions of nineteenth- and twentieth-century American art as well as exhibitions combining elements of the art, history and science of a given subject, but all in the context of the Hudson River Valley region. Some favorite past exhibitions— one on Bannerman Castle (see page 208), a wonderful show of kites created by artists called "Shaped by the Wind" and, from years ago, "Getting from Here to There," which explored the history and mechanics of bridges while displaying a large collection of paintings, drawings and photographs of bridges.

Then there's the 1876–77 Glenview Mansion and its impressive period rooms, including the very fine Eastlake-style sitting room, and lovely stenciled ceilings and the planetarium. But for me the highlights of the museum—after the exhibitions—are the Red Grooms installation, which opened in 1979 and is part of the gift shop, and the Hudson Riverama, a multimedia exhibit that depicts the entire length of the Hudson, from Lake Tear of the Clouds to the harbor in New York City. It includes a 31-foot-long scale model of the Hudson, interactive touch screen stations that give all kinds of river-related information, video displays, paintings, dioramas, aquariums … it's a cornucopia of information and absolutely fascinating. If you have kids, this is a must—they will love it.

This museum is fun to visit. It's quirky, and all the more stimulating because of it. To top it off, the museum café has wonderful views of the Hudson (but pedestrian food). The café is open Wednesday through Sunday, 12–3.

The Donald M. Kendall Sculpture Gardens at PepsiCo ■ Purchase. Open: Daily to sunset. Admission: Free.

Phone: 914-253-2001. Web site: www.gardenvisit.com/ge/a.pepsi.htm

This garden features one of the finest collections in twentieth-century sculpture in the country. Louise Nevelson, Henry Moore, Alexander Calder, David Smith, Jean Dubuffet … they're all here. So are George Segal, Claes Oldenburg, Isamu Noguchi and Robert Davidson. Equally spectacular, the collection of 45 sculptures is set in a 165-acre landscape of splendid gardens planted by Russell Page (1906–85) from 1980 until his death, and continued by François Goffinet.

The Gardens first. Space limits me from more than a mention of some of the joys and surprises you will come across, but a stroll along The Golden Path, which binds the whole together, will bring you to such special spots as woodlands filled with pink and white azaleas, a grove of 13 different species of birch, a Stream Garden with lush ferns and flowering plants and, my favorite site, the Perennial Border and Waterlily Pools with a pavilion as a resting place to enjoy not only the border and waterlilies but also a collection of daylilies.

The sculpture filling this exquisite space is worthy of its setting. What is particularly pleasant is to wander from space to space getting different views of such enormous pieces as Robert Davidson's "Totems," or coming across August Rodin's 1881 "Eve" just beyond a tunnel of flowering cherry and crabapple trees, or seeing David Wynne's "Grizzly Bear" loom over your view toward the lake as you start your tour. You can spend anywhere from two hours to the entire day here, and although it is a joy in every season, quite naturally it looks its best in spring and summer.

Finally, do note the PepsiCo headquarters building, which was designed by Edward Durell Stone (1902–78) and was completed in 1970. It is one of his better efforts.

Neuberger Museum of Art ▪ Purchase College, State University of New York, Purchase. Open: Tuesday–Friday 10–4, Saturday and Sunday 11–5. Closed: Monday. Free gallery tours on Tuesdays, Wednesdays and Thursdays at 1, Sundays at 2 and 3. Phone: 914-251-6100.

Philip Johnson designed this spacious museum (78,000 square feet) that dates from 1974. The collections of more than 5,000 works of art are something to behold and owe a great deal to the generosity of Roy R. Neuberger, who made his pile in money management and has had a long-time love affair with American art of the twentieth century. Neuberger wanted his collection to go to a teaching institution and chose SUNY Purchase. The result: A major visual arts center with a prestigious collection of twentieth-century American and European art, ancient art and African art.

Milton Avery, Mr. Neuberger's favorite painter, is represented by 20 canvases. But there are so many other artists as well that just to list some of the names in the collection should give you a hint of its breadth: Lyonel Feininger, Edward Hopper, Georgia O'Keeffe, Arthur Dove, Frank Stella, Jackson Pollock, Ben Shahn, Jack Levine, Mark Rothko, Larry Rivers, Josef Albers … you get the idea. There are even two paintings by Thomas Cole as well as works by Alfred Bierstadt and Maurice Prendergast, but the overwhelming majority of paintings are modern.

My own favorite work is "Threnody" (1973) by Cleve Gray. Gray was born in New York City in 1918 and commissioned by the museum to paint this series of enormous panels. The room that they fill is vast—100 feet by 60 feet by 22 feet high—and Gray chose to fill it with 14 abstract, glowing figures in burningly brilliant colors against a luminous black background. The room itself is in semidarkness with individual lights concentrated on the figures, shifting male-female forms whose torsos bend and sway in an extraordinary dance of death and life. I think it is one of the great pieces of American art created in the 1970s and, without any question, well worth a special trip to see. Unfortunately, the museum does not keep it on permanent display. Therefore, I'd call in advance. If it's not on view, ask when it will be. Then go as soon as possible. No one with even the slightest interest in contemporary art can afford to miss this monumental and deeply moving masterpiece.

The Newington–Cropsey Foundation Gallery of Art and Cultural Studies Center and the Jasper Francis Cropsey Home and Studio ■ Hastings-on-Hudson. Both are open by appointment only, and their hours are different.

Phone: 914-478-7990, web site; www.newingtoncropsey.com (Newington-Cropsey), 914-478-1372 (Home and studio).

The gallery is dedicated to the works of the Hudson River painter Jasper Cropsey (1823–1900), who spent the latter part of his life (1885–1900) in the enchantingly designed Gothic Revival cottage, now restored and open to visitors. As for the gallery, which lies below the house, it was built by Cropsey's great-granddaughter, Barbara Newington, who spent several million dollars to build the present foundation and gallery complex, which were designed by the architects Rodney Mims Cook, Jr., and Peter Polites in the classical style on the exterior, but with a Gothic Revival gallery. The two make for an interesting visit, but because hours can vary for each, it's a good idea to coordinate your appointments.

First, the house, which is painted a bright yellow, the gingerbread trim in white. The surrounding grounds have been prepared with great care, and the impression is charming. As for the interior, you enter on the lowest level where you will see a well-done, twenty-minute video explaining Jasper Cropsey and his art, and then you can look at Cropsey's artwork in that section. (The video also talks about Cropsey's ability as an architect and shows his designs for the Sixth Avenue Elevated stairways, waiting rooms and platforms in New York City, all long gone. What a pity one couldn't be saved. They were quite wonderful Victorian designs.) I've always liked Cropsey's work. Not the greatest of the Hudson River School, perhaps, and a lousy drawer of figures, but his landscapes are brilliantly colored—his snowscapes, for me, hold particular appeal—and his drawings in this section are really quite wonderful—look for the sheep as seen from the back, and the small grouping of ducks. Back upstairs to the main house, where you see the parlor, dining room and studio. The restoration has been very good and is as close to what the original looked like as it could possibly be. For example, the furniture Cropsey himself designed is all in place, and very little, if any, of the material is not original to Cropsey's time here. Cropsey's artistic work is everywhere, but the great surprise is the studio, wide and spacious, with its wonderful wooden inglenook. My favorite picture? A small study of a skunk cabbage with small flowers (primroses?) in the foreground. It really is worth a visit, and it's interesting to see the artist's work in situ and as he placed it.

Now for the foundation building and gallery. The building—a combination of various architectural styles that is handsome and Italian in its overall look—is set in a very attractive landscape, with a pond filled with ducks, small waterfalls, and so forth as well as some handsome sculptures. It looks rather incongruous because above this, on the top of the hill, are rather ordinary houses—far from the luxurious building in front of you. Once inside the octagonal, Gothic Revival gallery with its very high ceiling you will see the Cropsey paintings displayed in the nineteenth-century style of one on top of the other, and although they are well lit, it's difficult to study any details unless you have binoculars with you.

In brief, the two buildings form a unique entity unlike anything else in the Valley. If you are interested in Cropsey in particular and the Hudson River School in general, the two are a must. In any case, they are worth a visit.

Van Cortlandt House ■ Van Cortlandt Park (near Broadway and W. 246th Street). Open: Tuesday–Friday 10–3, Saturday and Sunday 11–4. Closed: Monday.

Phone: 718-543-3344. Web site: www.vancortlandthouse.org

Although not as beautiful or as magnificently restored as Van Cortlandt Manor (see page 229), this house, built in 1748, belonged to another branch of the same family and has a very definite charm of its own.

The 9-room house is more English than Dutch in feel (but do note the wonderful heads above the windows; typically Dutch) and is built of rubble stone with brick trim around the windows. Inside, much of the collection you see belonged to the family.

Some highlights: The East Parlor, with its handsome Georgian mantel and Massachusetts block-front secretary. In this same room you'll note an adequate portrait of Augustus Van Cortlandt by John Wesley Jarvis (1781–1840), an artist less famed for his paintings than for his sense of humor and for what were then euphemistically termed his "mysterious marriages."

In the East Parlor also can be found a pair of portraits (Frances White and her husband Archibald Bruce) by John Vanderlyn (see page 107). In the West Parlor is a handsome Hudson Valley Dutch kast, or chest, while the dining room contains a portrait of John Jacob Astor, a relative by marriage, after Gilbert Stuart, as well as my favorite things in the whole house: two huge teakwood eagles on either side of the fireplace, purportedly given to the family by the future English king, William IV, and a British admiral in thanks for the Van Cortlandts' hospitality.

The upstairs also has its moments, in particular the Dutch Room (a seventeenth-century bedroom) and the Washington Room, where—yes— he really did sleep. Best of all, though, at least when I've been there, you're allowed to wander about as you please, without a guide, enjoying the printed, self-guided tour.

Wave Hill ■ 675 West 252nd Street in the Bronx. Open: Mid-October to mid-April, Tuesday–Sunday 9–4:30; mid-April to mid-October, Tuesday–Sunday, 9–5:30.

Phone: 718-549-3200. Web site: www.wavehill.org

What a pleasant spot this is for the first-time visitor. Here is the only Hudson River estate open to the public within the boundaries of New York City, and it's very special. Arturo Toscanini lived here, as did Samuel Clemens and Theodore Roosevelt. All of them loved it, and once you've been here you'll know why.

The grounds sit high above the Hudson and offer a sweeping panorama of the Palisades across the river, the George Washington Bridge and, farther south, the city skyscrapers that seem in startling contrast to the pastoral landscape that surrounds you.

Wave Hill House was built in 1843 by William Lewis Morris, a New York lawyer. In 1866, William Henry Appleton, the publisher, bought it to use as a summer house. But its real period of glory came when George W. Perkins, a partner in J. P. Morgan & Company, purchased it in 1903 and, over a period of almost 20 years, assembled other neighboring properties until he had himself an estate of 80 acres. While he lived at Wave Hill, Perkins built 8 greenhouses and planted many varieties of exotic trees, using, as his chief gardener, a former royal landscape artist from Vienna. Not one to do things in a small way, Perkins also secured his "vista," for he was instrumental in helping to form Palisades Park in 1912. Perkins died in 1920. In 1960, his descendants donated 28 acres of the estate, its two houses and the magnificent gardens to New York City as a public cultural institution.

The landscaping you see today was begun in 1967, and now there are more than 600 species and varieties of trees and shrubs alone. The greenhouse, part of which is open to the public, has tropical and succulent plants, cacti, and an ever-changing display of flora. But the grounds themselves, full of pleasures and surprises, provide the major interest, with their huge trees, elms and maples, shading the lawns, their herb and flower gardens, and, perhaps best of all, a wild garden that leads up to a pretty gazebo from which the views are superb ... flowers everywhere! Below the houses, on a 10-acre plot, a forest project is underway to restore a native Bronx woodland.

In Wave Hill House there's a small gift shop and café, and the public rooms are devoted to art exhibitions, concerts and conferences.

THREE RIVER JOURNEYS

World Yacht Dining Cruises ■ Pier 81, west end of West 41st Street. Parking available. Year-round schedule. Phone: 212-630-8100. For detailed information go to the web site: www.worldyacht.com.

The "fleet" of this company is furnished and decorated with both elegance and comfort in mind. Without any question, this is the most luxurious and romantic way to cruise around Manhattan and would be an ideal way to show the city off to a newly arrived tourist—and even a jaded New Yorker. I recommend it.

New York Waterway ■ Pier 78. This company operates full-day cruises on the Hudson and a Historic Hudson Weekend Getaway Cruise. I think they do an excellent job. Phone: 800-53-FERRY. For detailed information, go to the web site: www.nywaterway.com.

Circle Line Sightseeing Cruises ■ Pier 83, west end of West 42nd Street. Phone: 212-563-3200. For a complete list of cruises and other information go to the web site: www.circleline42.com.

More than 50 million people have taken the 3-hour, 35-mile-long cruise around Manhattan, and although shorter cruises are available, this is the one to take. For many years, I had not been among them. More the fool me, for as I had been told ad nauseam by everyone who had taken it, this little trip is a must.

Before the trip, though, some tips. First, everyone rushes for seats on the open top deck. Don't. I did, but soon realized that, no matter how much the crew complains, everyone is going to stand, taking thousands of pictures, and it's soon like the subway at rush hour. So I went downstairs where there were fewer people and just as good a view for all of the east side of Manhattan after the Brooklyn Bridge. (Stand or sit on the port—left—side facing forward, if possible.) I would suggest remaining outside for the first part of the trip past the Statue of Liberty and up the East River to the Brooklyn Bridge and then going inside, returning on deck only for the part going back down the Hudson. Another good place is on the bow, where people tend to come and go, and you're more likely to get a good spot. Second, the commentators are wonderful, and do try to listen to some of their spiels.

At first I was a little disappointed after the boat began its run; New York City, New Jersey and the Hudson do not blend into a ravishing sight at this point, but then, as you move out into the Upper Bay and see Ellis Island and the Statue of Liberty and finally swing around to look at that world-famous view of Lower Manhattan in the sunlight, it's hard not to get a lump in your throat. On up to the Brooklyn Bridge (1883), designed by John Augustus Roebling (1806–69)—he died of tetanus after his foot was crushed by a wooden piling during the early days of the bridge's construction—and completed by his son, Washington (1837–1926). For me it's the most special bridge in the world and the best justification I know of to see the East River. Then up the East Side; basically dull if you know New York, but with one or two nice moments—the UN building, for instance. Things pick up, though, as you go through the Harlem River Ship Canal at Spuyten Duyvil and they race when you return back out onto the river, this "great romantic stream," as Henry James said, "such as could throw not a little of its glamour ... over the city at its mouth." "The sordid city," he added elsewhere, "has the honour, after all, of sitting there at the Beautiful Gate." He had his priorities exactly right: The river graces the city, not the other way around.

The first and most obvious glory is the Palisades Ridge, that unique landmark that extends for 50 miles and soars as high as 827 feet above the river. Here, from the river, it is a series of awe-inspiring columns, marching north over the horizon and south to the bay, an ultraglamorous setting from which the Hudson will make its dramatic exit. Then there's the George Washington Bridge (1931), a silvery, elegant 4,760-foot strand of steel that was designed by Othmar Hermann Ammann (1879–1965), a civil engineer also responsible for the Verrazano–Narrows Bridge (1964). For me the brilliance of the George Washington Bridge, aside from its basic beauty (Cass Gilbert served as consulting architect), is how well it suits the river; it does not bestride it, like some vulgar conqueror, nor does it hesitate tentatively at the great leap it must make. Rather it looks like a companion, a natural addition to the scene and one of the few man-made ones that neither uses, in the commercial sense, nor abuses the magnificence of its setting.

After that, it's a series of wonderful impressions as the great river passes Manhattan (*pace,* Henry James): There are The Cloisters and Grant's Tomb and Riverside Baptist Church and Morningside Heights and then the great skyscrapers ... and ... and, a little sadly, the Upper Bay, where the Hudson disappears from sight, still to run its final course to the edge of the Continental Shelf. There it will end at last, in one more burst of splendor, as an undersea falls. How I wish I could see that!

Where to Stay and Eat

Putnam, Orange and Westchester Counties
Area Codes: 845, 914

WHERE TO STAY

The Bird & Bottle Inn ▉ Route 9, Garrison 10524 (Putnam County). Phone: 845-424-2333. Web site: www.thebirdandbottleinn.com

This old clapboard inn, yellow with black trim, was established in 1761 and has just about everything an inn should have including fireplaces, beamed ceilings and wide plank floors. It's a visual delight. (For the food, see page 250.)

Castle on the Hudson ▉ 400 Benedict Avenue, Tarrytown (Westchester County). Phone: 914-631-1980.
Web site: www.castleonthehudsonhotel.com

Yup. It's a castle, all right. Lovely guestrooms, luxurious suites with wood-burning fireplaces, wonderful views of the Hudson River, swimming pool, tennis court ... and topped off by one of the best restaurants in the lower Hudson Valley, Equus (see page 249). Needless to say, this doesn't come cheap. But it's worth it.

Crabtree's Kittle House Inn ▉ 11 Kittle Road (Route 117), Chappaqua 10514 (Westchester County). Phone: 914-666-8044.
Web site: www.kittlehouse.com

This is a lovely inn and, again, offers excellent dining (see page 248). The house was built in 1790 and now offers 12 guest rooms, each attractive and comfortable. Not as opulent as Castle on the Hudson, but equally appealing in its own, more subdued way. And it's much more reasonable.

Hotel Thayer ■ West Point 10996 (Orange County).
Phone: 845-446-4731. Web site: www.thethayerhotel.com/

The Thayer, a Gothic-inspired hotel built in 1926, has been completely renovated and is the largest hotel (151 rooms) between New York and
Albany. All rooms have river views and are comfortable. Room sizes range
from double bedrooms to suites. It's a little stuffy, I think, a little on the
dreary side. Doesn't seem at all country, in any case. They have a good
Sunday brunch, but the food generally is uninspired.

Hudson House ■ 2 Main Street, Cold Spring 10516 (Putnam County).
Phone: 845-265-9355. Web site: www.hudsonhouseinn.com.

The Hudson Valley's most dramatic river setting. (For a description of
the inn, setting and food, see page 188.) Reserve in advance.

BED & BREAKFAST INNS

Pig Hill Inn ■ 73 Main Street, Cold Spring 10516 (Putnam County).
Phone: 845-265-9247. Web site: www.pighillinn.com. Some rooms have
a shared bath.

Very pretty, with a lovely terraced garden dining area and nine inter-
estingly decorated rooms—all of the antique furnishings, by the way, are
for sale, and five rooms have wood-burning stoves, while one has a fireplace—with stencilled walls executed by the stencilsmith next door. Henry
and Vera Keil are the owners, and they have created one of the more attractive B&B's in the area. P.S.: There also is a gift shop.

WHERE TO EAT: Some Favorites

Dozens of restaurants sprinkle the Lower Hudson, but I have only listed
those that, for one reason or another, I have truly enjoyed and feel can be
recommended, even with some reservations. In addition, prices at many of
them approximate those found in New York City and, again as in New
York, French cuisine predominates. I would also like to register a formal
complaint that the wine prices at French restaurants are ridiculously high
(again New York's baleful influence) and I now tend to stick to the house
wines, thereby saving a measurable percentage of my yearly income. At all
of my "favorites," reservations are generally essential.

The Arch ▮ Route 22 (1 mile north of 684), Brewster (Westchester County). Phone: 845-279-5011. Web site: www.archrestaurant.com

This physically unpretentious restaurant, with a flagstone terrace for outdoor dining in good weather, pretty garden and several small, cozy dining rooms inside (the main dining room has a fireplace), is particularly notable for its exquisite attention to service and detail as well as for excellent French cooking. The wine list is expensive, and so is the food, but if you wish to savor a special event in grand style, this is the place.

Blue Hill at Stone Barns ▮ 630 Bedford Road, Pocantico Hills (Westchester County). Phone: 914-366-9600.
Web site: www.bluehillstonebarns.com

This restaurant, an outpost of the extremely popular Blue Hill restaurant in Manhattan, is part of Stone Barns Center for Food and Agriculture, an 80-acre complex of gardens, pastures and woods, which I'll get to a little later. You can spend a very pleasant day at the Center, much less have an excellent meal.

As for the restaurant, it ranks as one of the best in the Valley. Using only fresh ingredients from the farm and from Valley providers, the menu changes constantly but the quality of both ingredients and preparation is first rate. The setting, cool and minimalist but sometimes with a bit too intrusive piped-in music, is right on target, and the service is friendly. The wine list is well chosen and reasonably priced—given what wines cost in restaurants—and the service people are knowledgeable about what is in the cellar. One minor caveat; at dinner every course is described as the waiter presents it at the table. That is, I think, a bore. Still, this is the place to go for a special occasion, but be warned—reservations are in great demand, and you should reserve as far ahead as possible—they accept reservations two months in advance. They also operate the Blue Hill Café, right next door, where you can get light snacks—panini, vegetable chips, trail mix, and so forth—to either eat at the tables there or in the courtyard or while you walk around the farm.

And now for the farm. Stone Barns Center is nonprofit and is, to quote from their excellent brochure, "a multi-purpose educational center … along with 50 miles of adjacent walking and riding trails. Our beautiful Norman-style barns were originally built in the 1930s by John D. Rockefeller Jr. … and have been lovingly renovated through the direction

and generosity of David Rockefeller and daughter Peggy Dulany."
Wandering around here is fascinating. You can visit a full half-acre of
greenhouses. Or hike the trail to Pocantico River and Sleepy Hollow or
one of the other trails. Or wander in the Herb Garden, source of herbs and
edible flowers used by the restaurant's chef. It's a fascinating place. I call it
Rockefeller Center North: Rural Division. For further information,
phone: 366-6200. Web site: stonebarnscenter.org

Buffet de la Gare ■ Hastings-on-Hudson (Westchester County).
Phone: 914-478-1671.

Inside the unpretentious building, the tiny interior is charming with
pressed-tin walls and ceiling, fresh flowers in abundance, a handsome old
oak bar, lace curtains, not to mention Victorian chandeliers and wall fixtures. As for the food, it's excellent. In fact, it seems to get better and better. The French menu is smallish, featuring eight entrées plus four
specials, but everything is first-rate and the selections avoid the obvious.
I would recommend duck ; it's always done to perfection. And if cassoulet
is on the menu, go for it; it's excellent. The wine list, for once, is reasonably priced and offers several nice selections. Overall, you will dine very,
very well in this pleasant bistro that could have been transported here
directly from France.

Crabtree's Kittle House ■ 11 Kittle Road (Route 117), Chappaqua
(Westchester County). Phone: 914-666-8044. Web site: kittlehouse.com

The food—New American—is delicious and serious but not pretentious. The same goes for the dining rooms. You can't go wrong eating here.
In fact, it's one of my favorite restaurants in the entire Valley. And the wine
list is extraordinary—there are, quite literally, several thousand labels. It
also is one of Bill Clinton's favorites. And the bar was originally a gift from
Fanny Brice to Dutch Shultz. Belly up with care.

La Crèmaillére ■ 46 Bedford–Banksville Road, Banksville (Westchester
County). Phone: 914-234-9647. Web site: www.cremaillere.com.

This, the doyenne of Westchester restaurants, offers charm, delicious
food and high prices. It also has an amazing wine list. Well worth it,
though, for a special occasion or if you just want to kick up your heels.

Equus ■ 400 Benedict Avenue, Tarrytown (Westchester County).
Phone 914-631-3646. Web site: www.castleonthehudsonhotel.com

Wow. This place is truly beautiful, and the food is very good—
American inspired. Expensive? You'd better believe it. Worth it? Yes—particularly if you're celebrating a special event. There are three dining rooms. My
favorite? It's a draw between the room that once belonged to Louis XIV or
the one with views of the garden, the Hudson, and the Manhattan skyline.

Finch Tavern ■ 592 Route 22, Croton Falls (Westchester County).
Phone: 914-277-4580.

Housed in a wonderful 1864 Victorian white-frame building with a
broad veranda, this has gone from a homey Italian restaurant to a sleek
twenty-first-century "tavern" with chic New American cuisine and a clientele to match. The staff is highly professional, the food first rate and the
cost is considerably less than the other restaurants in this section. Not for
a cheap date, but still you'll be able to afford the gas to get home.

Freelance Café and Wine Bar ■ 506 Piermont Avenue, Piermont
(Rockland County). Phone: 845-365-3250. Web site: www.xaviars.com
No credit cards.

This restaurant is owned by Peter Xavier Kelly, who owns the next-
door Xaviar's (see above). I like it very much because you can get either
small plates or large plates of the same entrée, the service and general
ambiance is relaxed and friendly and it's cheaper than Xaviar's. I also like
it because the food is very good, a combination of American, French and
Italian, and it all works. No reservations, so if you don't get there early, be
prepared to wait—it's worth it, and it's reasonable.

Restaurant X and Bully Boy Bar ■ 117 Route 303 (between Lake Road
and Route 9W) Congers (Westchester County). Phone: 845-268-6555.
Web site: www.xaviars.com

Of all Xavier Kelly's restaurants, this is my favorite. The rooms offer a
variety of settings from country to modern, there's a fireplace, the service
(as in all the Kelly restaurants) is impeccable … in short, this gets my vote
for No.1 in the Kelly empire. It really is good, and the menu and wine list
are amazing.

Plumbush ■ Route 9D, Cold Spring (Putnam County). Phone: 845-265-3904. Web site: plumbushinn.net. See page 190.

Xaviar's in Piermont ■ 506 Piermont Avenue, Piermont. Phone: 845-359-7007. Web site: www.xaviers.com. No credit cards.

Many readers rate this as the best restaurant in the Valley. I don't agree. It's excellent—really—but I find it a little too self-consciously "interesting," with a little too much emphasis on amazing the diner. It can best be called a contemporary American kitchen, and you will dine extremely well, but it is, somehow, too sleek. I should point out, though, that I'm very much in the minority. I also should tell you that the wine list is superb—750 selections—and with prices to match. Also see the Freelance Cafe and Xaviar's in Garrison.

OTHER RESTAURANTS WORTH NOTING

Vox (formerly Auberge Maxime) ■ Route 116, North Salem (Westchester County). Phone: 914-669-5450. Web site: www.vox-restaurant.com.

Homely on the outside, but within, the small dining room is both attractive and comfortable. The restaurant doesn't serve as fancy a menu as it used to. Now the food is simpler and well prepared, but I think the prices are rather steep for what you get.

The Bird & Bottle Inn ■ Route 9, Garrison (Putnam County). Phone: 845-424-2333. Web site: www.thebirdandbottleinn.com

The dining room, long and warmly lit by fireplaces, is appealing and offers a near-perfect setting for a romantic dinner. The food can be good, a combination of American and European, but it can be an up and down affair. And the service could be improved, too. But the primary reason to be here is still the romantic atmosphere.

Caravela ■ 53 North Broadway, Tarrytown (Westchester County). Phone: 914-631-1863.

A Portuguese-Brazilian restaurant that specializes in seafood and is decorated with tiles (surprise!) and so forth, I find the prices to be very high for what you get, although what you get is served in generous proportions and is generally well prepared. I also leave dehydrated; I think there's salt in everything. On the other hand, there's not too much of a choice in this immediate area.

Il Cenàcolo ■ 152 Route 52, Newburgh (Orange County). Phone: 845-564-4494.

This restaurant is a Tuscan treasure and worth a detour. "Absolutely first class," I was told, and indeed it is. If you like northern Italian food, this is the best I know of in the Valley, and it's also only moderately expensive.

Le Bouchon ■ 76 Main Street, Cold Spring (Putnam County). Phone: 845-265-7676.

Cold Spring has gone French. At least at this nice little restaurant offering classic brasserie food. And there's a terrace for summer and a cheerful fireplace for winter. Very pleasant.

Le Château ■ Route 35, junction Route 123, South Salem (Westchester County). Phone: 914-533-6631. Web site: www.lechateauny.com

Set on 32 acres with pleasant views, this brick-and-stone house was built by J. P. Morgan in 1907 as a gift for the rector of St. George's Episcopal Church in New York City. The interior is rich with paneling and fine craftsmanship. If only I could say as much for the food. The service is adequate but lacks that extra touch of the true professional. The menu is standard as is much of the cooking, but the specials can be quite good; one night, for instance, I had venison that was perfectly cooked and served in a creamy rich brown sauce. But the wild rice that accompanied it was overdone, the vegetables watery and unbuttered, the bread stale. You win one and you lose one—or three—but the restaurant is expensive and the food should be more carefully prepared and presented. On the other hand, lots of people love it.

Gasho ■ Route 32, Central Valley (Orange County).
Phone: 914-928-2277. Web site: www.gasho.com

There are brochures everywhere for this restaurant and its younger sibling in Hawthorne (914-592-5900), so I put off going for a long time thinking it would be mobbed with people and probably not very good. I was right on the first point, wrong on the second; the food is not only good, it's also very reasonably priced. Another surprise is that the restaurant itself is so very attractive. Located in a farmhouse that was moved here from Japan, then reconstructed, it's surrounded by flowers, a Japanese garden, waterwheels and a teahouse. The tables are communal, a grill in the center of each, and the food is cooked right there before you in one of those displays of Japanese dexterity in chopping, mincing and dicing that always makes me afraid one of the chef's fingers may wind up in my rice. The restaurant in Hawthorne is equally attractive and good. This is a find.

Hudson House ■ 2 Main Street, Cold Spring (Putnam County).
Phone: 845-265-9355. We site: www.hudsonhouseinn.com

As I mentioned earlier (see page 188), you do not come here for the food. It's passable, standard food, but the dining rooms are attractive, the service very pleasant, and the view spectacular. If you're there at lunch and get a window table, check out the gulls landing on the finial on top of the bandstand. For some reason one will alight there, then can't keep its footing and fly off, abandoning the position to the next one. Not very bright, gulls.

Painter's ■ 266 Hudson Street (Route 218), Cornwall-on-Hudson (Orange County). Phone: 845-534-2109.
Web site: www.painters-restaurant.com

This modest restaurant, where you can eat on the porch in the summer, has surprisingly good food. The dining room is homey/funky, with changing art by local artists and the expected good, bad and indifferent offerings, but it is pleasant to look at and it adds warmth to the surroundings. The food ranges from pasta to hamburgers to fish and salads, and everything I've had there has been more than acceptable. Better yet, the prices are very reasonable.

Purdys Homestead Restaurant ▓ 100 Titicus Road (at the crossroads of Routes 22 & 116), North Salem (Westchester County). Phone: 914-277-2301. Web site: www.purdyshomestead.4t.com.

Originally, this was the Box Tree, a wonderful restaurant. Now it is equally good and run by a couple, Maureen Brown-Steppe, the pastry chef, and her husband, Charles Steppe, who worked at some of the finest restaurants in New York. It shows. The three dining rooms, with three fireplaces, are attractive and welcoming, and the food is wonderful. As for the desserts—sublime is the only word. It's expensive, but it is consistently rewarding.

Riverview ▓ 45 Fair Street, Cold Spring (Putnam County). Phone: 845-265-4778. No credit cards.

On the river, and in the summer you can enjoy the view from the terrace. Be sure to make a reservation, though, since this is a favorite place of the locals and there only are 15 tables outside. One specialty on the imaginative menu is the Italian wood-oven pizza with a paper-thin crust and delicious toppings.

Valley Restaurant at the Garrison ▓ 2015 Route 9, Garrison (Putnam County). Phone: 845-424-2339. Web site: www.thegarrison.com

The setting is lovely—great views, and the terrace in summer is enchanting. The interior is welcoming—handsomely decorated and comfortable. The food is very good, and the service impeccable. The menu changes constantly to take advantage of what's available. But ... the meals I've had here have always been good, granted, but there's something that always keeps them from going over the top to "great." On a scale of 1 to 10, I'd give it a 7.

Wasabi ▓ 110 Main Street, Nyack (Rockland County). Phone: 845-358-7977.

The young chef-owner, Doug Nguyen, came as a child to this country from Vietnam. He is an extremely gifted chef, and if you like sushi and sashimi and Japanese food with an inventive twist, this place *is* definitely worth a trip. In fact, it *is* a trip, with a black ceiling and green and mustard-colored walls. It's very good.

About the Author

Tim Mulligan is an (almost) lifelong New Yorker. He was educated at Phillips Academy, Andover, Yale University and the University of Paris. He has been both an editor and writer for several national magazines and is also the author of *The Traveler's Guide to Western New England and the Connecticut River Valley* and *Virginia: A History and Guide.* He is the co-editor of *The Battle of Hampton Roads: New Perspectives on the USS Monitor and the CSS Virginia.*

Index